CAKES

150 BEST CAKE RECIPES OF ALL TIME

PAULA ISABELLA

Copyright © 2015

This book is dedicated to people who loves making cakes,
cupcakes, pies, cookies and other cool sweet stuffs.

BAKING HAS NEVER BEEN EASIER THAN THESE NOWADAYS.

The Golden Rule – always read the recipe entirely before starting out.

SUMMARY

INTRODUCTION

Making a very good cake could be quite tricky. It has to be aesthetically pleasing, it has to have a great topping, the perfect glaze (if you screw this part, which is usually very simple, but in my early stage I used to fail at making the glaze) and most importantly, a cake must be very very delicious. SWEET is the word.

If you make a cake for family members only, and you screw it, then you are not in such a big problem, but if you do it when you have guests, for a special occasion, then you are DEAD.

Don't worry, I am here to help you.

In this book you will find numerous recipes for both cakes and cupcakes. It is lessen of all non-essentials. There won't be many tips and how to, assuming you already know the basics of baking cakes, and you are not a beginner. However, I have two rules which I want you to respect to the letter before making any of these recipes.

Here they are:

Rule #1 Read the recipe entirely before going after Ingredients and pay very close attention to the preparation steps.

Rule #2 Follow the recipe! DO NOT try to improvise unless you are very experienced in this field.

You may be asking why do I emphasize this? Because I broken these two rules and the result was awful. Trust me, I know what I am saying.

BAKER'S TIPS

1. **Before beating the egg whites, let them come to the room temperature. It is very likely that if you beat them cold, they won't become fluffy.**
2. **Choose the Ingredients wisely.**
3. **Read the entire recipe before buying the Ingredients.**
4. **Don't rely solely on the baking time. Do a check for yourself.**

5. Do not speed the frosting process. One mistake and it can cause you a lot.
6. Frost the cupcakes once they are cooled down.
7. Serve them at the right temperature(varies from recipe to recipe).

Cupcakes are the best for serving guests. It is a very *versatile* dessert for they are literally small, sweet, aesthetically more pleasing that regular cakes.

ESPRESSO CUPCAKES

INGREDIENTS

CUPCAKES

- 1 cup butter, softened to room temperature
- 1 3/4 cup sugar
- 2 eggs
- 2 tsp. vanilla extract
- 1 cup buttermilk or 1 cup whole milk with 1 Tbs. lemon juice
- 1/2 cup strong coffee, cooled
- 2 cups flour
- 3/4 cup cocoa powder
- 1 tsp. baking soda
- 1 1/2 tsp. baking powder
- 1/2 tsp. salt

FROSTING

- 8 oz. bar cream cheese, cold
- 1/2 cup butter (1 stick), softened to room temperature
- 1 tsp vanilla extract
- 4 Tbs. Kahlua coffee liqueur
- 3 1/2 cups powdered sugar, measure then sift

TOPPING

- 1/2 to 3/4 cup Kahlua coffee liqeuer*
- 1 cup chocolate covered espresso beans

DIRECTIONS

1. Preheat oven to 350 degrees F. Line 3 muffin pans with cupcake liners. Beat together butter and sugar till light and fluffy. Slowly add eggs one at a time.
2. Sift together flour, cocoa powder, baking soda, baking powder and salt. Combine the buttermilk and coffee together. Alternate adding the flour mixture and buttermilk mixture.

3. Pour into the prepared pans. Bake for 12-15 minutes or until a toothpick inserted in the middle of the cupcake comes out clean. Let cool for at least 10 minutes then poke holes on top of each cupcake. Drizzle about 1/2 teaspoon of Kahlua over each cupcake.
4. With the mixer on a low speed, beat the cream cheese and butter till blended. Mix in vanilla and Kahlua. Slowly add the powdered sugar, a cup at a time.
5. Once all the powdered sugar is added, increase to a higher speed to whip up the frosting till light and fluffy. Transfer frosting into a piping bag.
6. Place the chocolate covered espresso beans inside a ziplock bag. Using a rolling pin, lightly crush them into smaller pieces. Pipe frosting on top of each cupcake.
7. Drizzle a little bit of Kahlua on top of the frosting. Sprinkle the crushed chocolate covered espresso beans on top of each cupcake.

ROASTED BERRY CUPCAKES

INGREDIENTS

ROASTED BERRIES

- 3 cups assorted berries
- 1/4 cup sugar

CUPCAKES

- 1/2 cup (1 stick) unsalted butter, softened at room temperature
- 3/4 cup granulated sugar
- 2 large eggs
- 1 teaspoon vanilla
- 1 1/3 cup cake flour
- 1 1/4 teaspoons baking powder
- 1/4 teaspoon kosher salt
- 1/2 cup buttermilk
- 1 cup roasted berries, drained

FROSTING

- 1/2 cup (1 stick) unsalted butter, softened at room temperature
- 1/2 cup cream cheese
- 3 cups confectioner's sugar
- 1-2 drops pink food coloring
- 1 cup mashed roasted berries

DIRECTIONS

1. Preheat the oven to 400°F. Line a small baking tray with parchment paper and scatter the berries in one layer on the tray. Sprinkle with the sugar and roast for about 15-20 minutes, or until the berries are soft and have released their juices. Remove from the oven and cool completely.
2. Take the roasted berries and drain some of the excess liquid. Mash the remaining berries using a fork and set this aside for the frosting.

3. Lower the oven temperature to 350°F. Prepare muffin trays by lining with cupcake liners.

4. In the bowl of a stand mixer with the whisk attachment, cream the butter until light and fluffy. Mix in the sugar until well incorporated, then add the eggs and vanilla, scraping down the sides of the bowl periodically.
5. In a small bowl, whisk together the cake flour, baking powder and salt. Add the flour to the egg mixture, mixing until just incorporated. Add the buttermilk and mix again until the batter is smooth, but take care not to over mix.
6. Remove the mixing bowl from the stand mixer and gently fold in the roasted berries. Spoon the batter into the muffin trays, about 3/4 full.
7. Bake for about 20 minutes, or until an toothpick inserted in the center come out with just a few moist crumbs. Set aside to cool before icing.

FROSTING

1. Whisk the butter, cream cheese and confectioner's sugar in a stand mixer with the whisk attachment on low speed. When the Ingredients start to come together, increase the speed to medium and let the icing mix for about 2 minutes.
2. Add the food coloring and mix again. Once the icing is smooth, remove the mixing bowl from the mixer.
3. Spoon the mashed berries into the bowl, then spoon the icing into a piping bag outfitted with a large decorating tip.

CHOCOLATE BUTTERCREAM CUPCAKES

INGREDIENTS

YELLOW CUPCAKES

- 3/4 cup (1 1/2 sticks or 169g) unsalted butter, room temperature
- 1 1/2 cups (300g) granulated sugar
- 3 extra-large (3/4 cup, 56g, or 6ounces) eggs, room temperature
- 2 teaspoons pure vanilla extract
- 1 teaspoon almond extract
- 1 1/4 cups (287g) sour cream, room temperature
- 2 1/2 cups (312g) cake flour
- 2 teaspoons baking powder
- 1/2 teaspoon baking soda
- 1/2 teaspoon salt

CHOCOLATE BUTTERCREAM

- 1 1/2 cups (340g) butter, at room temperature
- 4 cups (500g) powdered sugar
- 3/4 cup (94g) cocoa powder
- 4 tablespoons (60ml) heavy whipping cream
- 2 teaspoons vanilla extract
- pinch table salt

DIRECTIONS

1. Preheat the oven to 350 degrees F.
2. Cream the butter and sugar in the bowl of a stand mixer fitted with the paddle attachment for about 3 minutes or until light and fluffy.
3. With mixer on medium-low, add the eggs 1 at a time, allowing them to incorporate before adding next.
4. With mixer off, add the vanilla, almond extract, and sour cream. Turn mixer on low until incorporated then high for about 1 minute.
5. In a separate bowl, sift together the flour, baking powder, baking soda, and salt. Sift at least 2 times.

6. With the mixer on low, add the flour mixture to the batter until just combined. Remove bowl from mixer and finish stirring with a spatula to be sure the batter is completely mixed.
7. Using a 1/4 cup ice cream scoop or a measuring cup, divide batter into cupcake pans.
8. Bake for 16-20 minutes or until cupcake springs back when pressed in the center.
9. Chocolate Buttercream
10. In a the bowl of an stand mixer fitted with whisk attachment, whisk butter and sugar on medium-high speed until very pale and fluffy, or about five minutes.
11. Be sure to stop at least once and scrape the bowl.
12. With the mixer off, add in cocoa powder, vanilla, and salt.
13. Turn mixer on low and blend for about 30 seconds.
14. One tablespoon at a time, add in heavy cream.
15. Once all cream has been added and mixture is mostly combined, turn off the mixer and scrape down the sides of the bowl.
16. Now turn the mixer onto medium-high to high and whisk for 3-5 minutes or until mixture is light and fluffy. The frosting will be shiny and seem to have many large air bubbles throughout and this is exactly what we are going for.
17. Allow cupcakes to cool before frosting.

PUMPKIN CUPCAKES WITH MAPLE CREAM

INGREDIENTS

CUPCAKES

- 1 cup all purpose flour
- 1 teaspoon baking powder
- ½ teaspoon baking soda
- 1 teaspoon ground cinnamon
- ¼ teaspoon ground ginger
- ½ teaspoon nutmeg
- ½ teaspoon salt
- 2 eggs
- 1 cup canned pumpkin puree
- ¼ cup granulated sugar
- ½ cup brown sugar, lightly packed
- ⅓ cup vegetable oil

FROSTING

- 6 ounces cream cheese, at room temperature (
- 3 tablespoons unsalted butter, at room temperature
- 2 tablespoons pure maple syrup
- ½ teaspoon pure vanilla extract
- 2 cups powdered sugar
- For the salted maple glazed pecans:
- 4 tablespoons unsalted butter
- ½ cup brown sugar, lightly packed
- ½ teaspoon salt
- ¼ cup pure maple syrup
- 1 tablespoon milk
- ⅔ cup chopped, toasted pecans

DIRECTIONS

CUPCAKES

1. Preheat oven to 350. Grease a muffin pan or fill with 9 paper liners.

2. In a medium bowl, whisk together the flour, baking powder, baking soda, cinnamon, ginger, nutmeg and salt.
3. In a large bowl, whisk together the eggs, pumpkin puree, sugars and vegetable oil. Add the flour mixture to the wet Ingredients and stir until combined.
4. Divide the batter evenly between the 9 muffin cups and bake for 15-18 minutes, until a toothpick inserted in the cupcakes comes out clean.
5. Cool the cupcakes completely before spreading with frosting and topping with pecans.

FROSTING

1. Beat cream cheese, butter, maple syrup and vanilla extract until combined.
2. Slowly add in powdered sugar and beat until smooth.

PECANS

1. In a saucepan over medium-high heat, melt the butter. Once melted, whisk in the brown sugar and salt. Bring to a boil, reduce the heat to medium and continue to boil for 2 minutes, whisking frequently.
2. Add the maple syrup and boil 4 minutes longer, until the mixture has thickened, whisking frequently. Remove from the heat and immediately stir in the milk and pecans.
3. Pour onto a baking sheet that has been lined with foil. Allow to cool, then break into small pieces. Top the frosted cupcakes generously with the pecans.

VEGAN CHOCOLATE CUPCAKES

INGREDIENTS

CUPCAKES

- 1 1/2 cups (355 milliliters) Silk unsweetened original almond milk
- 1 1/2 teaspoons white vinegar
- 1/2 cup (113 grams) melted oil
- 2/3 cup (133 grams) brown sugar
- 1/2 cup (100 grams) granulated sugar
- 2 teaspoons vanilla extract
- 1 teaspoon espresso powder 2
- 1 1/2 cups (188 grams) flour
- 1/2 cup (58 grams) cocoa powder
- 1 1/4 teaspoons baking soda
- 3/4 teaspoon baking powder
- 1/2 teaspoon salt

FROSTING

- 1 cup (170 grams) semi-sweet chocolate chips
- 1/4 cup (60 milliliters) Silk unsweetened original almond milk
- 1/4 cup (56 grams) coconut oil
- 1 teaspoon vanilla extract
- 1/3 cup (40 grams) powdered sugar, sifted if lumpy4
- pinch of salt

DECORATING

- 16 chocolate peanut butter football truffles
- 1/2 cup naturally dyed shredded coconut

DIRECTIONS

CUPCAKES

1. Preheat the oven to 350 °F (175 °C) and line two muffin pans with a total of 16 cupcake liners.

2. In a large mixing bowl, stir together the almond milk and vinegar. Let sit for 5 minutes.
3. Stir in the melted coconut oil, brown sugar, granulated sugar, vanilla extract and espresso powder.
4. In a medium mixing bowl, stir together the flour, cocoa powder, baking soda, baking powder and salt. Add this to the wet mixture and stir just until combined.
5. Fill the liners slightly more than half-way full and bake for 16-18 minutes or until a toothpick inserted in the middle comes out clean or with some moist crumbs.
6. Let cool for 5 minutes and then turn out onto a wire rack to cool completely.

FROSTING

1. In a small saucepan over medium-low heat, mix together the chocolate chips, almond milk, coconut oil, and vanilla extract. Stir until melted and then gradually whisk in the powdered sugar until completely smooth.
2. Let the pan cool for about 15 and then place the pan in the refrigerator for about 10-20 minutes, stirring after every 5 minutes, or until firm enough to spread on the cupcakes.
3. Spread 1 tablespoon of frosting on top of each cupcake.

DECORATING

1. Sprinkle about 1 1/2 teaspoons of coconut grass over the frosting. Stick a toothpick in the football truffle and place on the cupcake. Can be kept at room temperature for about 4-6 hours.
2. Place in the refrigerator. Let come to room temperature (about 1-2 hours) before serving.

CHOCOLATE CUPCAKE WITH PUMPKIN BUTTERCREAM

INGREDIENTS

CUPCAKES

- 1/2 cup (1 stick or 115g) unsalted butter
- 2 ounces semi-sweet baking chocolate
- 2 large eggs, at room temperature
- 3/4 cup (150g) granulated sugar
- 2 teaspoons vanilla extract
- 1/2 cup (115g) sour cream, room temperature
- 1/2 cup (42g) unsweetened cocoa powder
- 3/4 cup (95g) all-purpose flour
- 1/2 teaspoon baking soda
- 1 teaspoon baking powder
- 1/4 teaspoon salt

PUMPKIN BUTTERCREAM

- 1/2 cup butter (113g), room temperature
- 1/2 cup (110g) pumpkin puree
- 1 teaspoon vanilla
- 3 cups (380g) confectioners sugar
- 1 tablespoon pumpkin spice

DIRECTIONS

CUPCAKES

1. Preheat the oven to 350F degrees. This recipe makes 12-14 cupcakes, so prepare one with cupcake liners.
2. Melt the butter and chocolate together in the microwave. Microwave in 30-second increments, stirring in between each time. Set aside.
3. In the bowl of a stand mixer with the whisk attachment; add the eggs, sugar, vanilla, and sour cream and whisk on medium speed until smooth.
4. In a medium sized bowl, sift the cocoa powder, flour, baking soda, baking powder, and salt together until thoroughly combined.

5. Add the cooled butter/chocolate to the stand mixer and whisk until smooth, about 30 seconds.
6. Slowly add in the flour mixture, about 1/4 cup at a time with the stand mixer on low.
7. Fill the cupcake liners 2/3 of the way full with batter. Bake for 15-18 minutes.

PUMPKIN BUTTERCREAM

Place all Ingredients in bowl of stand mixer with paddle attachment and turn on to low speed.

Once all Ingredients are combined, turn mixer speed to medium-high and mix for 2-3 minutes.

MOCHA CUPCAKES

INGREDIENTS

- 1/2 c (118 ml) strong brewed coffee, room temp
- 1 1/2 tsp espresso powder
- 1/2 c (118 ml) whole milk
- 1 tsp vanilla extract
- 1 1/3 c (189 g) flour
- 1/3 c (30 g) cocoa powder
- 1 tsp baking powder
- 1/2 tsp baking soda
- 1/4 tsp salt
- 1/2 c (118 g) butter, room temp
- 1/2 c (99 g) granulated sugar
- 1/2 c (71 g) brown sugar
- 1 egg, room temp

SWISS MERINGUE BUTTERCREAM

- 1 1/2 c (300 g) sugar
- 7 egg whites
- 27 Tbsp (381 g) unsalted butter, room temp
- 2 Tbsp instant coffee
- 2 Tbsp warm water

DIRECTIONS

1. Preheat the oven to 350F. Line a cupcake pan with 12 liners and set aside.
2. Mix the espresso powder/instant coffee granules into the brewed coffee. Add the milk and vanilla set aside to cool.
3. In a small bowl, combine the flour, cocoa powder, baking powder, baking soda and salt. Set aside.
4. In a separate medium-sized bowl, beat the butter until creamy. Add the sugars and beat until light and fluffy, about five minutes.
5. Add the egg and beat until fully incorporated, scarping down the sides and the bottom of the bowl.
6. Add about 1/3 of the flour mixture to the batter, and mix slowly to combine. Scrape down the sides and add half of the coffee mixture. Scrape down the sides of the bowl

again and continue alternating wet and dry, ending with dry. Mix just until combined.
7. Scoop batter into the prepared liners. Bake 17-20 minutes or until the cupcakes spring back when pressed. Cool on a rack in pans for 3 minutes, then remove the cupcakes from the pans and allow to cool thoroughly before frosting.

SWISS MERINGUE BUTTERCREAM

1. In a double boiler, cook the egg whites and sugar over medium heat, whisking constantly, until the sugar is completely dissolved.
2. Pour into another bowl and whip on high speed until room temp.
3. On a medium-low speed, add the butter, waiting until each piece is completely incorporated before adding the next.
4. While it's beating, combine the water and instant coffee. Pour into whipped buttercream as you would an extract, and beat to combine.

APPLE PIE CUPCAKES

INGREDIENTS

- 4 tablespoons unsalted butter
- 2 large Granny Smith apples, peeled, cored and diced in to 1/4-inch cubes
- 1/2 teaspoon ground cinnamon
- 1/8 teaspoon salt
- Juice of half lemon (about 1 1/2 tablespoons)
- 1/4 cup all purpose flour
- 1/4 cup + 2 tablespoons packed brown sugar
- 1/4 cup chopped walnuts
- 1 can (12.4 oz) Pillsbury refrigerated cinnamon rolls
- whipped cream
- caramel-flavored syrup

DIRECTIONS

1. Heat oven to 400°F. Lightly spray 8 regular-size muffin cups with cooking spray.
2. In 10-inch skillet, melt 2 tablespoons butter over medium-high heat. Add apples; cook about 5 minutes, stirring occasionally, until softened.
3. Sprinkle with 2 tablespoons brown sugar, the cinnamon and salt. Cook 5 minutes longer or until tender. Stir in lemon juice.
4. Meanwhile, in small bowl, mix butter, flour, 1/4 cup of brown sugar and walnuts with fork or hands until crumbly. Set aside.
5. Separate dough into 8 rolls. Flatten each into 4-inch round; place in muffin cup. Divide apple filling evenly onto rolls in muffin cups. Divide flour mixture evenly over apples.
6. Bake 10 to 12 minutes or until bubbly and tops are lightly browned. Cool slightly before removing from muffin cups.
7. Cool completely, about 30 minutes.Serve cupcakes topped with whipped cream and a drizzle of syrup.

CINNAMON ROLL CUPCAKES

INGREDIENTS

- 2 1/4 tsp or 1 packet (1/4 oz./7 g) dry active yeast
- 1/2 cup sugar, divided
- 1 cup warm milk (approximately 110 degrees Fahrenheit)
- 2 eggs, room temperature
- 1/3 cup butter, melted
- 1 tsp salt
- 4 1/2 cups bread flour
- 1 cup brown sugar, packed
- 2 1/2 Tbsp ground cinnamon
- 1/3 cup butter, softened

DIRECTIONS

1. Dissolve the yeast and 1/4 cup of the granulated sugar in the warm milk in a large bowl and let stand for about 10 minutes until foamy.
2. Mix in the eggs, butter, salt, and other 1/4 cup of granulated sugar. Add flour and mix until well blended and the dough forms a ball. Put in a bowl, cover and let rise in a warm place until doubled in size.
3. After the dough has doubled in size, turn it out onto a lightly floured surface, cover and let rest for 10 minutes. In a small bowl, combine brown sugar and cinnamon. Line cupcake pan with cupcake liners, and lightly spray over the top of them with cooking spray.
4. Roll dough into a 12x22 inch rectangle. Spread dough with 1/3 cup butter and sprinkle evenly with sugar/cinnamon mixture. Roll up dough and cut into 24 rolls.
5. Place each roll in a cupcake liner. Cover and let rise until nearly doubled, about 30 minutes. Meanwhile, preheat oven to 400 degrees Fahrenheit.
6. Bake rolls in preheated oven until golden brown, about 10-12 minutes. Let rolls cool completely before frosting.

PEPPERMINT CUPCAKES

INGREDIENTS

CUPCAKES

- 2 2/3 cups all-purpose flour
- 2/3 cup unsweetened cocoa powder
- 2-3 tsp. espresso powder
- 2 tsp. baking powder
- 1 tsp. baking soda
- ½ tsp. salt
- 1 cup whole milk
- 1 cup strong brewed coffee
- 1 tsp. peppermint extract
- 1 cup (2 sticks) unsalted butter, at room temperature
- 1 cup granulated sugar
- 1 cup light brown sugar
- 2 large eggs

FROSTING

- 6 large egg whites
- 1¾ plus 2 tbsp. granulated sugar
- 1½ cups (3 sticks) unsalted butter, at room temperature
- 4 tsp. peppermint extract
- 1-2 tsp. vanilla extract

DIRECTIONS

1. To make the cupcakes, preheat the oven to 350° F. Line two cupcake pans with paper liners.
2. In a medium bowl, combine the flour, cocoa powder, espresso powder, baking powder, baking soda and salt; stir together. Combine the milk, coffee and peppermint extract in a liquid measuring cup.
3. In the bowl of a stand mixer fitted with the paddle attachment, combine the butter and sugars. Beat on medium-high speed until light and fluffy, 2-3 minutes, scraping down the sides of the bowl as needed. Blend in the eggs one at a time.
4. Alternately mix in the dry and liquid Ingredients, beginning and ending with the dry Ingredients and mixing just until incorporated.
5. Divide the batter evenly between the prepared cupcake liners. Bake 18-20 minutes, or until a toothpick inserted in the center comes out clean. Let cool in the pan 5-10 minutes, then transfer to a wire rack to cool completely.

FROSTING

1. Combine the egg whites and sugar in a heatproof bowl set over a pot of simmering water. Heat, whisking frequently, until the mixture reaches 160° F and the sugar has dissolved.
2. Transfer the mixture to the bowl of a stand mixer fitted with the whisk attachment. Beat on medium-high speed until stiff peaks form and the mixture has cooled to room temperature, about 8 minutes.
3. Reduce the speed to medium and add the butter, 2 tablespoons at a time, adding more once each addition has been incorporated.
4. Stir in the peppermint and vanilla extracts and mix just until incorporated, then pipe or spread the frosting onto the cupcakes.
5. Remove about half of the frosting to a bowl. Take the remaining frosting in the mixing bowl, add red gel coloring and mix until you have achieved the desired shade. Fit a pastry bag with a large tip. Fill one side of the pastry bag with the white frosting, and then fill in the other side with the red frosting Pipe a test streak until you see both colors coming out of the tip.

GREEN CUPCAKES

INGREDIENTS

- 1 pkg. (2-layer size) white cake mix
- 2 oz. BAKER'S Semi-Sweet Chocolate, melted
- 1 Tbsp. green food coloring
- 4 oz. (1/2 of 8-oz. pkg.) Cream Cheese, softened
- 1 jar (7 oz.) Marshmallow Creme
- 1 tsp. vanilla
- 1 tub (8 oz.) Whipped Topping, thawed

DIRECTIONS

1. Heat oven to 350°F.
2. Prepare and bake cake batter as directed on package for 24 cupcakes, blending melted chocolate and food coloring into batter before spooning into prepared muffin cups. Cool completely.
3. Beat cream cheese, marshmallow creme and vanilla in large bowl with mixer until blended. Add the whipped topping; beat just until blended.
4. Spoon whip mixture into resealable plastic bag. Cut corner off one bottom corner of bag; use to pipe whip mixture onto tops of cupcakes.

STRAWBERRY CHEESECAKE CUPCAKES

INGREDIENTS

GRAHAM CRACKER CRUST

- 1 ¼ cups graham cracker crumbs
- 1/3 cup sugar
- 5 tablespoons unsalted butter, melted

CUPCAKES

- 2 1/2 cups sifted cake flour
- 1 tablespoon baking powder
- 1/2 teaspoon salt
- 1 cup milk, at room temperature
- 2 large egg whites, at room temperature
- 1 whole egg, at room temperature
- 1 teaspoon vanilla extract
- 1/4 teaspoon almond extract
- 1 1/2 cups sugar
- 8 tablespoons (1 stick) unsalted butter, at room temperature
- 1/2 cup heavy cream, cold

CHEESECAKE FILLING

- 1 (8 ounce) package cream cheese, at room temperature
- ¼ cup (4 tablespoons) unsalted butter, at room temperature
- ½ teaspoon vanilla extract
- 1 ¼ cups confectioners' sugar, sifted

STRAWBERRY BUTTERCREAM FROSTING

- ¾ cup (1.5 sticks) unsalted butter, at room temperature
- 3 cups confectioner's sugar, sifted
- 1/2 cup fresh strawberries
- 1/2 teaspoon vanilla extract
- For the strawberry topping:
- 1 cup diced strawberries

- ¼ cup graham cracker crumbs

DIRECTIONS

CUPCAKES

1. Preheat the oven to 350 degrees F. Line 2 muffin pans with cupcake liners.
2. In a medium bowl combine the flour, baking powder and salt. In a glass measuring cup, whisk the milk, eggs, vanilla and almond extract.
3. In an electric mixer fitted with the paddle attachment, cream the butter and sugar on medium speed until pale and creamy, about 5 minutes. Alternate additions of the flour mixture and liquid mixture, beginning and ending with the flour mixture (3 dry additions, 2 wet), beating after each addition until incorporated. Continue mixing on medium speed for 2 minutes.
4. Chill a clean stainless mixer bowl in the freezer for 5 minutes. Return bowl to mixer fitted with the whisk attachment and then whisk the heavy cream on medium-high speed until soft peaks form.
5. Fold whipped cream into the cake batter.
6. Divide the batter evenly among cupcake liners (about 2/3 full) and bake until a toothpick comes out with only a few crumbs, about 16-18 minutes. Remove from pan and let cool on wire racks. Repeat with second muffin pan.

GRAHAM CRACKER CRUST

1. In a small mixing bowl, combine the graham cracker crumbs, sugar and melted butter; mix well with a fork. Drop about 1 tablespoon of the graham cracker mixture in the bottom of each cupcake liner and press down to line the bottom.
2. Bake for 5 minutes. Remove from the oven, and maintain the oven temperature.

FILLING

1. In the bowl of a stand mixer fitted with the paddle attachment beat the cream cheese and butter until creamy.
2. Add the vanilla then gradually add the confectioners' sugar.
3. Beat until well combined.

STRAWBERRY FROSTING

1. Puree the strawberries in a food processor. Strain the puree through a fine mesh sieve placed over a bowl to remove the seeds. In an electric mixer fitted with the paddle attachment, combine butter and half of the sugar.
2. Beat on low speed until well blended. Add the other half of the sugar and two tablespoons of strawberry puree, mixing until combined.
3. Increase speed to medium and add additional puree, a tablespoon at a time, until desired color and flavor is reached. Add vanilla and beat on high for about 30 seconds to lighten the frosting.

ASSEMBLE

1. Remove a small amount of the center part of the cupcake using a cupcake corer or pairing knife.
2. Divide the cheesecake filling evenly among the cupcakes, filling the hole in the middle of the cupcake. Pipe frosting around the edge of each cupcake, leaving a well for the strawberry topping.
3. Divide strawberry topping among cupcakes and sprinkle with graham cracker crumbs.

RASPBERRY CHEESECAKE CUPCAKES

INGREDIENTS

CRUST

- 3/4 cup + 2 Tbsp graham cracker crumbs
- 1 1/2 tsp granulated sugar
- 3 1 /2 Tbsp salted butter, melted

RASPBERRY SWIRL

- 4 oz fresh raspberries
- 2 Tbsp granulated sugar

CHEESECAKE FILLING

- 3/4 cup granulated sugar
- 1 Tbsp all-purpose flour
- 2 (8 oz) pkg cream cheese, softened well but not melted
- 1 tsp lemon zest
- 2 large eggs
- 1 tsp vanilla extract
- 1/4 cup sour cream

DIRECTIONS

CRUST

1. Preheat oven to 325 degrees. In a mixing bowl, using a fork, stir together graham cracker crumbs and sugar, then pour in melted butter and stir until evenly moistened.
2. Add 1 slightly heaping tablespoonful to 12 paper lined muffin cups. Press crust firmly into an even layer.
3. Bake in preheated oven 5 minutes then remove from oven and allow to cool.

RASPBERRY SWIRL

1. Add raspberries and 2 Tbsp granulated sugar to a food processor and pulse until well pureed, about 30 seconds - 1 minute.
2. Press mixture through a fine mesh strainer into a bowl.
3. Set aside.

CHEESECAKE FILLING

1. In a mixing bowl, whisk together granulated sugar and flour. Add cream cheese and lemon zest using an electric hand mixer, blend mixture just until smooth.
2. Mix in eggs one at a time. Stir in vanilla and sour cream just until combined.
3. Tap bowl forcefully against countertop, about 10 times, to release large air bubbles. Divide mixture evenly among cups over crust layer, adding about 1/3 cup to each and filling nearly full. Jiggle pan to level cheesecake filling then dollop about 5 small circle of raspberry sauce over each cupcake, about 3/4 tsp total over each one.
4. Using a toothpick, swirl raspberry filling with cheesecake mixture to create a marbled design. Bake in preheated oven 22 - 25 minutes until cupcakes are puffed and nearly set.
5. Remove from oven and allow to cool completely, then chill in refrigerator 3 hours, until set. Store in refrigerator in an airtight container.

CHOCOLATE PUMPKIN CUPCAKES

INGREDIENTS

CUPCAKES

- 1½ cup flour
- 1 teaspoon baking powder
- ¼ teaspoon baking soda
- ¾ teaspoon pumpkin spice
- ½ teaspoon salt
- ½ cup brown sugar
- ½ cup granulated sugar
- ½ cup canola oil
- 2 eggs
- ¾ cup pumpkin puree
- 1 teaspoon vanilla

GANACHE

- 3 ounces (1/2 cup) semi sweet chocolate
- 6 tablespoons whipping cream

FROSTING

- 4 ounces cream cheese, room temperature
- ¼ cup butter (1/2 stick), room temperature
- ½ teaspoon vanilla
- ¼ teaspoon cinnamon
- Pinch of nutmeg
- Pinch of salt
- 2 cups powdered sugar

DIRECTIONS

CUPCAKES

1. Preheat oven to 350 degrees and line a muffin tin with 12 paper cupcake liners.

2. In a mixing bowl, combine flour, baking powder, baking soda, pumpkin spice, and salt together. Set aside.
3. In the bowl of a standing mixer fitted with the paddle attachment, mix sugars together until there are no lumps. Mix in the oil and then the eggs one at a time. Add the pumpkin and vanilla and mix well. Gradually mix in the dry Ingredients until combined.
    Spoon batter into the cupcake liners filling ¾ full (about ¼ cup).
4. Bake for 20-25 minutes until toothpick comes out clean.
5. Let cupcakes cool in muffin tin for 5 minutes and then allow to cool completely on a wire rack.

GANACHE

1. Microwave heavy whipping cream for 45 seconds and then add the chocolate chips and let it sit for 2 minutes and then whisk together until smooth.
2. Allow to sit and cool for 5 minutes and then spoon about 1 teaspoon onto the top of each cupcake. Let the ganache cool and set for about 10 minutes before piping on frosting.

FROSTING

1. Beat cream cheese and butter together until smooth. Mix in the vanilla and then add the cinnamon, nutmeg, salt, and the powdered sugar a little at a time mixing on low.
2. Cream until fluffy and smooth. Place frosting in a piping bag fitted with a star tip and pipe on top of the ganache covered cupcakes.

MANGO & VANILLA CUPCAKES

INGREDIENTS

- 1 & ⅓ cup all-purpose flour
- ½ tsp baking powder
- ¼ tsp baking soda
- ¼ tsp salt
- ½ cup unsalted butter, melted and cooled
- 1 cup sugar
- 1 large egg
- ¼ cup coconut flavored yogurt (or vanilla)
- ¾ cup milk
- 1 tsp vanilla

BUTTERCREAM

- ¾ cup unsalted butter, room temperature
- ½ cup mango puree ¼ tsp salt
- ½ tsp vanilla extract
- 4 cups icing sugar

DIRECTIONS

1. Preheat oven to 350°F and line a muffin pan with 12 paper liners.
2. In a large bowl, toss together flour, baking powder, baking soda and salt.
3. In a medium bowl, whisk the melted butter with the sugar. Add the egg, yogurt, milk and vanilla. Stir together, then gently pour into the dry Ingredients. Mix until smooth and try not to over mix.
4. Fill the paper liners ¾ full with batter and bake for about 18-20 minutes or until a toothpick inserted into the centre comes out clean. Let cupcakes cool completely before frosting.

BUTTERCREAM

1. Whip the butter until light and fluffy. Add the mango puree, salt and vanilla, mix until somewhat incorporated. Add the icing sugar, one cup at a time, blend until smooth.

CUPCAKES WITH RASPBERRY BUTTERCREAM

INGREDIENTS

CUPCAKES

- ½ cup unsalted butter, softened
- ¾ cup sugar
- 2 eggs plus one egg yolk, room temperature
- ½ teaspoon vanilla extract
- 1½ cups all purpose flour
- ¼ teaspoon salt
- 1½ teaspoons baking powder
- 4 ounces milk, room temperature

RASPBERRY BUTTERCREAM

- 1 cup fresh raspberries
- ½ cup unsalted butter, softened
- 2 cups powdered sugar

DIRECTIONS

CUPCAKES

2. Preheat oven to 350 degrees. In a stand mixer with the paddle attachment cream butter and sugar until fluffy.
3. Add in eggs and vanilla extract. Mix to combine.
4. In a separate bowl mix together the dry Ingredients. Combine the flour, salt, and baking powder.
5. Alternatively add the dry Ingredients and milk in two parts to the egg mixture.
6. Fill a cupcake lined pan with batter ⅔ of the way up.
7. Place in the oven and bake for 12-15 minutes.
8. Allow the cupcakes to cool completely before frosting.

RASPBERRY BUTTERCREAM

1. Add raspberries to a food processor. Pulse until they become a thick sauce.

2. Push the raspberry puree through a sieve to extract the juice and get rid of the seeds. Set raspberry sauce aside.
3. In a stand mixer with the paddle attachment cream butter on high for about 2-3 minutes to get a creamy fluffy texture.
4. Add in the powdered sugar and raspberry sauce on low speed until combined.
5. Pipe the icing onto cool cupcakes and decorate as desired. Cupcakes can be stored on the counter at room temperature for a day or two and in the refrigerator for up to 5 days.
6. Top with a raspberry.

TOFFEE CUPCAKE

INGREDIENTS

CUPCAKE

- 1 cup (4.5 ounces) all purpose flour
- 1 cup plus 2 tablespoons (7.3 ounces) sugar
- 1/3 cup plus 2 tablespoons (1.5 ounces) Unsweetened Natural Cocoa Powder
- 1/2 teaspoon baking soda
- 1/4 teaspoon salt
- 1/2 cup (1 stick) unsalted butter, melted and warm
- 2 large eggs
- 1 teaspoon pure vanilla extract
- 2 tablespoon instant coffee granules
- 1/2 cup hot coffee
- 1/2 cup chocolate covered toffee bits

CARAMEL FROSTING

- 5 large egg whites
- 11/2 cup granulated sugar
- 4 sticks unsalted butter, diced and softened
- 1/4 teaspoon salt
- 1 tablespoon vanilla
- 1/3 cup caramel sauce

CHOCOLATE DIPPING SAUCE

- 2/3 cups dark chocolate
- 2 tablespoons heavy cream
- 4 tablespoons powdered sugar, sifted
- 5-8 tablespoons water, warm

DIRECTIONS

CUPCAKE

1. Position a rack in the lower third of the oven. Heat the oven to 350 degrees.

2. In a large bowl, combine and mix together flour, cocoa powder, sugar, baking soda and salt. Add in butter, eggs, and vanilla and beat for one minute. Scrape down the sides of the bowl and add the instant coffee granules and hot coffee, beat until batter is smooth, about 20-30 seconds.
3. Divide it evenly among the lined cups. Bake 18-22 minutes just until a toothpick inserted into a few of the cupcakes comes out clean. Set the pan on a rack to cool.
4. Frost the cupcakes when they are completely cool. Store and serve at room temperature.

CARAMEL FROSTING

1. Combine egg whites and sugar in a bowl placed over simmering water. Bring mixture to 150 degrees F while whisking constantly.
2. Transfer mixture to stand mixer bowl, fitted with a whisk attachment and beat on medium speed until mixture cools and doubles in volume.
3. Add butter in one piece at a time, mixing to incorporate after each addition. The mixture may appear clumpy and almost curdled looking-this is normal.
4. Keep mixing and it will become even and smooth again. Add salt and vanilla and mix to combine. Add caramel sauce and mix to combine.

CHOCOLATE DIPPING SAUCE

1. Place chocolate and heavy cream in a bowl over simmering water. Let chocolate and cream sit for 2-3 minutes to melt without stirring.
2. Slowly stir mixture to combine. Add powdered sugar and mix to combine. Add water one tablespoon at a time, mixing after each addition until pouring consistency is reached. Set aside and let sauce cool to warm.

ASSEMBLE

1. To frost the cupcakes: Fill a pastry bag fitted with a large round tip and start piping from the outside working in to the center to create one even layer.
2. Freeze cupcakes for 20 minutes before dipping in warm chocolate sauce, so that the frosting does not melt. Remove cupcakes and dip in warm chocolate sauce, and then rim with chocolate covered toffee bits.
3. Return cupcakes to freezer for five minutes for chocolate to set. Remove from freezer and finish piping frosting on top.

KIT KAT CUPCAKES

INGREDIENTS

CUPCAKES

- 1 cup all-purpose flour
- 1 cup sugar
- ⅓ cup unprocessed cocoa powder
- 1 teaspoon baking soda
- ½ teaspoon baking powder
- ½ teaspoon salt
- 1 egg, at room temperature
- ½ cup buttermilk, at room temperature
- ½ cup hot coffee or hot water
- ¼ cup vegetable oil
- 1½ teaspoons vanilla extract

FROSTING

- 1 cup (2 sticks) unsalted butter, at room temperature
- 3-4 cups powdered sugar
- 2 teaspoons pure vanilla extract
- Pinch of salt
- 2-3 tablespoons heavy cream
- 6-7 snack size Kit Kats, chopped finely

DIRECTIONS

CUPCAKES

1. Preheat oven to 350 degrees F. Line muffin tins with cupcake liners. Sift together all the dry Ingredients into a large bowl. In a medium bowl, combine all the wet Ingredients, including egg, using a whisk. Be sure to whisk the last into the wet Ingredients to avoid scrambling with the hot coffee.
2. Using a mixer, mix the dry Ingredients on low speed for 1 minute. Stop the mixer and add the wet Ingredients. Mix for 2 minutes on medium speed and scrape down the sides and bottom of bowl. Mix for additional minute on medium speed.
3. The batter will be thin. Divide evenly among the cupcake liners.

4. Bake for 12-15 minutes or until a toothpick inserted in the center comes out almost clean.
5. Cool cupcakes on wire racks completely. Meanwhile you could start on the frosting.

FROSTING

1. Whip butter on medium speed for about 2-3 minutes in the bowl of a stand mixer fitted with the paddle attachment until light and creamy.
2. Add the powdered sugar, vanilla extract, salt and heavy cream and mix on low for 1 minute until combined. Increase speed to medium-high and whip for 6 minutes. Add in the chopped Kit Kats and mix until combined.
3. Use frosting immediately to frost cooled cupcakes.

TWO COLORS

INGREDIENTS

CHOCOLATE CAKE

- 1 Box Devil's Food Cake mix
- 3 eggs
- ½ C. oil
- 1 C. milk
- 1/3 C. sour cream
- 2 tsp. vanilla extract

VANILLA CAKE

- 1 Box White Cake mix
- 3 eggs
- 1/3 C. oil
- 1 C. milk
- 1/3 C. sour cream
- 1 Tbsp. vanilla extract

STRAWBERRY BUTTERCREAM

- 2 C. butter, softened
- ¼ C. strawberry puree
- 2 tsp. vanilla extract
- 6-8 C. powdered sugar

DIRECTIONS

1. Preheat your oven to 350 degrees and line pans with cupcake liners.
2. Sift both cake mixes into two separate bowl and set aside.
3. Chocolate Cake: In a large bowl, combine eggs, oil, milk, sour cream and vanilla extract. Add cake mix and stir until smooth.
4. Vanilla Cake: In another large bowl, combine eggs, oil, milk, sour cream and vanilla extract. Add cake mix and stir until smooth.
5. Place a small scoop of chocolate batter in the side of each cupcake liner. Then, place a small scoop of vanilla batter next to the chocolate.
6. Bake for 16-20 minutes, or until an inserted knife comes out clean.

7. Strawberry Buttercream: Beat butter for 2 minutes, scrape down bowl and beat again. Add strawberry puree and vanilla extract. Slowly add powdered sugar until you reach your desired consistency.

8. Pipe buttercream onto cooled cupcakes and top with a fresh strawberry.

ICE CREAM CUPCAKES

INGREDIENTS

CUPCAKES

- 1⅔ Cup All-Purpose Flour
- 2 Teaspoon Baking Powder
- 1 Cup White Sugar
- 1 Cup Butter, Softened
- 3 Eggs
- ⅔ Cup Buttermilk
- 2 Teaspoons Vanilla Extract
- ½ Cup Rainbow Sprinkles
- Pinch of Salt, To Taste

VANILLA BUTTERCREAM

- 1⅔ Cups Powdered Sugar
- 2 Teaspoons Vanilla Extract
- ½ Cup Butter, Softened
- 1 Tablespoon Whole Milk
- Pinch of Salt, To Taste

DECOR

- 1 Cup Milk Chocolate Chips
- 1 Tablespoon Vegetable Oil
- Rainbow Sprinkles

DIRECTIONS

CUPCAKES

1. Preheat oven to 350 degrees F. Line a cupcake tin with paper wrappers.
2. In a large bowl, cream butter and sugar together. Stir in eggs, milk, and vanilla.
3. Add in salt and baking powder. Gradually stir in flour a little at a time until just combined.
4. Fill each wrapper 2/3 of the way full and bake for 20-25 minutes .

5. Cool completely.

VANILLA BUTTERCREAM

1. Cream butter. Stir in vanilla and salt.
2. Gradually add powdered sugar a little at a time, adding milk as needed.

ASSEMBLE

1. In a microwave safe bowl, melt chocolate chips for 30-60 seconds or until smooth.
2. Remove from heat and stir in vegetable oil.
3. Use an ice cream scoop to place icing onto the top of each cupcake. Shape with a knife as needed.
4. Spoon chocolate on top of the frosting. Top with rainbow sprinkles.

BANANA & CHOCOLATE CUPCAKES

INGREDIENTS

CUPCAKES

- 1 1/2 cups (212g) all-purpose flour
- 1/2 tsp baking soda
- 1/4 tsp salt
- 6 Tbsp (3 oz) unsalted butter, softened
- 3/4 cup (165g) granulated sugar
- 1 large egg
- 1 large egg yolk
- 1/2 tsp vanilla extract
- 3/4 cup mashed overripe Chiquita bananas
- 1/2 cup (120ml) buttermilk
- 1/2 cup (86g) mini semi-sweet chocolate chips, plus more for garnish
- 1 1/2 Chiquita bananas sliced, for garnish

FROSTING

- 8 oz cream cheese, nearly at room temperature
- 1/2 cup (4 oz) unsalted butter, nearly at room temperature
- 2 1/2 cups (310g) powdered sugar
- 1 tsp vanilla extract

DIRECTIONS

CUPCAKES

1. Preheat oven to 350 degrees. In a mixing bowl whisk together flour, baking soda and salt for 20 seconds. In the bowl of an electric stand mixer fitted with the paddle attachment, whip together butter and granulated sugar until pale and fluffy.
2. Mix in egg then mix in egg yolk and vanilla. Blend in mashed bananas. Add 1/3 of the flour mixture then mix just until combined, pour in 1/2 of the buttermilk and mix just until combined, repeat process with flour and buttermilk once more.
3. Finish by adding in remaining 1/3 of the flour mixture and the chocolate chips and mix just until combined. Scrape down sides and bottom of bowl and fold batter.

4. Divide batter among 12 paper lined muffin cups, filling each about 3/4 full. Bake in preheated oven until toothpick inserted into center of cupcake comes out clean, about 20 - 25 minutes.

FROSTING

1. In the bowl of an electric stand mixer cream together cream cheese and butter until smooth.
2. Mix in powdered sugar and blend until light and fluffy.

ASSEMBLE

3. Cool in pan several minutes then transfer to a wire rack and cool completely. frost with cream cheese frosting, top with 2 banana slices and sprinkle with chocolate chips.
4. Store in refrigerator in an air tight container and allow to rest at room temperature about 5 - 10 minutes before serving.

PUMPKIN CHOCOLATE CUPCAKES(2ND VERSION)

INGREDIENTS

CHOCOLATE BATTER

- ⅓ cup flour
- 2 tablespoons cocoa powder
- ¼ teaspoon baking soda
- ¼ teaspoon instant espresso powder
- 4 teaspoons neutral-flavored oil
- ½ teaspoon vanilla extract
- ¼ packed cup light brown sugar
- ⅓ cup buttermilk
- 1 large egg yolk

PUMPKIN BATTER

- 7 tablespoons flour
- ½ teaspoon baking powder
- ⅛ teaspoon baking soda
- ¼ teaspoon salt
- ½ teaspoon cinnamon
- ¼ teaspoon freshly grated nutmeg
- ¼ teaspoon ground ginger
- 1 large egg white
- ½ cup canned pumpkin puree
- ¼ packed cup light brown sugar
- 3 tablespoons neutral-flavored oil
- 3 tablespoons granulated sugar

VANILLA BUTTERCREAM

- 4 tablespoons unsalted butter, softened
- 1½ cups powdered sugar
- ½ vanilla bean, scraped
- ¼ teaspoon vanilla extract
- pinch of salt
- 1-2 tablespoons heavy cream

DIRECTIONS

Preheat the oven to 350, and line 6 cups in a muffin pan with liners.

CHOCOLATE BATTER

1. Whisk together the flour, cocoa powder, baking soda and espresso powder. Set aside.
2. Whisk together the oil, vanilla, brown sugar, buttermilk, and egg yolk. Set aside.

PUMPKIN BATTER

1. Whisk together the flour, baking powder, baking soda, salt, and spices. Set aside.
2. Whisk together the egg white, pumpkin, brown sugar, oil, and granulated sugar. Set aside.
3. When ready to fill the pan, mix the dry Ingredients for the chocolate cupcakes into its wet Ingredients.
4. Mix the dry Ingredients for the pumpkin cupcakes into its wet Ingredients.
5. Layer the batters in the cupcake liners.
6. Bake the cupcakes for 17-20 minutes, or until a toothpick inserted comes out with only moist crumbs.
7. Let the cupcakes cool in the pan for 1 minute, and then move to a cooling rack to cool completely.

FROSTING

1. Beat the butter until light and fluffy, about 1-2 minutes. Slowly add the powdered sugar, vanilla bean, vanilla extract, and salt while continuously beating.
2. Add the heavy cream, starting with just 1 tablespoon of the cream, and add more if needed.
3. Frost the cupcakes with the vanilla bean frosting, and serve.

APPLE CIDER CRANBERRY CUPCAKES

INGREDIENTS

CUPCAKES

- 2 cups all-purpose flour
- 1 teaspoon baking powder
- 1 teaspoon Saigon cinnamon
- ½ teaspoon kosher salt
- ½ cup unsalted butter, melted and cooled
- 1 cup light brown sugar, packed
- 4 large eggs
- 1 teaspoon vanilla extract
- 1 cup apple cider, natural & fresh

FROSTING

- 8 ounces cold cream cheese
- ½ cup unsalted butter, cold but still firm
- 1/8 teaspoon kosher salt
- ½ teaspoon Saigon cinnamon
- 3 ½ cups powdered sugar, sifted
- ½ teaspoon vanilla
- heavy cream if needed
- Spiced Apple Cider Cranberry Sauce

CINNAMON SUGAR PIE CRUSTS

- Your favorite pie crust
- ¼ teaspoon Saigon Cinnamon
- ¼ cup sugar + more for rolling

DIRECTIONS

CUPCAKES

1. Preheat the oven 350°. Line standard muffin tins with cupcake liners.

2. Whisk flour, baking powder, cinnamon and salt together in a medium bowl and set aside.
3. Using a hand mixer beat together the butter and sugar on medium-high speed until thick and lighter in color, 2-3 minutes.
4. Add the eggs one at a time, beating well after each addition. Add the vanilla with the last egg. Scrape down the sides of the bowl between each addition.
5. Alternately add flour and apple cider in three additions on low speed beginning and ending with flour, scraping down the sides of the bowl as needed.
6. Scoop or pour the batter into the liners ¾ full. Bake in preheated oven for 15-20 minutes.
7. Remove from tins immediately and let cool on a wire rack. They must be completely cool before frosting.

FROSTING

1. Using the paddle attachment of your stand mixer, beat cream cheese, butter, salt and cinnamon on medium-high speed until smooth and creamy, approximately 2-3 minutes.
2. Reduce speed to low and gradually add the powdered sugar, mixing until incorporated. Add the vanilla after the last addition and mix until incorporated.

3. PIE CRUSTS

4. Sprinkle a generous amount of sugar over a solid surface. Roll out your pie crusts in granulated sugar.
5. Cut out little leaves or shapes and place 1 inch apart on a baking tray.
6. Sprinkle generously with the cinnamon sugar mixture. Bake in preheated oven for 15-20 minutes or until they puff up and are brown around the edges.

BUTTERED CUPCAKES

INGREDIENTS

- 3 1/4 cup sifted cake flour
- 4 1/2 teaspoons baking powder
- 1/2 teaspoon salt
- 1 teaspoon vanilla extract
- 1 cup + 2 tablespoons whole milk
- 1/2 cup + 6 tablespoons softened butter
- 1 3/4 cups sugar
- 5 egg whites (room temperature)
- 24+ buttered pop corn jelly belly beans

FROSTING

- 5 egg whites (room temperature)
- 1 cup + 2 tablespoons sugar
- small pinch of salt
- 2 cups softened butter
- 1/2 teaspoon vanilla extract
- yellow food color

DIRECTIONS

1. Sift together the cake flour, baking powder and salt. Set aside.
2. With an electric mixer, or stand mixer, beat the egg whites until stiff peaks begin to form. Set aside.
3. With an electric mixer, or stand mixer cream the softened butter until smooth. Scrape down the sides of the bowl, add the sugar and beat again until the mixture begins to looked whipped.
4. Begin adding the flour mixture and milk in intervals, mixing in between. Add in the vanilla extract as well.
5. Fold the whipped egg whites into the batter using a rubber spatula. Cut through the batter down the center, then swiftly stir to one side. Keep mixing in this manner until nearly no lumps remain and the batter looks cohesive in texture.
6. Spoon batter into prepared baking cups. Add a jelly bean the center of each cupcake.
7. Bake at 350° for 20-22 minutes for standard size, and 17-18 minutes for mini size cupcakes.

FROSTING

1. Combine the egg whites and sugar in a metal or glass mixing bowl. Set this over a pot of simmering water. Whisk until the egg whites are slightly warmed and the sugar and completely dissolved.
2. Using an electric mixer or stand mixer, beat the egg whites until stiff, glossy peaks form.
3. With the mixer running on low, add the softened butter a few tablespoons at a time.
4. Turn the mixer up a few notches to whip the batter for a few seconds.

BAR CUPCAKES

INGREDIENTS

CUPCAKES

- 1½ cups all purpose flour
- 1½ teaspoons baking powder
- ½ teaspoon salt
- 1 cup sugar
- ½ cup butter, at room temperature
- 2 eggs
- 1 teaspoon vanilla extract
- 1 cup buttermilk

MILKY WAY FROSTING

- 12 oz (about 12 fun-sized) Milky Way candy bars
- ⅓ cup butter
- 1½ tablespoons milk
- 1 teaspoon vanilla
- 2 cups powdered sugar
- additional chopped or cut Milky Way candy bars, for garnish

DIRECTIONS

Preheat the oven to 325F. Line 18 cupcake tins with paper liners.

In a bowl, whisk together the flour, baking powder and salt.

In the bowl of a stand mixer, beat together the sugar and the butter until light and fluffy, about 2 minutes. Add in the eggs, one at a time, beating well after each addition. Scrape the sides of the bowl as needed. Beat in the vanilla.

Add one-third of the flour mixture, beat to combine, then half of the buttermilk. Repeat with another third of the flour and the remaining buttermilk, followed by the remaining flour, beating just until combined between each addition.

Divide the mixture between the 18 cups, filling each about ⅔ full. Bake until a tester comes out clean, about 18 minutes. Remove from the pans and cool completely.

1. Bring a small saucepan with about 1 inch of water to a simmer. Combine the candy bars, butter and milk in a large heat-proof bowl and set over the simmering water. Cook for 10-12 minutes, stirring frequently, until the candy bars have melted and the mixture is smooth.
2. Remove the bowl from the heat and stir in the vanilla. Add the powdered sugar and beat with a hand mixer until the mixture is smooth.
3. Let the mixture sit for 10 to 15 minutes until just warm to the touch. Transfer the frosting to a piping bag fitted with a large round tip. Pipe the frosting onto the cooled cupcakes.
4. Top with a candy bar piece.

CHOCOLATE CHIP COOKIE DOUGH CUPCAKES

INGREDIENTS

COOKIE DOUGH

- 1 1/2 cups flour
- 1/4 tsp. baking soda
- 1/4 tsp. salt
- 1/2 cup softened, unsalted butter
- 1/4 cup white sugar
- 1/4 cup brown sugar
- 2 tsp. vanilla
- 1 egg, at room temperature
- 1 cup semi-sweet chocolate chips

CHOCOLATE CUPCAKES

- 1/2 cup plus 1 tbsp. cocoa powder
- 1/2 cup plus 1 tbsp. hot water
- 2 1/4 cups all-purpose flour
- 3/4 tsp. baking soda
- 3/4 tsp. baking powder
- 1/2 tsp. salt
- 2 sticks plus 1 tbsp. (17 tbsp. total) butter, at room temperature
- 1 2/3 cups granulated sugar
- 3 large eggs, at room temperature
- 1 tbsp. vanilla extract
- 3/4 cup sour cream

FROSTING

- 3 sticks unsalted butter, room temperature
- 3/4 cup light brown sugar
- 1 tsp. kosher salt
- 2 1/2 cups powdered sugar
- 2 1/2 tsp. vanilla
- 1 cup flour
- 3-4 tbsp. milk

DIRECTIONS

COOKIE DOUGH

1. Mix the flour, baking soda, and salt in a bowl and set aside. In another bowl, beat the butter and sugars until they are light and fluffy, about 2 to 3 minutes.
2. Add the egg and vanilla and stir until mixed, about 1 minute. Gradually add flour and mix until a dough forms. Fold in the chocolate chips. Form dough into no larger than tbsp.-sized balls and freeze.

CUPCAKES

1. Preheat the oven to 350 F. Line 2 standard cupcake pans with paper liners. In a glass liquid measuring cup, combine the cocoa powder and hot water and whisk until smooth.
2. In a medium bowl whisk together the flour, baking soda, baking powder, and salt; set aside.
3. In a medium saucepan over medium heat, combine the butter and sugar.
4. Cook, whisking occasionally, until the mixture is smooth and the butter is completely melted. Transfer the mixture to the bowl of an electric mixer and beat on medium-low speed until the mixture is cool, about 4-5 minutes.
5. Add the eggs one at a time, mixing well after each addition and scraping down the sides of the bowl as needed. Blend in the vanilla and then the cocoa mixture until smooth. With the mixer on low speed, add the flour mixture in three additions alternating with the sour cream, beginning and ending with the dry Ingredients and mixing each addition just until incorporated.
6. Place one frozen cookie dough ball in each paper liner of one tray.
7. Divide the batter evenly between the prepared liners, filling no more than 2/3 full. If you live at a high altitude or have had overflowing cupcakes in the past, err on the side of filling the liner of one cupcake 1/2 full and baking it alone first to judge how the cupcake will rise in the oven.
8. Bake the cupcakes for about 18-20 minutes. Remove the cupcakes to a wire rack to cool completely.
9. Repeat process with remaining cake batter and cookie dough. Cool cupcakes to room temperature before frosting, about 1 hour.

FROSTING

1. Beat butter, brown sugar, and salt together with mixer until light and fluffy, 3-4 minutes. Add powdered sugar and vanilla until combined.

2. Add flour and mix until just combined. If necessary, add 1 tbsp. milk at a time until desired consistency is reached.

LEMON MERINGUE CUPCAKES

INGREDIENTS

CUPCAKES

- 240ml / 1 cup almond milk
- Juice and zest from 1 medium lemon
- 150g / 1¼ cup self-raising flour
- 2 tbsp corn starch
- 80ml / ⅓ cup mild olive oil
- 150g / ¾ cup caster sugar
- 1 tsp vanilla extract

LEMON CURD

- Juice from 2 large lemons (to make about 120ml / ½ cup)
- 120ml / ½ cup almond milk
- 150g / ¾ cup caster sugar
- 2 tbsp corn starch
- 1 tbsp dairy-free butter

FROSTING

- Liquid from a 400g tin of chickpeas
- 50g / ½ cup icing sugar
- ½ tsp cream of tartar
- 1 tsp vanilla extract

DIRECTIONS

LEMON CUPCAKES

1. Preheat the oven to 170c and line a cupcake tray with liners.
2. Mix the almond milk and lemon juice & zest together in a large bowl and leave to for a few minutes.
3. Meanwhile, mix the flour and corn starch together in a separate bowl.
4. Add the oil, sugar and vanilla extract to the almond milk and then the flour mixture. Stir everything until just combined.

5. Divide equally between 12 cupcake cases and bake for 20-25 minutes until golden brown and spongey to the touch.
6. Leave to cool completely before coring the centre of the cupcakes.

LEMON CURD

Whilst the cupcakes are baking, make the curd by mixing the lemon juice, half of the almond milk, sugar, and corn starch together in a small saucepan.

Continually whisk over medium heat until it starts to boil. The mixture should start thickening.

Remove from heat and whisk in the rest of the almond milk and dairy-free butter.

It should be a smooth, thick, runny consistency. Leave it to cool in the fridge where it will thicken some more.

Once cooled, pour into the centre of the cupcakes until it reaches the brim.

FROSTING

1. In a stand mixer, whisk the chickpea water on high for a few minutes, until it starts to turn frothy
2. Slowly add in the icing sugar, a little at a time.
3. Add the cream of tartar.
4. Keep whisking on high speed for approximately 10 minutes until the mixture forms stiff peaks.
5. Add the vanilla and whisk again for another minute.
6. Add the mixture to a piping bag fitted with a large star nozzle. Pipe swirls on top of the cupcakes.

NUTELLA CHEESECAKE CUPCAKES

INGREDIENTS

- 12 Oreos, finely crushed
- 1 1/2 Tbsp salted butter, melted
- 6 Tbsp granulated sugar
- 1 1/2 Tbsp all-purpose flour
- 12 oz cream cheese, well softened
- 2 large eggs
- 1/4 cup milk
- 1/4 cup sour cream
- 1/2 tsp vanilla extract
- 1/2 cup Nutella

TOPPING

- 1 cup heavy cream
- 3 Tbsp powdered sugar
- 1/4 c chopped, toasted hazelnuts
- chopped chocolate, for garnish

DIRECTIONS

1. Preheat oven to 325 degrees. In a mixing using a fork, blend together crushed Oreos and butter. Divide mixture evenly among 12 paper lined muffin cups, adding a heaping 1 Tbsp to each. Press crumbs into an even layer. Bake in preheated oven 5 minutes. Remove from oven and allow to cool while preparing filling.
2. In a mixing bowl whisk together granulated sugar and flour. Add in cream cheese and using an electric hand mixer, whip just until smooth. Blend in eggs. Add in milk, sour cream and vanilla and mix just until combined, then add in Nutella and mix just until combined.
3. Tap bowl forcefully against countertop about 30 times to release some of the air bubbles. Divide mixture among muffin cups, pouring over crusts and filling each cup nearly full, about 1/4 cup batter in each. Bake in 325 degree oven 20 - 24 minutes until centers only jiggle slightly.
4. Remove from oven and allow to cool at room temperature 30 minutes, then cover loosely with plastic wrap or foil and transfer to refrigerator and chill 3 hours. Serve with sweetened whipped cream, hazelnuts, chopped chocolate or chocolate. Store in refrigerator in an airtight container.

5. In a mixing bowl, using an electric hand mixer, whip heavy cream on high speed until soft peaks form. Add in powdered sugar and whip until stiff peaks form. Store in refrigerator.

SWEET POTATO CUPCAKES

INGREDIENTS

- 1 1/2 cups firmly packed brown sugar
- 1/3 cup butter, room temperature
- 2 eggs
- 1 tsp vanilla
- 2 3/4 cups all purpose flour
- 1 Tbsp baking powder
- 1 tsp pumpkin pie spice
- 3/4 tsp salt
- 3/4 cup whole milk
- 1 cup cooked sweet potatoes
- 1/3 cup bourbon

CANDIED PECANS

- 1 cup sugar
- 1 cup water
- pecan halves

VANILLA GLAZE

- 2 cups sifted confectioner's sugar
- 1 Tbsp butter, room temperature
- 1 tsp vanilla
- 3-4 Tbsps milk

SYRUP

- 1 1/2 cup sugar
- 1/2 cup water
- 1 tsp butter
- 2 tsp vanilla
- 2 Tbsp bourbon

DIRECTIONS

1. Preheat oven to 350 degrees.
2. Line cupcake trays with 24 baking cups.
3. Whisk together flour, baking powder, pumpkin pie spice and salt in a large bowl.
4. In another large mixing bowl, mix brown sugar, butter and eggs until fluffy.
5. Add sweet potatoes and vanilla. Mix well.
6. Add 1/3 of flour mixture to sugar mixture until combined. Add bourbon. Add second 1/3 of flour mixture. Add milk. Add final 1/3 flour mixture.
7. Mix well with each addition.
8. Fill baking cups.
9. Bake for 12-15 minutes or until done.
10. Cool completely.

CANDIED PECANS

1. Add equal parts sugar and water to a pot. Add pecans. Simmer for about six minutes. Drain syrup off.
2. In a deep fryer at about 375 degrees add pecans to oil. Heat for about 30 seconds to a minute or until frying noise.
3. Lay on parchment paper lined tray and cool slightly.
4. Sprinkle some extra sugar on top to make them prettier.
5. Allow to dry completely.

VANILLA GLAZE

1. In a medium bowl, mix sugar and butter. Add vanilla.
2. Add milk 1 Tbsp at a time until you get the desired consistency.
3. Mix until smooth.

SYRUP

1. In a small saucepan, bring sugar and water to a boil.
2. Boil for five minutes and add remaining Ingredients. Cook until a syrupy consistency.
3. Add one candied pecan to each cupcake if you don't eat them all first.

CHOCOLATE MOCHA CUPCAKE

INGREDIENTS

CUPCAKE

- 1 cup (4.5 ounces) all purpose flour
- 1 cup plus 2 tablespoons (7.3 ounces) sugar
- 1/3 cup plus 2 tablespoons (1.5 ounces) Cocoa Powder
- 1/2 teaspoon baking soda
- 1/4 teaspoon salt
- 1/2 cup (1 stick) unsalted butter, melted and warm
- 2 large eggs
- 1 teaspoon pure vanilla extract
- 2 tablespoon instant coffee
- 1/2 cup hot coffee
- 1/2 cup crushed Whoppers

CHOCOLATE SWISS MERINGUE

- 5 large egg whites
- 11/2 cup sugar
- 4 sticks unsalted butter, diced and softened
- 1/4 teaspoon salt
- 1 tablespoon vanilla
- 2 tablespoons unsweetened cocoa powder
- 10 ounces bittersweet chocolate, melted and cooled

CHOCOLATE SAUCE

- 2/3 cups dark chocolate
- 2 tablespoons heavy cream
- 4 tablespoons powdered sugar, sifted
- 4-5 tablespoons water, warm

DIRECTIONS

CUPCAKE

1. Add flour, cocoa powder, sugar, baking soda, and salt in a bowl and mix thoroughly to combine. Add in the butter, eggs, and vanilla and beat on medium speed for one minute.
2. Add instant coffee and half of the hot coffee into the mixture and beat for 20 seconds. Scrape the sides of the bowl and add remaining coffee. Beat for 20-30 seconds until the batter is smooth. The batter will be thin enough to pour.
3. Divide it evenly among the lined cups. Bake 18-22 minutes just until a toothpick inserted into a few of the cupcakes comes out clean. Set the pan on a rack to cool. Frost the cupcakes when they are completely cool.

CHOCOLATE SWISS MERINGUE

1. Combine egg whites and sugar in a bowl placed over simmering water. Bring mixture to 160 degrees F while whisking constantly.
2. Transfer mixture to stand mixer bowl, fitted with a whisk attachment and beat on medium high speed until mixture cools and doubles in volume and forms stiff peaks; about 10-12 minutes.
3. Add butter in one piece at a time, mixing to incorporate after each addition. The mixture may appear clumpy and almost curdled looking-this is normal. Keep mixing and it will become even and smooth again. Add salt and vanilla and mix to combine. Add cooled chocolate and mix to combine.

CHOCOLATE SAUCE

1. Place chocolate and heavy cream in a bowl over simmering water. Let chocolate and cream sit for 2-3 minutes to melt without stirring.
2. Stir slowly mixture to combine. Add powdered sugar and mix to combine. Add water 1 tablespoon at a time, mixing after each addition until pouring consistency is reached. Set aside and let sauce cool to warm.

ASSEMBLY

1. Frost cooled cupcakes. Freeze frosted cupcakes for ten minutes. Drizzle chocolate pour over chocolate frosting.
2. Sprinkle crushed Whoppers on chocolate sauce. Finish with a small swirl of frosting and a Whopper.

CARAMEL APPLE CUPCAKES

INGREDIENTS

CUPCAKES

- 1 2/3 cups all purpose flour
- 1/2 cup brown sugar
- 1/2 cup sugar
- 1/4 tsp baking soda
- 1 1/4 tsp baking powder
- 1 tsp cinnamon
- 1/8 tsp nutmeg
- 3 egg whites
- 2 tsp vanilla extract
- 1/2 cup sour cream
- 1/2 cup milk
- 3/4 cup salted butter, slightly melted
- 1 large apple, chopped

BUTTERCREAM

- 1 cup butter
- 1 cup shortening
- 8 cups powdered sugar
- 3/4 cup + 2 tbsp caramel sauce

DIRECTIONS

1. Preheat oven to 350 degrees.
2. Whisk together flour, sugars, baking soda, baking powder, cinnamon and nutmeg in a large mixing bowl.
3. Add egg whites, vanilla extract, sour cream, milk and butter and mix on medium speed just until smooth. Do not over mix.
4. Stir in chopped apples
5. Fill cupcake liners about 3/4 full.
6. Bake 17-19 minutes.
7. Allow to cool for 1-2 minutes, then remove to cooling rack to finish cooling.

8. To make the buttercream, combine butter and shortening and mix until smooth. Add 4 cups of powdered sugar and mix until smooth.
9. Add caramel sauce and mix until smooth. Add remaining powdered sugar and mix until smooth.
10. Top cupcakes with icing and a drizzle of caramel.

DULCE DE LECHE CUPCAKES

INGREDIENTS

- 2 tablespoons canola oil
- 1 stick unsalted butter, melted and slightly cooled
- 1/2 cup semi-sweet chocolate chips
- 1/2 cup granulated sugar
- 1/2 cup light brown sugar
- 2 large eggs + 1 large egg yolk, at room temperature
- 1/2 teaspoon vanilla
- 3/4 cup + 3 tablespoons all-purpose flour, not packed
- 1/2 teaspoon baking soda
- 1 teaspoon baking powder
- 1/2 cup unsweetened cocoa powder
- 3/4 teaspoon salt
- 1/2 cup full fat sour cream
- 1/2 cup boiling water
- 1/2 cup dulce de leche

BUTTERCREAM

- 1 stick unsalted butter, VERY soft
- 3 cups confectioners sugar, sifted
- 3/4 cup unsweetened cocoa powder, sifted
- 3 tablespoons half and half, more if needed
- 1 heaping tablespoon dulce de leche
- 1/2 teaspoon salt

TOPPING

- Dulce de leche, for drizzling
- Flaky Sea Salt

DIRECTIONS

CUPCAKES

1. Preheat the oven to 350 degrees (F). Line a 12-cup cupcake/muffin tin with cupcake liners and lightly spray the liners with non-stick spray.
2. Melt the oil, butter,and chocolate together in the microwave, heating in 30 second increments, and stirring between increments each time. Whisk mixture until completely smooth. Set aside to cool.
3. In a medium sized bowl combine the flour, baking soda, baking powder, cocoa powder, and salt; stir together until thoroughly combined; set aside.
4. In a large bowl, whisk together the eggs, yolk, sugars, and vanilla; beat until smooth. Add the cooled oil/butter/chocolate mixture and whisk until smooth.
5. Add half of the flour mixture, then half of the sour cream. Repeat the process until everything is added, and be sure to mix until just combined.
6. Quickly stir in the hot water until evenly combined.
7. Divide the batter among the 12 liners in your prepared pan. Bake for 16-18 minutes.
8. Once cooled, use a small sharp knife to carve out a small hole on the top of each not carving too wide or deep. Fill each hole with 1-2 teaspoons of dulce de leche.

BUTTERCREAM

1. Sift together the confectioners sugar and cocoa powder, whisking well.
2. Using a mixer beat the butter on medium-high speed until creamy; about 2 minutes. Reduce speed to low and slowly add the sifted sugar/cocoa powder, alternating with the half and half; add in the dulce de leche and salt.
3. Once all of the Ingredients have been added, beat on medium-high speed until light and creamy and combined; at least 2 minutes. Add more cream to the frosting if it seems too thick; add a touch more sugar to the frosting if it seems too thin.
4. Frost cooled, filled cupcakes and top with more dulce de leche and flaky sea salt.

CHEESECAKE CUPCAKES

INGREDIENTS

- 2 pkg. (8 oz. each) Cream Cheese, softened
- 1 cup granulated sugar
- 1 tsp. butter extract
- 2 eggs
- 12 vanilla wafers
- 1 cup seedless raspberry jam
- 1 pt. fresh raspberries
- 2 Tbsp. powdered sugar for dusting

DIRECTIONS

1. Heat oven to 350°F.
2. Place a paper cupcake liner in each of 12 muffin cups.
3. Beat cream cheese with a hand-held electric mixer until fluffy. Add granulated sugar and butter extract, beating well. Add eggs, one at a time, beating well after each addition.
4. Place a vanilla wafer, flat-side down, in each muffin cup. Spoon cream cheese mixture over wafers. Bake for 20 minutes.
5. Allow tarts to cool completely. When cool, top each cheesecake cupcake with 1/2 Tbsp. of raspberry jam and fresh raspberries. Dust with powdered sugar.

PUMPKIN PIE CUPCAKES

INGREDIENTS

- 3 tbsp coconut flour
- 1 tsp pumpkin pie spice
- 1/4 tsp baking powder
- 1/4 tsp baking soda
- Pinch salt
- 1 cup pumpkin puree
- 1/3 cup Swerve Sweetener

- 1/4 cup heavy cream
- 1 large egg
- 1/2 tsp vanilla

DIRECTIONS

1. Preheat oven to 350F and line 6 muffin cups with paper liners.
2. In a small bowl, whisk together the coconut flour, pumpkin pie spice, baking powder, baking soda, and salt.
3. In a large bowl, whisk pumpkin puree, sweetener, cream, egg, and vanilla until well combined. Whisk in dry Ingredients.
4. Divide among prepared muffin cups and bake 25 to 30 minutes, until just puffed and barely set. Remove from oven and let cool in pan.
5. Refrigerate for at least one hour before serving. Dollop whipped cream generously on top.

MINT & CHOCOLATE CUPCAKES

INGREDIENTS

CHOCOLATE CUPCAKES

- 105 grams (3/4 cup) plain flour
- 20 grams (1/4 cup) cocoa powder
- 20 grams (1/4 cup) dutch processed cocoa powder
- 1/2 teaspoon baking soda
- 1/2 teaspoon baking powder
- 100 grams (1/2 cup) caster sugar
- 45 grams (1/4 cup) brown sugar
- 115 grams (1/2 cup or 1 stick) unsalted butter
- 2 large eggs
- 1 teaspoon vanilla extract
- 120 ml (1/2 cup) buttermilk

MINT FROSTING

- 115 grams (1/2 cup or 1 stick) unsalted butter, softened
- 435 grams (3 and 1/2 cups) icing or powdered sugar
- 3 tablespoons milk
- 1 teaspoon peppermint or mint extract
- A few drops of green food colouring
- 6 whole mint chocolate cookie or biscuit, cut in half

DIRECTIONS

1. Preheat the oven to 180C (360 F). Line a 12 hole muffin tin with patty cases. In a large mixing bowl, sift the flour, cocoa powders, baking soda, baking powder and then add the sugars and give it a stir. Pop the butter into the microwave for a short burst, 10 seconds or so at a time, until it is melted.
2. Give it a stir with a fork to eliminate any lumps. In a separate mixing bowl, add the eggs, vanilla and butter and whisk together until smooth.
3. Then add the wet mixture into the dry mixture, along with the buttermilk and gently fold until just combined.

4. Spoon the mixture into the prepared patty cases and pop into the oven. Bake for 18-20 minutes or until just cooked through. Set cakes out onto a wire rack and leave to cool completely.

MINT FROSTING

1. Add the butter to a large mixing bowl and beat with an electric mixer until pale and creamy. Gently sift in the icing sugar, one cup at a time. Add a tablespoon or two of milk to help loosen up the mixture. Add the mint extract and continue to beat.
2. Add a tablespoon of milk if needed. The icing should be nice and creamy but thick enough to hold its shape. Add in green food colouring until it reaches your desired colour. Pipe the icing onto the cupcakes using a piping bag and a large star tip. Top each cupcake with half a chocolate mint cookie.

PUDDING CUPCAKES

INGREDIENTS

- 1 3.4-ounce box instant chocolate pudding mix
- 1 3/4 cup whole milk
- 12 ounce container whipped topping, thawed, divided use
- 24 chocolate cupcakes, baked and cooled
- 15 chocolate sandwich cookies, crushed into crumbs
- 24 Campfire Ghoster Roasters

DIRECTIONS

1. In a large bowl, beat pudding mix and milk on medium speed until thoroughly combined and thickened. Fold 1 cup whipped topping into the pudding until no streaks remain. Cover and refrigerate for one hour.
2. Using a sharp paring knife, or an apple corer, core the center of each cupcake. Reserve the cake pieces that were removed.
3. Fill a piping bag or large zip-top bag with the chilled pudding.
4. Pipe pudding into the center of each cupcake. Cover the pudding with reserved cake pieces that you cored from the cupcake.
5. Fill a large piping bar or large zip-top bag with remaining whipped topping.
6. Pipe whipped topping onto cupcakes. Sprinkle each cupcake with crushed cookies and top with a Campfire® Ghoster Roaster.
7. Refrigerate cupcakes until ready to serve.

HALLOWEEN CUPCAKES

INGREDIENTS

CHOCOLATE CUPCAKES

- ½ cup boiling water
- ¼ cup unsalted butter, softened
- 1 cup sugar
- ⅓ cup good quality cocoa powder
- 1½ cups all purpose flour
- ½ teaspoon salt
- ½ teaspoon baking powder
- ½ teaspoon baking soda
- 1 large egg, beaten
- ½ cup sour cream
- 1 teaspoon vanilla extract

BUTTERCREAM FROSTING

- 1⅓ cups unsalted butter, softened
- 8oz marshmallow fluff (about 2 cups)
- 1 tablespoon vanilla extract
- 1 teaspoon heavy cream
- 2⅔ cups confectioners sugar
- 24 mini chocolate chips (for eyes)

DIRECTIONS

CHOCOLATE CUPCAKES

1. Preheat over to 350 degrees.
2. Line a 12-count muffin tin with cupcake cups. Reserve.
3. In the bowl of a stand mixer, combine the butter, the sugar, the cocoa powder and the boiling water. Beat on low until smooth and the sugar is dissolved.
4. In a separate bowl, combine the flour, the salt, the baking powder and the baking soda. Reserve.
5. In a third bowl, beat the egg and add the sour cream and the vanilla extract. Whisk until smooth. Reserve.

6. With the mixer on low, add ½ the dry Ingredients to the butter/sugar/boiling water mixture. Then, add the egg/sour cream and finish with the remaining of the flour. Mix just until the flour is incorporated.
7. Pour the batter into the cupcake cups, about ⅔ full.
8. Bake the cupcakes for 20 to 25 minutes or until a toothpick inserted in the center of a cupcake comes out clean.
9. Cool in the pan for 5 minutes. Remove from the pan and cool completely before frosting.

FROSTING

1. In the bowl of a stand mixer, combine the butter and the marshmallow fluff. Beat until creamy and smooth.
2. Add the vanilla extract and the heavy cream and beat until incorporated.
3. With the mixer on low, slowly add the confectioners sugar. Once incorporated, turn the speed up and beat for 1 minute, until light and fluffy. Add a pinch of salt if the frosting is too sweet.
4. Frost cooled cupcakes and decorate with the eyes.

GLASS CUPCAKES(HALLOWEEN)

INGREDIENTS

CUPCAKES

- 2 cups all-purpose flour
- 2 cups sugar
- 2 tablespoons sugar
- 1 cup unsweetened dark cocoa powder
- 2 teaspoons baking soda
- 1 teaspoon baking powder
- 1/2 teaspoon salt
- 2 eggs
- 1 cup cold coffee
- 1 cup buttermilk
- 1/2 cup vegetable oil

FROSTING

- 1 cup unsalted butter, slightly softened
- 1 package cream cheese
- 2 teaspoons pure vanilla extract
- 4 to 4½ cups confectioners' sugar

GLASS

- ½ cup sugar
- ¼ cup light corn syrup
- parchment paper

BLOOD

- ½ cup corn syrup
- 1 tablespoons water
- 1 tablespoons of red food coloring
- 1 tablespoon of chocolate syrup
- 1 tablespoon of cornstarch

CUPCAKES

1. Preheat oven to 350 degrees. Place 24 liners in cupcake tin. In a large bowl, combine flour, sugar, cocoa, baking soda, baking powder and salt.
2. Make a well in the center and pour in the eggs, coffee, milk and oil. Mix until smooth; batter will be thin. Spoon into prepared cupcake pan.
3. Bake in the preheated oven 14-17 minutes, or until a toothpick inserted into the center of the cupcake comes out clean. Allow to cool completely.

FROSTING

1. Using an electric mixer and large bowl, beat butter until creamy. Add cream cheese and vanilla; beat until fully incorporated.
2. Gradually increase mixer speed to high and continue beating until light and fluffy, scraping down the sides of bowl as necessary with rubber spatula.
3. Gradually add 4 cups confectioners' sugar, beating on low speed (stir), until well combined. Add additional confectioners' sugar until desired consistency for piping. Beat on high speed until well combined and smooth while scraping down sides of bowl as necessary, about 1 to 2 minutes.
4. GLASS
   Mix sugar and corn syrup in a microwave-safe glass. Cover glass with plastic wrap and microwave 2 minutes Remove plastic wrap carefully to avoid steam. Stir and cover with a new piece of plastic wrap. microwave 1 minute.
5. Carefully pour onto parchment lined baking sheet, spread as thinly as possible, allow to cook completely, and break by smacking baking sheet on counter. Store shards in airtight container until ready to use.

BLOOD

1. Mix all of the Ingredients in the blender for a few seconds.

ASSEMBLY

2. Pipe icing on cupcake using an open star cupcake tip in a swirl working from the outside to the center. Add glass shards Drizzle with blood.

CORN CUPCAKES

INGREDIENTS

- 1 white cake mix
- 2 eggs
- 1 cup sour cream
- ½ cup milk
- ⅓ cup vegetable oil

GARNISH

- candy corns
- orange sprinkles

FROSTING

- 1 cup butter
- 4 cups powdered sugar
- ¼ teaspoon salt
- 1 teaspoon vanilla extract
- ⅓ cup heavy whipping cream

DIRECTIONS

3. Preheat oven to 350 degrees and line cupcake pan with paper liners.
4. Combine all Ingredients in a large bowl until incorporated. Scrape sides of bowl and then beat on medium-high speed for 3 minutes.
5. Divide batter in half and color one half orange and the other half yellow.
6. Fill paper liners with about 1-2 Tablespoons of yellow batter. Then top with 1-2 Tablespoons of orange batter. Bake according to cake mix package directions - about 15-18 minutes. Cool cupcakes.

FROSTING

7. In a mixing bowl, cream butter until fluffy. Add sugar and continue creaming until well blended. Add salt, vanilla, and whipping cream.
8. Blend on low speed until moistened. Beat at high speed until frosting is fluffy.

CUPCAKES WITH VANILLA BUTTERCREAM

INGREDIENTS

CUPCAKES

- 2¼ cups all-purpose flour
- ¾ cup unsweetened Dutch-process cocoa powder
- ½ cup granulated sugar
- ¾ cup brown sugar
- 1½ teaspoons baking soda
- ½ teaspoon salt
- 1 cup milk
- 1¼ cups original malted milk powder
- 1 cup vegetable oil
- 3 large eggs, at room temperature
- 1 cup sour cream, at room temperature
- 1 teaspoon vanilla extract

BUTTERCREAM

- 1½ cups unsalted butter, at room temperature
- ¾ cup original malted milk powder
- 2½ cups powdered sugar
- ½ teaspoon vanilla extract

DIRECTIONS

CUPCAKES

1. Preheat the oven to 350ºF. Line 30 muffin tins with cupcake liners.
2. In a large bowl, combine the flour, cocoa powder, granulated sugar, brown sugar, baking soda and salt. Whisk to combine.
3. Combine the milk and the malted milk powder in the bowl of a stand mixer and mix until the malted milk powder has dissolved. Add in the oil, then add in the eggs, one at a time, beating until combined.
4. Scrape down the sides of the bowl, then add in the dry Ingredients. Mix just until combined. Add the sour cream and vanilla, and mix just until combined.

5. Divide the batter between the prepared cups. Bake 20 minutes. Let cool completely before frosting.

BUTTERCREAM

1. Place the butter in the bowl of a stand mixer and beat until very light, about 2 minutes.
2. Add in the malted milk powder and mix another minute. Start adding in the powdered sugar, ½ cup at a time, until combined, then add in the vanilla.
3. Continue to beat for a couple more minutes, until light and fluffy.
4. Frost the cupcakes as desired.

CIDER&CARAMEL CUPCAKES

INGREDIENTS

CUPCAKES

- 1/3 cup butter
- 1 egg, room temperature
- 1 cup buttermilk, room temp
- 1 cup dark brown sugar
- 1/3 cup sugar
- 1/2 tablespoon vanilla extract
- 2 1/2 cups unbleached all-purpose flour
- 1/2 tablespoon cinnamon
- 1/2 teaspoon nutmeg
- 1 teaspoon salt
- 1 tablespoon baking soda
- 1 cup hard apple cider, room temperature

APPLE FILLING

- 3 tablespoons butter
- 2 large (or 3 small) Honey Crisp apples peeled, cored, and diced
- 1/4 cup dark brown sugar
- 1/4 teaspoon cinnamon
- 1/4 teaspoon kosher salt
- 1 1/2 teaspoons vanilla extract
- 1 teaspoon cornstarch
- 2 tablespoons whiskey

BUTTERCREAM

- 1 cup butter, at room temperature
- 3½ cups powdered sugar
- 1/4 teaspoon cinnamon
- 1 teaspoon vanilla extract
- 1-2 tablespoons whiskey

DIRECTIONS

CUPCAKES

1. Preheat oven to 350.
2. In a small saucepan, heat the butter over low-medium heat, whisking constantly. Once you see brown specks appear on the bottom, remove from the heat and continue whisking for 30 seconds. Pour into another bowl so that the butter doesn't continue to cook.
3. Once the butter is cool, add the buttermilk, egg, sugars and vanilla, and mix until well combined.
4. In a separate bowl, sift together the flour, cinnamon, nutmeg, salt, and baking soda.
5. Gradually add the flour to the wet Ingredients, scraping down the sides of the bowl after each addition.
6. Once the flour is fully incorporated, stir in the hard cider.
7. Line a muffin pan with liners, and spray them with non-stick spray. Fill each muffin tin slightly more than halfway with the batter.
8. Bake for 15-18 minutes, until a knife inserted in the center of a cupcake comes out clean.

FILLING

1. Melt the butter in a medium-sized saucepan over medium heat.
2. Add the apples, sugar, cinnamon, salt, and vanilla. Cook for about 10 minutes, until the apples are soft and have released their juices.
3. In a separate bowl, whisk together the whiskey with cornstarch, and then add to the pan with the apples and cook for about 3 minutes, until the liquid thickens. Set aside to cool.

FROSTING

1. Cream the butter for about 30 seconds. Add the powdered sugar, cinnamon, and vanilla extract. Beat on medium speed until creamy.
2. Add the whiskey and beat on high for 2-3 minutes, until fluffy and whipped.

ASSEMBLY

1. Core each cupcake with a cupcake corer, or with a knife angled at 45-degrees.
2. Fill the cupcake with apples, then top with buttercream, top the frosting with more apples.

PUMPKIN & CINNAMON BUTTERCREAM CUPCAKES

INGREDIENTS

- 1½ cups spelt flour
- ¾ cups organic cane sugar
- 1 teaspoon baking soda
- ½ teaspoon salt
- 1 teaspoon cinnamon
- ½ teaspoon ginger
- ⅛ teaspoon nutmeg
- pinch cloves
- 1 cup of pumpkin puree
- ⅓ cup organic canola oil
- 1 teaspoon vanilla extract
- 1 teaspoon apple cider vinegar
- ½ cup water

FROSTING

- 3 Tablespoons vegan buttery spread
- 2½ cups powdered sugar
- 1-2 Tablespoons unsweetened coconut milk
- ½ teaspoon cinnamon
- ½ teaspoon ginger
- pinch of cloves

DIRECTIONS

1. Preheat the oven to 350 degrees. Line a cupcake tin with paper liners.
2. In a medium bowl, whisk together the flour, sugar, baking soda, salt, cinnamon, ginger, nutmeg, and cloves. Set aside.
3. In a large bowl, combine the pumpkin puree, organic canola oil, vanilla, apple cider vinegar, and water. Stir well.
4. Add the dry Ingredients to the wet Ingredients and stir well to combine.
5. Spoon the batter into the cupcake liners, filling them about ⅔ full.
6. Bake at 350 degrees for about 16-18 minutes, or until a toothpick inserted in the center comes out clean.

1. Beat the buttery spread until fluffy. Sift the powdered sugar into the bowl and drizzle in a little coconut milk.
2. Alternate adding more sugar and milk until the frosting is thick and creamy.
3. Add the spices and mix again.
4. Spread or pipe frosting onto cooled cupcakes. Store leftover cupcakes in the refrigerator.

BLACK VELVET CUPCAKES

INGREDIENTS

CUPCAKES

- 1 cup granulated sugar
- 1/4 cup butter, room temperature
- 2 tbsp vegetable oil
- 1 egg
- 1 tsp black food coloring or soft gel paste
- 3 tbsp dark dutch-process cocoa powder
- 1 tsp pure vanilla extract
- 1/2 tsp salt
- 1/2 cup buttermilk, room temperature
- 1/2 tsp white vinegar
- 1 1/4 cup flour
- 1/4 tsp baking soda

FROSTING

- 1 8 oz. package of cream cheese, room temperature
- 1/4 cup butter, room temperature
- 3 1/2 cups powdered sugar
- 1 tsp pure vanilla extract
- 1 tsp black food coloring or gel paste

DIRECTIONS

CUPCAKES

1. Sift together the cocoa powder, flour, salt and baking powder in one bowl and set aside. Fitted with the whisk attachment, use your mixer to mix together the sugar, butter, oil and vanilla until fluffy.
2. Add the food coloring and beat to combine. Mix in the egg. Add 1/3 of the dry Ingredients and alternate with the buttermilk until all Ingredients are combined. Lastly, mix in the vinegar.

3. Distribute the batter among 12-14 cupcake liners and bake on 350 degrees for about 20 minutes until an inserted toothpick comes out clean. Remove from oven to cool on a wire rack.

FROSTING

1. To make this spooky black frosting, beat together the cream cheese and butter with a paddle attachment. Slowly mix in the powdered sugar until you reach your desired sweetness .
2. Then mix in the vanilla extract and black coloring until the frosting reaches its proper color.
3. Once the cupcakes have cooled, pipe the frosting onto the . Let in cool in the fridge.

PUMPKIN CUPCAKES

INGREDIENTS

CUPCAKES

- 2 cups all-purpose flour
- 1½ tsp ground cinnamon
- ½ tsp ground nutmeg
- ½ tsp ground ginger
- ¼ tsp ground cloves
- ½ tsp salt
- 2 tsp baking powder
- 1 tsp baking soda
- ½ cup butter, softened
- 1 cup light brown sugar, packed
- ⅓ cup granulated sugar
- 2 eggs
- 1 cup buttermilk
- 1 cup pumpkin puree
- 1 tsp vanilla extract

FROSTING

- 1 - ¼ oz packet of unflavored gelatin
- ¼ (scant) cup cool water
- 3 cups heavy whipping cream
- 2 tsp vanilla   extract
- ⅔ cup confectioners sugar

DIRECTIONS

CUPCAKES

1. Preheat the oven to 350 degrees.
2. Sift together the flour, spices, salt, baking powder, and baking soda; set aside.
3. Cream butter and both sugars with an electric mixer until light and fluffy.
4. Add the eggs one at a time.

5. Add the buttermilk and pumpkin puree, blending well and scraping down sides as needed.
6. Stir in the flour mixture, then the vanilla, mixing until just incorporated.
7. Divide the batter into cupcake wrapper lined cups of a muffin tray.
8. Bake about 15-18 minutes or until a toothpick comes out clean.
9. Cool in the pans for 5 minutes before removing to cool completely on a wire rack.

FROSTING

1. Combine gelatin and water in a small saucepan and let stand until thick.
2. Warm over low heat and stir until gelatin is softened and remove and cool, but do not allow to set.
3. Whip the heavy cream until thickened. Add confectioners sugar and vanilla, beating until it holds soft peaks.
4. Gradually add the gelatin to the whipped cream, beating constantly.
5. Continue to beat on med/high speed until it holds stiff peaks.
6. Frost cooled cupcakes immediately and serve, or refrigerate frosting until ready to use.

MINT&CHOCOLATE CUPCAKES

INGREDIENTS

CHOCOLATE CUPCAKES

- 75 g (2.7 oz.) butter
- ½ tsp. vanilla essence
- 100 ml (3.4 fl. oz.) hot water
- 150 ml (5.1 fl. oz.) whole milk
- 1 large egg, lightly beaten
- 300 g (10. 6 oz.) plain flour
- 100 g (3.5 oz.) dutch processed cocoa powder
- 1 tsp. bicarbonate of soda
- 1 tsp. baking powder
- 250 g (8.8 oz.) caster sugar
- Pinch of salt

MINT FROSTING

- 1 ½ (3 sticks) cups unsalted butter, softened
- 3 tbsp. heavy cream
- 1 tsp. vanilla extract
- 1 tbsp. peppermint essence
- ¼ tsp salt
- 3 cups (12 oz.) icing sugar
- 1 cup (6.2 oz.) dark chocolate chips
- 3 tbsp. fresh mint leaves, chopped

DIRECTIONS

CHOCOLATE CUPCAKES

1. Preheat an oven to 175 C (350 F). Line a 12 hole cupcake pan with cupcake liners.
2. Over a low heat, melt the butter. Once melted, remove from the heat and stir in the vanilla essence, water, milk and beaten egg. Set aside.
3. In a separate large bowl sift together the flour, cocoa powder, bicarbonate of soda, baking powder, sugar and salt.

4. In two batches, pour the liquid Ingredients into the bowl with the dry Ingredients and whisk until uniform, combined and smooth.
5. Divide the mixture evenly among the cupcake liners, filling them no more than ⅔rds full. Bake for 15 to 18 minutes or until a skewer inserted comes out clean. Leave to cool completely on a wire rack before frosting.

MINT FROSTING

1. Beat the butter, cream, vanilla, peppermint and salt together on medium speed until smooth, 2-3 minutes.
2. Reduce speed to low and slowly, in batches, add in the icing sugar. Beat until incorporated and smooth, 4 – 6 minutes.
3. Increase the mixer speed to medium-high and beat until the frosting is light and fluffy, 5 – 8 minutes. Add the chocolate chips and chopped mint leaves, and stir until just combined.

CHOCOLATE BLACKBERRY CUPCAKES

INGREDIENTS

- 10 ounces (285 grams) fresh blackberries
- 1 1/2 cups (190 grams) all-purpose flour
- 3/4 cup (150 grams) granulated sugar, divided
- 1/3 cup (60 grams) cocoa powder
- 2 teaspoons espresso powder
- 1 teaspoon baking soda
- 1/2 teaspoon salt
- 1 teaspoon vanilla extract
- 1/3 cup (78 ml) vegetable oil
- 1 cup (237 ml) milk of choice
- 6 ounces (170 grams) semi-sweet or bittersweet chocolate, chopped finely
- Fresh blackberries, for garnish

DIRECTIONS

In a large saucepan, combine the blackberries with 1/4 cup granulated sugar. Bring to a boil over medium heat and cook for about 10 minutes, stirring occasionally, until the berries burst and are swimming in their juices. Remove from heat.

Using a fine mesh strainer, strain out the liquid and save it for later use. Place the solid fruit back into the saucepan and set aside.

Preheat oven to 350 degrees F (180 degrees C). Line a cupcake pan with baking cups.

In a mixing bowl, whisk together the flour, sugar, cocoa, espresso powder, baking soda, and salt. Add the vanilla extract, oil, and milk. Using a spatula, mix the batter until smooth. Fold in the blackberry solids.

Divide batter evenly between 12 baking cups (about 3/4 full). Bake for 18-22 minutes, or until a toothpick inserted into the center comes out clean. Remove from baking pan and allow to cool to room temperature.

FROSTING

1. Place chopped chocolate into a mixing bowl. Warm the blackberry juice back up to boiling and pour over the chocolate, allowing it to set for 5 minutes before stirring until smooth.

2. Allow frosting to rest on the counter, stirring occasionally, until it cools down and thickens.
3. Beat the chocolate ganache for several minutes until it incorporates air and feels lighter.
4. Place frosting in a pastry bag and pipe frosting onto the cooled cupcakes. Garnish with fresh blackberries.

PEANUT BUTTER CUPCAKES

INGREDIENTS

CUPCAKES

- 1 cup all-purpose flour
- 1 teaspoon baking powder
- 1/4 teaspoon salt
- 6 tablespoons unsalted butter, at room temperature
- 3/4 cup chunky or smooth peanut butter
- 1 cup packed brown sugar
- 1 egg
- 1 1/2 teaspoons vanilla
- 1/2 cup milk

GANACHE

- 2 ounces bittersweet chocolate, chopped
- 1/2 teaspoon instant coffee granules
- 2 ounces heavy cream

PEANUT BUTTER BUTTERCREAM

- 1 cup unsalted butter, at room temperature (2 sticks)
- 1 cup powdered sugar, or more, to taste
- 1/8 teaspoon salt
- 1/2 teaspoon vanilla extract
- 3/4 cup peanut butter, at room temperature

DIRECTIONS

1. Heat the oven to 350 degrees. Line 12 muffin tin cups with paper cupcake liners.
2. Sift the flour, baking powder and salt in a medium bowl and set aside.
3. Using a stand mixer, beat the butter, peanut butter and brown sugar, on medium speed, until smooth and light in color, about 1 minute.
4. Mix in the egg. Add the vanilla and beat for 1 minute, or until the batter is smooth. On low speed, add the flour mixture in 3 additions and the milk in 2 additions, beginning

and ending with the flour mixture and mixing just until the flour is incorporated and the batter looks smooth.

5. Fill each paper liner with batter, about 1/3 inch below the top of the liner. Bake just until the tops feel firm and are lightly browned, about 20 minutes. There will be a few cracks on top. Cool the cupcakes for 10 minutes in the pan on a wire rack. Carefully remove cupcakes from pan to finish cooling.

GANACHE

1. Place the chocolate and coffee granules in a heatproof bowl. Heat the cream in a small sauce pan over medium heat, until it comes to a boil.
2. Pour the hot cream into the bowl with the chocolate and stir until completely mixed and glossy.

PEANUT BUTTER BUTTERCREAM

1. Beat everything in a bowl until smooth and blended.
2. Add in more powdered sugar, if needed, according to your preference.

ASSEMBLY

1. Spread a layer of chocolate ganache on top of the cupcake and then frost with the peanut butter buttercream.
2. Sprinkle with chopped nuts and chocolate sprinkles.

FUDGE CUPCAKES

INGREDIENTS

- 250 g butter (150 g for the cakes and 100 g for the frosting)
- 150 g sugar
- 3 large eggs
- 225 g self-raising flour
- 100 g mini fudge pieces (75 g for the cakes and 25 g for decorating the frosting)
- 200 g icing sugar
- 2 tablespoons of clear honey
- 2 tabs honeycomb pieces (for decor)

DIRECTIONS

FUDGE CUPCAKES

1. Pre-heat the oven 180 C.
2. Beat together the butter and sugar until light and fluffy.
3. Beat the eggs and gradually beat into the butter and sugar with a spoon or two of the flour to prevent curdling.
4. Fold in the rest of the flour to form a smooth thick batter. It needs to be thicker than a normal sponge mix otherwise the fudge pieces will sink.
5. Fold in 75 g of the fudge pieces and spoon the mixture evenly into 12 large muffin cases.
6. Bake for 20 minutes or until risen and golden brown.

FROSTING

1. Combine 100 g of butter with 200 g of icing sugar and 1 tablespoon of clear honey. If the mix is too dry then add the second spoon of honey.
2. Pipe or spread onto the cakes and sprinkle with the remaining 25 g of fudge pieces and the honeycomb pieces.

CHOCOLATE & COOKIE CUPCAKES

INGREDIENTS

COOKIE DOUGH

- 1 cup unsalted butter at room temperature
- 3/4 cup sugar
- 3/4 cup brown sugar
- 4 tbsp whole milk
- 1 tbsp vanilla
- 2 1/2 cups all-purpose flour
- 1/4 tsp. salt
- 1 cup mini chocolate chips

CUPCAKES

- 1 1/2 c unsalted butter, room temperature
- 1 1/2 cups light brown sugar, packed
- 4 large eggs, room temperature
- 2 2/3 cups all-purpose flour
- 1 tsp. baking powder
- 1 tsp. baking soda
- 1/4 tsp. kosher salt
- 1 cup whole milk, room temperature
- 2 tsp. vanilla extract

DIRECTIONS

COOKIE DOUGH

1. Combine the butter and sugars in a mixing bowl and cream on medium-high speed until light and fluffy.   Beat in milk and vanilla until incorporated and smooth.
2. Mix in the flour and salt until just combined. Stir in the chocolate chips.
3. Using a small scoop, shape the dough into balls or tubes. Freeze on a parchment lined baking sheet overnight.

PUMPKIN AND CHOCOLATE CREAM CUPCAKES

INGREDIENTS

- ¾ cup unsweetened cocoa powder
- 1½ cups all-purpose flour
- 1½ cups sugar
- 1½ teaspoons baking soda
- ¾ teaspoon baking powder
- 1 teaspoon salt
- 2 large eggs
- ½ cup warm water
- ¾ cup buttermilk
- 5 tablespoons safflower oil
- 1 teaspoon pure vanilla extract

FROSTING

- 7 tablespoons butter, softened
- 5 ounces cream cheese, softened
- ¾ cup pumpkin puree
- 2 ½ cups powdered sugar, sifted

DIRECTIONS

1. Preheat oven to 350 degrees. Line standard muffin tins with paper liners; set aside. In the bottom of a stand mixer, whisk together cocoa powder, flour, sugar, baking soda, baking powder, and salt.
2. Switch to the paddle attachment, turn the mixer on low and add eggs, warm water, buttermilk, oil, and vanilla, and mix until smooth.. Scrape down the sides and bottom of bowl to make sure everything is incorporated.
3. Divide batter evenly among muffin cups, filling each ⅔ full. Bake until tops spring back when touched, about 20 minutes, rotating once halfway through baking. Transfer to a wire rack; let cool completely.
4. In the bottom of a stand mixer, using the paddle attachment cream the butter and cream cheese until light and fluffy on a medium-high speed, about two to three minutes.
5. Add in pumpkin puree, mix another minute. Slowly add in powdered sugar, about a ½ cup at a time until fully incorporated. If the icing is not thick enough, add more

powdered sugar. Transfer to a ziplock bag or pastry bag. Chill for at least an hour or even overnight.

6. When cupcakes have cooled completely, pipe frosting. Store in the fridge. When ready to use, let sit at room temperature for 20 minutes.

RED VELVET CUPCAKES

INGREDIENTS

CUPCAKES

- 2½ cups all-purpose flour
- 1½ cups granulated sugar
- 1 teaspoon baking soda
- ½ teaspoon salt
- 1 tablespoon cocoa powder
- 1 cup vegetable oil
- ½ cup (1 stick) unsalted butter, room
- 1 cup buttermilk
- 2 eggs, room temperature
- 1 teaspoon distilled white vinegar
- Red food coloring

CREAM CHEESE FROSTING

- 16 ounces cream cheese, room temperature
- ½ cup (1 stick) unsalted butter, room temperature
- 3 heaping cups confectioners sugar
- 1 teaspoon vanilla

DIRECTIONS

1. Preheat oven to 350 degrees and line a cupcake pan with liners.
2. In a mixer fitted with a paddle attachment, mix together butter, oil, buttermilk, eggs, vanilla and vinegar. Mixture may be lumpy.

3. In a separate bowl, sift together flour, cocoa powder, salt and baking soda. With mixer on low-speed, gradually add dry Ingredients to the wet Ingredients. Mix until smooth and no longer lumpy, but careful to not over mix.

4. Add food coloring to your liking and stir to combine. Because of the cocoa powder, the cupcakes will be a dusty red color. If you want light or bright red cupcakes, omit the cocoa powder.

5. Fill cupcake liners about ⅔ full. For mini muffins, bake for 11 minutes, turning cupcakes half way through baking process. For regular size muffins, bake for about 20 minutes, turning half way through. Check doneness by inserting a tooth pick into cupcakes - if the toothpick comes out clean, they're done.

6. To make cream cheese frosting, add butter and cream cheese to a mixer and whip until creamy and completely combined. With mixer on low-speed, gradually add confectioners sugar until frosting is smooth and fluffy. Lastly, add vanilla and mix for a few seconds until combined. Frost cupcakes.

CLASSIC VANILLA CUPCAKES

INGREDIENTS

- 1 1/2 cups all-purpose flour
- 1 1/2 teaspoons baking powder
- 1/4 teaspoon fine salt
- 2 large eggs, at room temperature
- 2/3 cup sugar
- 1 1/2 sticks (6 ounces) unsalted butter, melted
- 2 teaspoons pure vanilla extract
- 1/2 cup milk

DIRECTIONS

1. Preheat the oven to 350 F and position a rack in the middle of the oven. Line one 12-cup standard muffin tin or two 24-cup mini-muffin tins with cupcake liners.
2. Whisk the flour, baking powder and salt together in a medium bowl.
3. In another medium bowl, beat the eggs and sugar with an electric mixer until light and foamy, about 2 minutes. While beating, gradually pour in the butter and then the vanilla.
4. While mixing slowly, add half the dry Ingredients. Then add all the milk and follow with the rest of the dry Ingredients. Take care not to overmix the batter. Divide the batter evenly in the prepared tin.
5. Bake until a tester inserted in the center of the cakes comes out clean, rotating the tin about halfway through, 18 to 20 minutes (10 to 12 minutes for minis). Cool the cupcakes on a rack in the tin for 10 minutes, and then remove from the tin. Cool on the rack completely.

SIMPLE PUMPKIN CUPCAKES

INGREDIENTS

FOR THE CUPCAKES

- 1 can pumpkin or 1 1/2 cups pumpkin puree
- 2 very ripe bananas
- 1/2 cup coconut sugar
- 1 1/2 tsp cinnamon
- 1/4 tsp ginger
- 1/4 tsp nutmeg
- 1/4 tsp sea salt

FOR THE WHIP TOPPING

- 1 can full fat coconut milk
- 2 T maple syrup
- 1 tsp vanilla beans

DIRECTIONS

1. Preheat oven to 350.
2. In a food processor, combine all the cupcake Ingredients and blend until smooth.
3. Spoon the mixture into lined muffin pans.
4. Bake for 20-25 minutes.
5. Let these cool completely before removing from the muffin liners. Since they are soft like pumpkin pie.
6. To make the whip topping, open up your can of coconut milk that has been in the fridge overnight. Scoop the fatty white part off and place in a mixing bowl with the vanilla and maple syrup. Use the whipping attachment and whip the coconut into a cream. Scoop a little on top of each muffin.

THE GOLDEN CUPCAKE

INGREDIENTS

YELLOW CAKE

- 20-24 Golden Oreos
- 1 box yellow cake mix
- 3 eggs
- 1/3 C. oil
- 3/4 C. sour cream
- 1/2 C. milk or butter milk
- 2 tsp. vanilla extract

CREAM CHEESE FROSTING

- 8 oz. cream cheese
- 1/2 C. butter, softened
- 2 tsp. vanilla extract
- 1 Tbsp. milk
- 3-4 C. powdered sugar
- Extra Golden Oreos for decoration

DIRECTIONS

1. Preheat oven to 350 degrees and line pans with cupcake liners.
2. Place an Oreo on the bottom of each liner.
3. Sift cake mix into a large bowl to remove any lumps.
4. Add eggs, oil, sour cream, milk and vanilla extract and stir until smooth.
5. Fill cupcake liners (over Oreos) until about 3/4 full.
6. Bake for 15-20 minutes or until an inserted knife comes out clean. (Depending on your oven you may want to bake on a higher rack to not burn the Oreos on the bottom, some ovens get extra hot from below, so be careful!)
7. Let cool.
8. Cream Cheese Frosting: Beat cream cheese and butter until smooth. Add vanilla extract, milk and 2 cups. powdered sugar

an beat again. Continue to add more powdered sugar until you reach your desired consistency.

9. Pipe onto cooled cupcakes and top with an extra Golden Oreo.

BERRIES CUPCAKE WITH MASCARPONE

INGREDIENTS

MINI CORNMEAL CAKES

- 3/4 cup + 2 tablespoon (100 grams) unbleached all-purpose flour
- 1/4 cup (30 grams) stone ground yellow cornmeal
- 1/2 cup + 3 tablespoons (140 grams) granulated sugar
- 1 and 1/2 teaspoons baking powder
- 1/4 teaspoon kosher salt
- 3 large whole eggs
- 10 tablespoons (145 grams or 5 ounces) unsalted butter, very soft

WHIPPED MASCARPONE FROSTING

- 1/2 cup (113 grams) mascarpone cheese
- 1/2 cup (120 mL) chilled heavy cream
- 3 tablespoons (24 grams) powdered sugar
- 1/2 teaspoon pure vanilla extract

ASSEMBLY

- powdered sugar, for dusting
- fresh raspberries and blackberries (roughly 2 ounces of each)
- fresh lemon zest, for garnish

DIRECTIONS

1. Prepare the mini cornmeal cakes: Preheat the oven to 375 degrees Fahrenheit. Line a standard muffin tin with 11 liners. Set aside. In a medium bowl, whisk together the all-purpose flour, cornmeal, granulated sugar, baking powder, and salt. Set aside.
2. In a stand mixer, fitted with a paddle attachment, combine the whole eggs and softened butter. Add all of the dry Ingredients to the bowl. Turn on the mixer to medium speed

(4) and beat the batter for 2 minutes, or until all of the Ingredients are evenly incorporated and batter is smooth.

3. Divide the batter evenly among the lined muffin cups. The batter should be reach about half-way up each cup. Bake at 375 degrees for 14 to 16 minutes, or until the cornmeal cakes are golden brown and springy to touch. Remove from the oven and allow to cool in the baking tin, on a rack, for 5 minutes. Remove the cornmeal cakes from the tin and allow to cool to room temperature on a cooling rack.

4. Prepare the whipped mascarpone: In a clean mixer bowl, fitted with a paddle attachment, combine the mascarpone cheese, heavy cream, powdered sugar, and vanilla extract. Beat at low speed, slowly increasing to medium speed, until mixture thickens and forms soft peaks.

5. Using a spoon, add a dollop of whipped mascarpone in the center of each cooled cornmeal cake. Using a fine-meshed sieve, dust the cakes lightly with powdered sugar.

6. Top each cake with a mixture of fresh blackberries and fresh raspberries, and freshly grated lemon zest. Serve immediately.

BLACK CUPCAKE

INGREDIENTS

FOR THE BROWNIE LAYER

- 4 large eggs
- 2 cups sugar, sifted
- 8 ounces / 2 sticks melted butter
- ½ cup cocoa, sifted
- 2 vanilla beans, seeds only
- ¾ cups flour, sifted
- ½ teaspoon kosher salt
- ½ teaspoon pumpkin spice

PUMPKIN BUTTERCREAM

- 2½ sticks unsalted butter, room temperature
- 3 cups confectioners sugar
- 3 tablespoons pumpkin puree
- ½ teaspoon pumpkin spice
- 5 drops orange gel color

DIRECTIONS

1. Adjust oven rack to middle position and heat oven to 300 degrees F. Line a standard muffin/cupcake tin with paper or foil liners.
2. In a mixer fitted with the whisk attachment, beat the eggs at medium speed until fluffy and light yellow, add the sugar and beat until combined. Add remaining Ingredients, and mix to combine.
3. Pour the batter evenly into the cupcake tins and bake for 40 minutes. Check for doneness by inserting a toothpick into the center of the cupcake, it should come out with just a few crumbles attached.
4. When done, remove from oven and transfer cupcakes to a cooling rack. Cool cupcakes to room temperature before frosting.

5. Using the wire whisk attachment of a stand mixer, whip the butter on medium-high speed for 5 minutes, stopping to scrape the bowl once or twice.
6. Reduce the speed to low and gradually add the confectioner sugar and pumpkin spice. Once incorporated, increase the speed to medium-high and add the pumpkin puree and gel color, mixing until combined. Whip at medium-high speed until light and fluffy, about 2 minutes, scraping the bowl as needed.
7. Unused buttercream can be stored in the refrigerator in an airtight container. Let it come to room temperature and then give it a quick whip in the mixer before using it.
8. If the frosting is too soft, add more sugar - ½ cup at a time, if the frosting is too tough add some milk, 1 tablespoon as a time.
9. Transfer frosting to a piping bag and decorate the cupcakes, garnish with sprinkles.

SNICKERS CUPCAKES

INGREDIENTS

CHOCOLATE CUPCAKES

- 1 1/2 C. all-purpose flour
- 1 C. unsweetened cocoa powder
- 1 tsp. baking soda
- 1 1/2 tsp. baking powder
- 1/2 tsp. salt
- 4 eggs, at room temp
- 1 C. sugar
- 1 C. brown sugar, packed
- 2/3 cup oil
- 1 C. buttermilk or milk
- 1 Tbsp. vanilla extract

CHOCOLATE PEANUT BUTTER FROSTING

- 3/4 C. butter softened
- 1/2 C. peanut butter, creamy
- 1/2 C. unsweetened cocoa powder
- 2 tsp.vanilla extract
- 2-3 Tbsp. milk
- 3-4 C. powdered sugar
- Snickers bars and caramel sauce

DIRECTIONS

1. Preheat oven to 350 degrees and line pans with cupcake liners.
2. In a medium bowl, combine cocoa flour, cocoa powder, baking soda, baking powder and salt. Set aside.
3. In a large bowl, combine eggs, sugar, brown sugar, oil, buttermilk and vanilla extract.
4. Pour half the dry Ingredients into the wet and stir. Then add the rest of the dry Ingredients and stir again. Don't over mix.

5. Fill cupcake liners 2/3 full and bake for 18-22 minutes or until an inserted knife comes out clean. Let cool.
6. Frosting: Beat butter and peanut butter until smooth. Add cocoa powder, vanilla extract and 2 Tablespoons milk. Slowly add in powdered sugar until thick. If it becomes thick like cookie dough, stream in more milk!
7. Pipe onto cooled cupcakes and top with Snickers and caramel sauce.

CHOCOLATE & ORANGE CUPCAKES

INGREDIENTS

CUPCAKES

- 1 1/2 cups all-purpose flour
- 2/3 cup dark cocoa powder
- 1 1/3 cups granulated sugar
- 1 teaspoon baking soda
- 1/2 teaspoon baking powder
- 1/2 teaspoon salt
- 2 large eggs
- 1/3 cup vegetable oil
- 1 teaspoon vanilla extract
- 2/3 cup milk
- 2/3 cup hot water

FROSTING

- 1 cup unsalted butter (2 sticks)
- 7 cups confectioners sugar, sifted
- 1/2 cup milk
- 1 teaspoon vanilla extract
- 2 teaspoons orange extract
- Orange food coloring

DIRECTIONS

1. Preheat oven to 350°F and line muffin tins with cupcake liners.
2. In a large bowl, whisk the flour, cocoa powder, sugar, baking soda, baking powder, and salt together.
3. Add the eggs, vegetable oil, vanilla extract, and milk to the bowl with the dry Ingredients and mix until just combined.
4. Pour in the hot water and mix on medium speed with the hand mixer for about 1-2 minutes. Batter will be very liquidy.

5. Fill cupcake liners about 2/3 full and bake in the oven for 15-17 minutes or until a toothpick inserted in the middles comes out clean.
6. Remove cupcakes from oven, let cool for about 5 minutes. Then place cupcakes on a cooling rack to cool completely.
7. Make frosting.
8. Cut butter into cubes and put into a stand mixer bowl fitted with the paddle attachment. Mix on medium speed for 30 seconds.
9. Add 4 cups of the sifted confectioners sugar, the milk, vanilla and orange extracts. Mix on low for 10 seconds so the sugar doesn't fly everywhere, then turn mixer up to medium speed for 5 minutes.
10. Scrape the sides and bottom of the bowl in case any butter stuck to bottom or sides of bowl and didn't get mixed in. Then add the rest of the confectioners sugar and mix again on low speed for 10 seconds. Add 2 drops of orange food coloring, then up the speed to high for 2-3 minutes.
11. Prepare your piping bag with a large round tip, fill piping bag with frosting, then pipe large dollops onto each cupcake.
12. Top each cupcake with a chocolate orange slice and/or some orange peel.

HAT CUPCAKES

INGREDIENTS

CHOCOLATE CUPCAKES

- 105 grams (3/4 cup) plain flour
- 40 grams (1/2 cup) cocoa powder
- 1/2 teaspoon baking soda
- 1/2 teaspoon baking powder
- 100 grams (1/2 cup) caster sugar
- 45 grams (1/4 cup) brown sugar
- 115 grams (1/2 cup or 1 stick) unsalted butter
- 2 large eggs
- 1 teaspoon vanilla extract
- 120 ml (1/2 cup) buttermilk

MARSHMALLOW FROSTING

- 4 egg whites, room temperature
- 200 grams (1 cup) caster sugar
- 1/4 teaspoon cream of tartar
- 1 teaspoon vanilla extract

CHOCOLATE COATING

- 300 grams (2 cups) good quality dark chocolate, pieces
- 2 tablespoons vegetable oil

DIRECTIONS

1. Preheat the oven to 180C (360 F). Line a 12 hole muffin tin with patty cases. In a large mixing bowl, sift the flour, cocoa powder, baking soda, baking powder and then add the sugars - give it a little stir. Pop the butter into the microwave for a short burst, 10 seconds or so at a time, until it is just melted. Give it a stir with a fork to eliminate any lumps.
2. In a separate mixing bowl, add the eggs, vanilla and butter and whisk together until smooth. Then add the wet mixture

into the dry mixture, along with the buttermilk and gently fold until just combined.

3. Spoon the mixture into the prepared patty cases and pop into the oven. Bake for 18-20 minutes or until just cooked through. Set cakes out onto a wire rack and leave to cool completely.
4. To make the marshmallow frosting, fill a medium saucepan with a few inches of water and pop on a medium heat.
5. In a small heatproof bowl, add your eggs whites, caster sugar and cream of tartar. Whisk together. Then pop the bowl over the saucepan, ensuring the bottom of the bowl does not touch the water. As the egg whites heat, whisk gently by hand the entire time. You'll want to heat the egg whites to 50 C / 120 F which you can test by sticking a candy thermometer into the mixture or go by feel (the mixture should be hot to the touch) - should be around 5-6 minutes or so.
6. Then remove the bowl from the saucepan and place the mixture in the base of a stand mixer (or simply use a hand beater) and beat on medium speed for approximately 5 minutes or until the mixture is fluffy, white and voluminous. Add the vanilla and beat for 30 seconds or so.
7. Then grab your piping bag fitted with a large round or star shaped tip. Fill with the marshmallow fluff and pipe tall swirls onto each cupcake. Pop the cupcakes into the freezer for at least 20 minutes for the frosting to firm up slightly. Then its time for the chocolate.
8. Melt your dark chocolate and oil over the stove using the boiler method. Place a few inches of water in a medium saucepan and then place a medium bowl over the top, with the chocolate and oil inside. Ensure that the bottom of the bowl does not touch the water, then place on a medium heat. Gently stir as the steam melts the chocolate until silky and smooth. Place the chocolate in a deep and high sided container.
9. Gently dip each cupcake upside down right into the chocolate, let the chocolate drip off gently and then place the right side up onto a wire rack. Continue with all the cupcakes and leave them to harden slightly at room temperature for about 20 minutes before placing in the fridge to firm completely. These

cupcakes keep quite well for 2-3 days, simply store in the fridge.

CUPCAKES WITH MINT BUTTERCREAM

INGREDIENTS

FOR THE CHOCOLATE CUPCAKES

- ⅔ Cup Cocoa Powder
- 1 Tsp Baking Soda
- 1 Cup Water, Boiling
- ½ Cup Butter, Melted
- 5 Tablespoons Vegetable Oil
- 1½ Cups White Sugar
- 2 Teaspoons Vanilla Extract
- ½ Teaspoons Salt
- 4 Eggs
- ½ Cup Heavy Creamy
- 1½ Cups All Purpose Flour

FOR THE MINT CHOCOLATE CHIP BUTTERCREAM

- 1½ Cups Butter, Softened
- 2 Teaspoons Mint Extract
- 2 Teaspoons Vanilla
- 5 Cups Powdered Sugar
- 1 Tablespoon Whole Milk
- 1 Cup Mini Chocolate Chips
- Green Food Coloring
- Pinch of Salt, To Taste

DIRECTIONS

1. Preheat oven to 350 degrees F. In a large mixing bowl mix cocoa powder and baking soda. Pour boiling water over the mixture and stir until combined.
2. In a separate large mixing bowl mix melted butter, oil, sugar, vanilla, salt, and eggs until combined. Blend in cocoa mixture and heavy cream.
3. Gradually stir in flour a little at a time and stir until just combined.

4. Divide batter evenly between lined cupcake bakers. Bake for 20-22 minutes or until a tooth pick inserted in the center comes out clean. Cool completely.
5. For the Mint Chocolate Chip Buttercream:
6. Stir butter until light and fluffy. Stir in mint and vanilla extracts.
7. Gradually stir in powdered sugar a little at time, adding milk as needed.
8. Stir in food coloring if desired. Fold in mini chocolate chips.
9. Scoop a generous amount of frosting onto the cupcakes with an ice cream scoop.

CHOCOLATE CUPCAKES WITH STRAWBERRY BUTTERCREAM

INGREDIENTS

STRAWBERRY BUTTERCREAM

- 1 cup butter
- 1 two-pound bag powder sugar (about 7-8 cups)
- 2 teaspoons strawberry extract
- 4 tablespoons milk
- dash salt
- 1-2 drops pink food coloring

VANILLA BUTTERCREAM

- 1 cup (2 sticks) unsalted butter, softened
- 6-8 cups confectioner's sugar
- 1/2 cup milk
- 2 teaspoons vanilla extract

CHOCOLATE BUTTERCREAM

- 1 cups unsalted butter (2 sticks) at room temp.
- 4 cups powdered sugar
- 1/2 cup good quality cocoa powder
- 1/2 teaspoon table salt
- 2 teaspoons vanilla extract
- 1/2 cup whole milk or heavy cream

DIRECTIONS

1. Put room temperature butter, strawberry extract, and salt into mixer. Add in powder sugar one cup at a time, alternating with the milk until you have used it all.
2. Add in food coloring a drop at a time to determine desired color.
3. If your frosting is too thick you can certainly add more milk.

4. In a large mixing bowl, combine 4 cups of confectioner's sugar with butter.
5. Stir in milk and vanilla.
6. On medium speed, beat until smooth and creamy 3-5 minutes. Gradually add remaining sugar 1 cup at a time until desired consistency. You may not use all the sugar.
7. Place room temperature butter and vanilla into a stand mixer and beat at medium-high for about three minutes. You want it to appear lighter and fluffier.
8. While butter is in mixer add powdered sugar, cocoa, and salt to a bowl and mix with a whisk. (sift)
9. With mixer off, add in one cup of the powdered sugar and cocoa mixture. Turn mixer on to low and then slowly add in remaining powdered sugar mixture, one cup at a time.
10. With mixer still on low, add in milk. Turn mixer to medium high and blend for at least two minutes.
11. Frosting will appear very light, but it will darken as it sets.

CUPCAKES WITH LEMONFROSTING

INGREDIENTS

LEMON CUPCAKES

- 1 1/3 cups (185g/6.5 oz.) all-purpose flour
- 1 teaspoon baking powder
- 1/4 teaspoon salt
- 1 cup (200g/7 oz.) granulated sugar
- 1 tablespoon lemon zest
- 1/2 cup (1 stick/113g) unsalted butter, softened
- 2 large eggs
- 1 teaspoon pure vanilla extract
- 1/4 cup plus 2 tablespoons (90 ml) whole milk
- 2 tablespoons (30ml) freshly squeezed lemon juice

LEMON BUTTERCREAM FROSTING

- 1/2 cup (1 stick/113g) unsalted butter, softened
- 1 1/2 – 2 1/2 cups (180g-280g) powdered sugar, sifted
- 1 tablespoon heavy cream or whole milk
- 1 tablespoon freshly squeezed lemon juice
- 2 teaspoons lemon zest

DIRECTIONS

1. For the cupcakes: Preheat oven to 350F/180C. Line a muffin tin with cupcake liners. Set aside.
2. In a medium bowl, sift together flour, baking powder, and salt. In another small bowl, toss together sugar and lemon zest until combined.
3. Using a mixer fitted with the paddle attachment, beat together butter and lemon-sugar mixture on medium speed until light and fluffy, about 2-3 minutes. Scrape down the sides and bottom of the bowl as necessary. On medium speed, beat in eggs, one at a time, beating well after each addition. Add vanilla extract and beat until combined. With the mixer on low speed, add half of the dry Ingredients and beat just

until combined. Add milk and lemon juice and beat until combined. Add the other half of the dry Ingredients and beat slowly until just combined.

4. Divide batter evenly between the cups, filling them about 3/4 full. Bake for 15-20 minutes (or 8-10 minutes for mini cupcakes), until a toothpick inserted into the center comes out clean or with just a few moist crumbs. Allow cupcakes to sit for 10 minutes, then remove from pan and allow to cool completely on a wire rack.

5. Unfrosted cupcakes can be kept tightly covered at room temperature for up to 3 days, or in the freezer for up to 2 months. Thaw, still covered, on the counter or overnight in the fridge.

6. For the frosting: In the bowl of an electric mixer fitted with the paddle attachment, beat butter on medium speed until smooth, creamy, and the consistency is similar to mayonnaise, about 2 minutes. Add 3/4 cup (90g) sugar and beat well until smooth. Add cream, lemon juice, and lemon zest and beat until combined and smooth. Add another 3/4 cup sugar and beat until completely smooth and fluffy. Beat in more sugar as needed, until desired consistency (thick enough to pipe). Frost cupcakes once they've cooled.

7. If you wish to add lemon curd filling: Once the cupcakes have cooled, cut a 1/2-inch (1.5cm) hole in the center of each cupcake using a spoon or melon baller. Spoon about a teaspoon of lemon curd into the hole, then frost the cupcakes.

PUMPKIN AND MAPLE CREAM CUPCAKES

INGREDIENTS

CAKE

- 1 c. vegetable oil
- 4 eggs
- 1 c. sugar
- 1 c. brown sugar
- 1 (15-16oz) can pure pumpkin
- 2 tsp. baking soda
- 2 tsp. baking powder
- 1 tsp. salt
- 2 c. flour
- 1 tsp. cinnamon
- 1 tsp. ginger
- 1 tsp nutmeg
- 24 cupcake liners

FROSTING

- 8 oz cream cheese, softened
- 1/4 c. butter, softened
- 1 tsp. vanilla extract
- 1 1/2 tsp. maple extract
- 3 c. powdered sugar

DIRECTIONS

1. In a mixer combine oil, eggs, both sugars, and pumpkin.
2. In a separate bowl whisk together baking soda, baking powder, salt, flour, cinnamon, ginger, and nutmeg. Slowly add the flour mixture to the liquid mixture till combined.
3. Add cupcake liners to tins and fill 2/3 of the way full with batter. Bake for 18-20 minutes at 350°. Cool completely before frosting.

4. To make the frosting, combine cream cheese and butter with an electric hand mixer until smooth; add vanilla extract and maple extract.
5. Add powdered sugar one cup at a time until combined. Frost cupcakes when cooled.

CHEESECAKE CUPCAKES

INGREDIENTS

MINI CHEESECAKE CUPCAKES

- 1 cup graham cracker crumbs
- 4 tablespoons unsalted butter, melted
- 2 tablespoons sugar
- 16 ounces cream cheese, softened
- ½ cup sour cream
- ¼ cup sugar
- 2 eggs
- 1 teaspoon vanilla extract
- caramel sauce or strawberry sauce for topping, optional
- 3 Ingredient Strawberry Sauce
- 1 cup strawberries, halved
- ½ teaspoon lemon juice
- 2 teaspoons sugar

EASY CARAMEL SAUCE

- 2 cups light brown sugar
- 1 stick plus 4 tablespoons unsalted butter
- 1 cup heavy cream
- 2 teaspoons vanilla extract
- sea salt for serving, if desired

1. DIRECTIONS

2. Mini Cheesecake Cupcakes
3. Preheat oven to 325 degrees.
4. Line a muffin pan with paper liners.
5. Combine graham cracker, butter and sugar in a small bowl. Texture should be similar to wet sand. Divide crust evenly into the bottom of the lined muffin tin.
6. Bake for 5-6 minutes or until golden brown.
7. Take out of the oven and cool completely.

8. Meanwhile assemble the cheesecake filling. Beat cream cheese in a stand mixer with the paddle attachment.
9. Add in sour cream, sugar, eggs and vanilla. Mix until combined. Make sure to scrap the sides of the bowl.
10. Pour cheesecake mixture into cooled muffin tin. It will be about 2 tablespoons of filling each. Fill almost all the way to the top.
11. Place in the oven and bake for 20 minutes or until the cheesecakes are set. They will still giggle a bit. Do not over cook them. If they start to crack they are getting over cooked.
12. Allow them to cool in the muffin tin completely. Place in the refrigerator to chill and serve cold with your favorite toppings.

INGREDIENT STRAWBERRY SAUCE

1. Add strawberries, lemon juice and sugar to a small saucepan. Simmer on low for 15 minutes, mashing up strawberries with the back of a wooden spoon. Take off heat and allow to cool.
2. Place in a food processor and pulse until creamy and thick. Place back in the fridge and serve cold.

EASY CARAMEL SAUCE

1. Add all of the Ingredients except for the vanilla to a saucepan. Cook over low-medium heat until thickened stirring occasionally. About 8 minutes. If the sauce isn't getting a lot thicker turn up the heat a bit and keep and eye on it making sure to whisk constantly. (The sauce will thicken as it cools in the refrigerator).
2. Stir in vanilla.
3. Take off of the heat and allow to cool in the saucepan. Transfer to a container and place in the refrigerator to firm up and cool.

VEGAN CHOCOLATE CUPCAKE

INGREDIENTS

- 1 cup of almond milk or any non-dairy/dairy milk
- 1/2 cup pumpkin puree
- 3/4 cup packed light brown sugar
- 1 tsp vanilla extract
- 1 cup whole wheat flour
- 1/3 cup unsweetened cocoa powder
- 1/2 tsp baking powder
- 3/4 tsp baking soda
- 1/4 tsp salt

CHOCOLATE GANACHE

- 4 oz bitter/semi sweet chocolate squares, chopped
- 2 tbsp Earth Balance butter

DIRECTIONS

1. Preheat oven to 350 degrees F. Line a 12 cup muffin tin with cupcake liners and spray a light coat of non-stick cooking spray.
2. In a small bowl, mix wet Ingredients and set aside.
3. In a bigger bowl, sift all dry Ingredients.
4. Gently pour wet Ingredients into dry Ingredients and mix to incorporate. Do not overmix.
5. Using a medium ice-cream scoop, divide batter evenly into lined muffin tin.
6. Bake for 18 – 20 minutes or until a toothpick inserted in center comes out clean.
7. Allow to cool on a wire rack for a few minutes before removing to cool completely.
8. Heat a saucepan with some water on medium high heat. Once water boils, turn down the heat to low. Place a bowl over the saucepan, add chocolate squares and butter. Stir to combine and allow chocolate to completely melt with the help of steam.

9. Once cupcakes are completely cool, dunk each with chocolate ganache and sprinkle on some of your favorite festive sprinkles.
10. Allow ganache to cool and harden completely before sinking in your fangs.

CUPCAKES WITH CARAMEL

INGREDIENTS

- 70g salted butter
- 170g plain flour
- 250g caster sugar
- 50g cocoa powder
- 1tbsp baking powder
- A pinch of salt
- 210ml milk
- 2 eggs

FOR THE FROSTING

- 670g icing sugar
- 210g salted butter (partially melted)
- 70ml milk
- 30g tinned caramel

FOR THE FILLING...

- 100g tinned caramel

DIRECTIONS

1. Pre-heat your oven to 180 degrees C
2. Combine all the Ingredients and whisk until smooth.
3. Pop into 12 cupcake cases, they should fill 3/4 of each case.
4. Put in the oven and cook for 22 minutes
5. Combine the icing sugar, butter and milk until smooth.
6. Then add in the tinned caramel until smooth and even in colour.
7. Once the cupcakes are completely cooled take a knife and cut a hollow out of each cupcake.
8. Keep the cut out 'top' of the cake.
9. In the hollow, put about a teaspoon of caramel into each cake.
10. Place the 'top' back on and repeat for all the cupcakes.
11. Once complete it's time to ice the cupcakes, just scoop on a generous amount of icing and decorate as you wish.

DARK CUPCAKES

INGREDIENTS

- 1/4 cup finely chopped hazelnut pieces
- Sugar Cone
- sugar cones
- 1/4 cup dark chocolate
- dark chocolate vermicelli sprinkles or sprinkles of choice
- hot fudge sauce

NUTELLA FROZEN CUSTARD

- 1 qt of Edy's vanilla frozen custard
- Nutella
- brownie pieces that you took out of the sugar cones
- 1/4 cup sugar cone crumb topping that you made earlier

DIRECTIONS

1. Preheat oven to 325 degrees. Mix the brownie mix per package DIRECTIONS and fold in the chopped hazelnuts. If you are using free standing baking cups like ours this recipe will make 6 large and 6 small. Place the baking cups on a baking sheet. If you are making 2 sizes, place each size on their own baking sheet since the small size take less time to bake. Using a 1.5 tablespoon cookie scoop add 2 scoops of the batter to the large baking cups and 1 scoop to the small. In my oven the small size took about 20 minutes and the large took 30 minutes.

2. While the brownies are baking take 6 sugar cones and cut them about 2.25" of the way down with a clean pair of kitchen scissors. Some pieces may break and that is okay since we will be using them for the sugar cone bits topping. Set aside the top and small tip of the cone.

3. Take the broken sugar cone pieces and crumble them into smaller bits. If you don't have around 1/2 cup of pieces you can break up another sugar cone as you will be adding the sugar cone bit topping to the frozen custard and using it as a

garnish on the brownie cupcakes. Spread the sugar cone pieces on a sheet of parchment paper. Place the dark chocolate in a quart size freezer bag and melt in the microwave for 1 minute on 50% power. If the chocolate is not fully melted heat for 20 more seconds on 50% power, repeat until fully melted. Snip off a tiny piece of the corner off the bag and drizzle the chocolate over the sugar cone pieces. Add vermicelli dark chocolate sprinkles (or sprinkles of choice) to the chocolate before it sets up and set aside to let harden. Once hardened break up the pieces to create the crumble topping.

4. By this time the brownies might be ready to come out of the oven. Set aside the small size brownies. While the larger brownie cupcakes are still warm from the oven take the top larger piece of the sugar cone and carefully press it completely down into the brownie. Gently give it a little twist like you would do with a cupcake corer. Pull the cone back out of the brownie and push the brownie piece that is now inside the cone out, set aside for the frozen custard mixture. Place the sugar cone back into the brownie cupcake. Do this to all of the larger brownie cupcakes. Add a tablespoon of hot fudge into the cavity of the sugar cookie cone in the brownie. The hot fudge does not need to be heated for this step. Now it is time to make the frozen custard mixture to fill the sugar cones that are in your brownies!

5. Slightly soften the frozen custard. Scoop out about 1/3 of the container into a small mixing bowl. Add about 1/4 cup of sugar cone crumbles you made earlier, a few tablespoons of Nutella and the reserved brownie pieces from the sugar cones (broken into smaller pieces) to the frozen custard. Mix until combined. Scoop the frozen custard mixture into the cavities of the sugar cones.

6. Fill until you reach the top of the cone and use a knife level the custard to the top of the cone. If the custard has become too soft place the brownie cupcakes in the freezer until they firm up or until serving. Place the extra frozen custard back in the freezer to use with the small brownie cupcakes.

7. When you are ready to serve your Brownie Sundae Nutella Cupcakes pull them out of the freezer. Place a few

tablespoons of hot fudge sauce in a quart size freezer bag and heat in the microwave for 30 seconds on 50% power.

8. You only need to soften it slightly. Snip the corner of bag off. Squeeze the hot fudge sauce onto the top of the brownie to cover it as shown in one of the pictures above. Add some of the sugar cone topping. For the top of the cone sticking out of the brownie add some dark chocolate vermicelli sprinkles or more of the sugar cone topping. Top with a Ferrero Rocher hazelnut chocolate to finish. If you are not eating them immediately place them back in the freezer until 5 to 10 minutes before serving.

COCONUT & LEMON CUPCAKES

INGREDIENTS

CUPCAKES

- 3 cups all-purpose flour
- 1 tablespoon baking powder
- ½ teaspoon salt
- 2 sticks unsalted butter
- 2 cups sugar
- 4 large eggs
- 1 cup half and half
- 1 tsp. vanilla
- 1½ tsp. coconut extract

FROSTING

- 1 stick butter, softened
- 4 oz. cream cheese, softened
- 1 tsp. vanilla
- 1 tsp. lemon extract
- 3-4 Tbsp. half and half
- 4 cups powdered sugar

DIRECTIONS

1. Preheat oven to 350 degrees. Line twenty-four muffin cups with paper or foil liners, and set aside.
2. Whisk together flour, baking powder, and salt in a medium bowl, and set aside.
3. Combine butter and sugar in a large bowl; beat until pale and fluffy, about 2 minutes. Add eggs one at a time, mixing well after each addition. Add vanilla and coconut extract. Beat in flour mixture and milk in three alternating batches, beginning and ending with flour mixture. After each addition, beat until just combined, scraping down sides and bottom of bowl as necessary.

4. Fill prepared muffin cups with about ¼ cup batter. Bake, rotating pans once, until cupcakes are just golden brown and spring back to the touch, 18 to 20 minutes. Let cupcakes cool about 5 minutes, then turn them out onto a cooling rack. Frost as desired.
5. To make frosting: beat butter and cream cheese until smooth and fluffy (about 3-4 minutes). Add remaining Ingredients and mix until smooth.

CHOCOLATE & COCONUT CUPCAKES

INGREDIENTS

FOR THE CUPCAKES

- 1 cup coconut flavored rum
- 1 cup (2 sticks) unsalted butter
- 3/4 cup unsweetened cocoa powder
- 2 cups all-purpose flour
- 1 1/4 cups sugar
- 3/4 teaspoon salt
- 1 1/2 teaspoons baking soda
- 2 large eggs
- 2/3 cup greek yogurt

FOR THE FROSTING

- 1 cup butter, softened
- 4 1/2 – 4 cups powdered sugar
- 1/4 cup coconut rum
- 1 tablespoon vanilla

DIRECTIONS

1. Preheat oven to 350 degrees F.Line 2 standard cupcake pans with 24 liners.In a large saucepan over medium heat, simmer coconut rum and butter.Slowly whisk cocoa powder into saucepan until mixture is creamy.

2. Remove from heat and allow to cool.Meanwhile, whisk sugar, flour, salt and baking soda in a large bowl.In a separate bowl, beat eggs and greek yogurt with an electric mixer. Slowly add coconut rum and cocoa mixture. Combine on low speed.Slowly add flour and sugar mixture, combining on low speed until completely incorporated.Fill baking cups three-fourths full. Bake for about 22 minutes. Cool.To make the frosting cream butter until smooth. Gradually add powdered sugar, alternating with rum and vanilla, until desired consistency is reached.

CHOCOLATE CREAM CHEESE CUPCAKES

INGREDIENTS

- 2 cups shredded zucchini
- 3 eggs
- 2 cups granulated sugar
- ¾ vegetable oil
- 2 teaspoons vanilla
- 2 cups all-purpose flour
- ⅔ cup unsweetened cocoa powder
- 1 teaspoon baking soda
- 1 teaspoon salt
- ½ teaspoon baking powder

CHOCOLATE CREAM FROSTING

- 8 oz package cream cheese, room temp
- ½ cup unsalted butter, room temp
- 3 cups powdered sugar
- ½ cup unsweetened cocoa powder
- ¼ tsp salt
- 1 tsp vanilla

DIRECTIONS

1. Preheat oven to 325 degrees. Line 24 muffin cups with liners or spray with non stick cooking spray and set aside.
2. In a large bowl, mix together zucchini, eggs, sugar, oil, and vanilla. Add flour, cocoa powder, baking soda, salt, and baking powder. Spoon the batter into the prepared pan filling them about half way.
3. Bake for 25 minutes or until a toothpick comes out clean. Cool cupcakes on wire racks.
4. To make the chocolate cream cheese frosting: In a large bowl beat together the cream cheese and butter until creamy. Add powdered sugar, cocoa powder and salt and vanilla. Continue beating until smooth and whipped. Frost cupcakes.

COCONUT CUPCAKES WITH LEMON CURD

INGREDIENTS

CUPCAKES

- 2 cups cake flour
- 1 ½ teaspoons baking powder
- ¾ teaspoon salt
- 2 sticks softened butter
- 1 ½ cups sugar
- Seeds of 1 vanilla bean
- ¾ cup + ⅛ cup coconut milk
- 1 egg yolk
- 4 egg whites
- 1 cup shredded, sweetened coconut

ASSEMBLY

- 1 batch lemon curd or a scant ¾ cup lemon curd
- 1 cup cold heavy cream
- 2 tablespoon sugar
- ¼ teaspoon pure vanilla extract
- 1 cup unsweetened flaked coconut

DIRECTIONS

1. Preheat oven to 350 degrees and line a regular muffin tin with liners.
2. Sift flour, baking powder and salt in a medium bowl. Set aside.
3. Cream butter and sugar in the bottom of a stand mixer until creamy, about two minutes. Add vanilla bean. Mix until combined. Add egg yolk, mix until combined.
4. With the mixer on low add in flour and coconut alternating each in three batches.
5. In a separate dry bowl, use an electric mixer to beat the egg whites until medium stiff peaks form.
6. Fold coconut until batter.

7. Gently fold egg whites into batter, making sure to not deflate.
8. Fill cupcake liners ¾ of the way full and bake for 24-25 minutes turning cupcakes halfway through. Depending on how your oven cooks it could be a minute or two less or more, the cupcakes are done when a wooden skewer comes out with a few crumbs attached.
9. Let cool.
10. In the bottom of the same stand mixer fitting with the whisk, add sugar and cream, whisk on a medium-high speed until whipped cream is formed, and be careful to not over mix. Whisk in vanilla. Set aside in fridge until ready to use.
11. Toast coconut in a small sauté pan over a low heat on the stove. BE CAREFUL the oils in the coconut can cause it to burn quickly; the toasting process should only take about 30 seconds.
12. When cupcakes are cool, spread about two teaspoons of lemon curd on the top. Pipe whipped cream on top of lemon curd and then sprinkle with toasted coconut.

TRIPLE CHOCOLATE CUPCAKES

INGREDIENTS

FOR THE CRUST

- 1 1/2 cups graham cracker crumbs
- 2 tablespoons granulated sugar
- 1 teaspoon kosher salt
- 5 tablespoons unsalted butter, melted and cooled

FOR THE DOUBLE CHOCOLATE CUPCAKES

- 1 cup all-purpose flour
- 1/2 cup graham flour
- 1 1/4 cups natural unsweetened cocoa powder
- 1 1/2 teaspoons baking soda
- 1/2 teaspoon baking powder
- 3/4 teaspoon kosher salt
- 2 ounces 70% cocoa chocolate, finely chopped
- 1 cup boiling water
- 1 cup buttermilk
- 1/2 teaspoon pure vanilla extract
- 2 large eggs
- 1/2 cup vegetable oil
- 2 1/4 cups granulated sugar

FOR THE CHOCOLATE BUTTER FROSTING

- 4 ounces 70% cacao chocolate, finely chopped
- 4 tablespoons (1/2 stick) unsalted butter, cut into 1-inch cubes
- 1 teaspoon light corn syrup

FOR THE MARSHMALLOW MERINGUE ICING

- 1 1/2 cups granulated sugar

- 1/4 teaspoon cream of tartar
- 1/4 cup water
- 3 large egg whites
- 1 teaspoon pure vanilla extract

DIRECTIONS

FOR THE DOUBLE CHOCOLATE, DOUBLE GRAHAM CUPCAKES

1. Center a rack in the oven and preheat to 350 (F). Prepare 2 muffin trays by lining each cavity with cupcake liners.
2. In a medium bowl, use a rubber spatula to stir together 1 1/2 cups graham cracker crumbs, 2 tablespoons granulated sugar, 1 teaspoon kosher salt and 5 tablespoons melted and cooled unsalted butter until evenly coated.
3. Use a 1 tablespoon measuring spoon to portion out a tablespoon sized scoop of the mixture in the bottom of each baking cup. Use your fingers (or one of these nifty tart tampers) to press down the graham cracker crumbs to the bottom of each liner until they form a solid crust. Bake in the preheated oven for 5 minutes to allow the base to harden, before transferring to wire racks to cool for a minimum of 15 minutes. While the graham cracker crusts are cooling, make the chocolate cake batter. Be sure to keep the oven on!
4. To make the chocolate cake batter, whisk together 1 cup all-purpose flour, 1/2 cup graham flour, 1 1/4 cups natural unsweetened cocoa powder, 1 1/2 teaspoons baking soda, 1/2 teaspoon baking powder and 3/4 teaspoon kosher salt in medium bowl until fully incorporated. Set aside.
5. Place 2 ounces finely chopped 70% cocoa chocolate in a medium, heatproof bowl and pour 1 cup boiling water over the chocolate. Whisk until the chocolate is melted, and allow the mixture to cool for 15 minutes.
6. In a liquid measuring cup, whisk together 1 cup buttermilk and 1/2 teaspoon pure vanilla extract. Set aside.
7. In the bowl of a freestanding electric mixer fitted with a whisk attachment, whisk 2 large eggs on medium-high speed until light and foamy, about 2 minutes. Reduce the mixer speed to its lowest setting and slowly pour in 1/2 cup vegetable oil, whisking for 30 to 60 seconds until combined.

8. With the mixer still on low, slowly pour in the cooled chocolate mixture into the egg mixture. Once the chocolate has been added, slowly pour in the buttermilk and vanilla mixture. Add 2 1/4 cups granulated sugar and continue to whisk until the batter is smooth and liquid, about 2 minutes.

9. Stop the mixer. Remove the bowl from the mixer and add the dry Ingredients. Use a rubber spatula to mix into the liquid Ingredients until just incorporated, scraping down the sides of the bowl and lifting and folding in from the bottom and center of the bowl. Whisk until the dry Ingredients are just incorporated — at this point, the batter will still look a little lumpy, but that's okay.

10. Pour the batter through a fine-mesh sieve over a large bowl to remove any lumps. Use a rubber spatula to press against any solids left in the sieve to push through as much batter as possible, but no need to overdo it. Disregard the remaining large lumps.

    Use a 1 tablespoon sized cookie dough scoop to divide the strained batter evenly between the graham-crusted cupcake liners, filling each cup up to two-thirds full with batter. Bake in the preheated oven for 25 to 30 minutes, or until a skewer inserted into the center of a cupcake comes out clean and the cupcake tops spring back when gently poked. Transfer the pans to a wire rack and allow to cool completely in the pan. When the cupcakes have cooled completely, make the chocolate ganache and marshmallow meringue frostings.

FOR THE CHOCOLATE BUTTER FROSTING

1. In a small, heavy bottomed saucepan over medium-low heat, melt together 4 ounces finely chopped chocolate, 4 tablespoons unsalted butter, and 1 teaspoon corn syrup, using a rubber spatula to stir constantly until completely melted and combined. Remove from heat and allow to cool in room temperature for about 20 minutes until mixture thickens to a spreadable consistency.

2. Once the mixture is spreadable, work quickly and use a small offset icing spatula to spread about 1 1/2 teaspoons of chocolate on the top of each cupcake. If the frosting hardens too much and becomes difficult to work with, reheat over

medium-low heat, whisking constantly until the mixture becomes spreadable again.

FOR THE MARSHMALLOW MERINGUE ICING

1. In a medium, heavy bottom saucepan over medium-low heat, combine 1 1/2 cups granulated sugar, 1/4 teaspoon cream of tartar and 1/4 cup of water. Whisk constantly until the sugar starts to dissolve, continuing to do so until the mixture reaches 240 (F) as measured by a candy thermometer. When the mixture reaches 240 (F), it should be syrupy. Immediately transfer to a heatproof liquid measuring cup and work quickly to make sure that it maintains its temperature.

2. In the bowl of a freestanding electric mixer fitted with a whisk attachment, combine 3 large egg whites and 1 teaspoon pure vanilla extract. With the mixture on medium speed, slowly pour the fresh sugar syrup down the side of the mixer bowl. When all the syrup is added, turn the mixer speed to medium-high and whisk until the icing becomes thick and holds a firm peak. Continue to whisk until the icing is just slightly warm and very thick, about 10 minutes total. DO NOT CONTINUE TO BEAT FOR LONGER THAN 10 MINUTES, otherwise the icing will thicken too much, become cement-like and impossible to spread and pipe.

3. Use immediately by transferring to a piping bag with a large round tip. Pipe a generous dollop of icing onto each cupcake. Once the cupcakes have all been frosted, use a culinary chef's torch to gently toast each dollop to give it that pretty toasted look.

ROOT BEER CUPCAKES

INGREDIENTS

- 1 1/2 cups root beer
- 1/4 cup butter
- 3/4 cups cocoa
- 2 cups brown sugar
- 3/4 cup sour cream
- 2 eggs
- 1 tsp vanilla extract
- 2 cups all purpose flour
- 2 1/2 tsp baking soda

BOURBON CREAM BUTTERCREAM

- 1/2 cup unsalted butter, softened
- 1/2 cup shortening
- 4 cups powdered sugar
- 1/2 tsp salt
- 4 tbsp Bourbon Cream liquor

DIRECTIONS

1. Pre heat oven to 325
2. Combine root beer and butter in a saucepan, once butter has melted, remove from heat. In a separate bowl, whisk together sour cream, eggs and vanilla. Add to cooled root beer and whisk until combined. Add in the cocoa and the sugar, mixing well. In a separate bowl, whisk together the flour and the baking soda. Add this to your root beer mixture, whisking until flour is incorporated. Batter will be very runny, but will bake up nicely. Fill cupcake liners about 3/4 full. This made pouring into my cupcake liners much easier. Bake in preheated oven for 15-17 minutes or until your cupcakes spring back when touched. Remove from oven and let cool completely before frosting.

FOR THE BUTTERCREAM

1. Combine softened butter and shortening in a large mixing bowl. Beat until very fluffy, about 10 minutes. Add in powdered sugar one cup at a time, mixing well after each addition. Add in the salt. Add in your bourbon cream. This is something you may have to taste as you go along . 4 tbsp to half of my buttercream added a subtle flavor. You may want to add more if you want the bourbon to be more pronounced. Mix buttercream until creamy.

FUNFETTI CUPCAKES

INGREDIENTS

- 2 cups all purpose flour
- 2 tbs baking powder
- 1/2 tsp salt
- 1/2 cup unsalted butter, melted
- 1 and 1/2 cup granulated sugar
- 2 eggs
- 1 and 1/2 tsp vanilla extract
- 1 and 1/4 cup milk
- 1/2 cup red, white, and pink sprinkles

DIRECTIONS

2. Preheat oven to 350F. Line muffin pan with paper cupcake tins (preferably Valentine's Day ones).
3. In a bowl, mix together flour, baking powder and salt. Set aside.
4. In a separate bowl, mix melted butter and sugar well. Mixture should be light and fluffy.
5. Add in eggs and vanilla extract and beat well. Whisk in milk.
6. Slowly add in flour mixture to the wet mix. Whisk just until combined.
7. Add sprinkles into mixture. Gently fold in just until sprinkles are scattered throughout the batter.
8. Pour batter into lined cupcake pan. Fill cupcake cups 3/4 of the way.
9. Bake cupcakes 15 to 20 minutes or until a toothpick inserted in the center of the cupcake comes out clean. Allow to cool before frosting.

FLOURLESS CHOCOLATE CUPCAKES

INGREDIENTS

- 8 oz. Chocolate Chips, 60% cacao content or higher
- 14 tablespoons (1¾ sticks) Butter, diced
- 2 tablespoons Currant Jelly
- 4 large Eggs
- ¼ cup Sugar
- 1 tablespoon Vanilla Extract
- 1 tablespoon Creme de Cassis

FOR THE CHANTILLY CREAM

- 2 cups Heavy Whipping Cream
- ¼ cup Sugar
- 3 tablespoons Creme de Cassis
- Fresh Cherries and Currants to garnish
- Chocolate Shavings, to garnish

DIRECTIONS

1. Preheat the oven to 325 degrees. Line a muffin tin with 12 cupcake wrappers.
2. Place the chocolate, butter, and jelly in a saucepan. Melt over medium/low heat, stirring well, until chocolate is melted and the mixture is well combined. Remove from heat and cool to lukewarm, stirring often, about 10 minutes.
3. While the chocolate mixture is cooling, whisk the eggs, sugar,creme de cassis, and vanilla in a large bowl until well blended, about 1 minute. Gradually whisk in the cooled chocolate mixture.
4. Divide the batter among baking wrappers.
5. Bake in the preheated oven for 12-15 minutes, or until puffy and slightly cracked on top.
6. Remove and let cool on a wire rack. Place in the refrigerator and chill until firm and cold.
7. Place the heavy cream and ¼ cup sugar in a bowl and beat with an electric mixer until stiff peaks form. Add the creme de cassis to the cream and beat in just until combined.

8. Place the cream in a piping bag fitted with a large star tip and pipe on top of the chilled cakes.
9. Garnish with 1 cherry each, fresh currants, and chocolate shavings.

DOUBLE CHOCOLATE CUPCAKES

INGREDIENTS

CUPCAKES

- ¼ cup cocoa powder
- 1 cup all-purpose flour
- ½ teaspoon baking soda
- ½ teaspoon baking powder
- ¼ teaspoon salt
- 2 large eggs, room temp
- 1 cup granulated sugar
- ⅓ cup melted coconut oil
- 2 teaspoons vanilla extract
- 1 tsp instant coffee mixed with 1 tsp warm water
- ½ cup buttermilk
- ½ cup mini chocolate chips, plus more for topping

FROSTING

- 2 Tbsp milk
- 1 Tbsp matcha powder
- 1 stick (1/2 cup) butter, room temp
- 3 cups icing sugar

DIRECTIONS

1. Preheat the oven to 350°F. Line a 12-cup muffin pan with cupcake liners; set aside. If you have a second muffin pan, line 4 more cups with liners, if not, simply bake the first batch and then reuse the pan for the rest of the batter.
2. In a medium bowl, whisk together the cocoa powder, flour, baking soda, baking powder, and salt; set aside.
3. In a large bowl, whisk together the eggs, sugar, oil, vanilla, and coffee mixture until smooth.
4. Add in half the dry Ingredients to the wet Ingredients, then half the buttermilk, mixing until smooth. Repeat with

remaining dry Ingredients and buttermilk. Add in chocolate chips and stir until just combined.

5. Pour batter into cupcake liners, filling about ⅔ of the way. Bake 18-20 minutes until a toothpick inserted in the centre comes out clean. Remove from oven and let cool completely.

6. Make frosting: in a small bowl, combine the matcha powder and milk and stir until a smooth paste forms. It is important that you get rid of any clumps as best you can. In a mixing bowl, beat together the butter until smooth. Add in icing sugar and matcha mixture and beat until thickened. Transfer to a piping bag and frost the fully cooled cupcakes. Top with mini chocolate chips, if desired.

EGG NOG CUPCAKES

INGREDIENTS

CUPCAKES

- 1 (16 ounce) box white cake mix
- 1¼ cups egg nog
- 2 eggs
- ½ teaspoon ground nutmeg
- ½ teaspoon vanilla extract

FROSTING

- ½ cup butter, softened to room temperature
- ¼ cup egg nog
- 1 teaspoon vanilla
- ½ teaspoon ground nutmeg
- 4 to 5 cups powdered sugar

DIRECTIONS

1. Preheat oven to 350 degrees F.
2. In a large bowl, combine cake mix, egg nog, eggs, nutmeg and vanilla. Whisk together until just combined.
3. Spoon batter into a mini cupcake pan filled with paper liners or sprayed with nonstick cooking spray. Fill each cupcake ⅔ of the way full.
4. Bake for 8-10 minutes, or until barely golden brown.
5. Remove from oven and let cool completely.

FOR THE FROSTING

1. In a large bowl, cream together butter, egg nog, vanilla, and nutmeg.
2. Mix in powdered sugar one cup at a time.
3. Spread or pipe frosting onto cooled cupcakes.

CHOCOLATE & PEANUT BUTTER CUPCAKES

INGREDIENTS

CHOCOLATE CUPCAKES

- 1/4 cup cocoa powder
- 1/2 cup flour
- 1/2 tsp baking powder
- 1/4 tsp baking soda
- 1/8 tsp salt
- 1/2 stick butter, room temperature
- 6 tbsp sugar
- 1 egg
- 1/2 tsp vanilla
  - tbsp sour cream
- 1 tbsp melted chocolate, cooled

PEANUT BUTTER CUPCAKES

- 1/2 cup & 1 tbsp flour
- 1/4 tsp baking soda
- 1/2 tsp baking powder
- 1/4 tsp salt
  - tbsp peanut butter
- 2 tbsp vegetable oil
- 1/4 cup brown sugar
- 1/4 cup buttermilk
- 1 egg
- 1/4 tsp vanilla

CHOCOLATE BUTTERCREAM

- 1 stick butter
- 1/2 cup vegetable shortening
- 3/4 cup cocoa
- 2-2.5 cups powdered sugar

PEANUT BUTTER CREAM

- 1 stick butter
- 1/2 cup vegetable shortening
- 3/4 cup peanut butter
- 2-4 cups powdered sugar

DIRECTIONS

CHOCOLATE CUPCAKES

1. Preheat the oven to 350º F. Line a muffin tin with 12 cupcake liners.
2. In a small mixing bowl, combine the cocoa powder, flour, baking powder, baking soda and salt. Gently mix using a spoon.
3. In a larger mixing bowl, combine the butter and sugar, beat using an electric mixer until fluffy. Add in the eggs and vanilla, lightly beat.
4. Add in the sour cream and melted chocolate, mix by hand using a spatula.
5. Add half of the flour mixture to the wet Ingredients, do not dump it in, rather take spoonfuls of the flour mixture and gently shake it over the wet Ingredients, as if you were sifting in the flour. Fold in the mixture until no flour remains. Repeat with the other half of the flour, folding it in and scraping the sides and bottom of the bowl to incorporate everything. Set aside.

PEANUT BUTTER CUPCAKES

1. In a bowl combine the flour, baking soda, baking powder, and salt. In a separate bowl, combine the peanut butter, oil, and brown sugar, beat together using an electric mixer. Add in the egg and vanilla, beat again. Add the flour mixture and buttermilk, alternating between the two and mixing by hand until everything is incorporated.
2. Begin to add the batter into the pan, alternating between chocolate and peanut butter. Fill the cupcake liners almost completely full with batter.

3. Place the pan in the middle of the oven and bake for 15-17 minutes or until a toothpick inserted in the center comes out clean.
4. Allow the cupcakes to cool for about 3 minutes in the pan, then take them out and allow them to cool upside down on a cooling rack. This will help create cupcakes with a dome top.
5. Allow the cupcakes to cool completely before adding the frosting.

CHOCOLATE BUTTERCREAM

1. In a mixing bowl, combine the butter and vegetable shortening, beat using an electric mixer until fluffy. Add in the cocoa powder, and gently mix by hand with a spatula.
2. Begin to add the powdered sugar, 1 cup at a time, mixing by hand first, then with the electric mixer. Continue adding powdered sugar until the frosting tastes good to you.

PEANUT BUTTERCREAM

1. In a mixing large bowl, combine the butter and vegetable shortening, beat using an electric mixer until fluffy.
2. Add in the peanut butter, beat using electric mixer.
3. Begin to add the powdered sugar, 1 cup at a time, mixing by hand first, then with the electric mixer. Continue adding powdered sugar until the frosting tastes good to you.

FROSTING

1. In a piping bag fit with a wilton 6B piping tip, do your best to add chocolate buttercream to one side of the bag and peanut butter buttercream to the other. Push the buttercream down into the bag. Pipe the buttercream onto the cupcakes, starting on the outside edge and working your way into the center, progressively stacking the frosting as you get to the center.

CHOCOLATE CUPCAKES WITH CARAMEL

INGREDIENTS

CHOCOLATE CUPCAKES

- 1/2 cup salted butter
- 1 cup sugar
- 2 eggs
- 1/2 tsp vanilla extract
- 6 tbsp water
- 6 tbsp cocoa powder
- 1 cup all purpose flour
- 1/2 tsp baking soda
- 6 tbsp Kahlua

KAHLUA ICING

- 1/2 cup salted butter
- 1/2 cup shortening*
- 4 cups powdered sugar
- 4-5 tbsp kahlua
- caramel sauce
- sea salt

DIRECTIONS

2. Preheat oven to 350 degrees.
3. Beat butter and sugar until light in color and fluffy, about 2-3 minutes.
4. Add eggs, one at a time, beating just until blended.
5. Add vanilla, water and cocoa powder to another bowl and whisk until smooth.
6. Add chocolate mixture to batter and mix until combined. Scrape down the sides of the bowl as needed to make sure everything is well combined.
7. Combine flour and baking soda in a separate bowl.
8. Alternate adding the flour mixture and kahlua to the batter. Begin by adding half of the dry mix, then mix well. Add the

kahlua and mix well, scrapes down the sides as needed. Add the remaining flour mixture and beat until smooth.

9. Fill cupcake liners about half way. Bake for 16-18 minutes, or until a toothpick inserted comes out with a few crumbs.
10. To make icing, beat butter and shortening until smooth.
11. Add 2 cups of powdered sugar and beat until smooth.
12. Add 4 tbsp Kahlua and remaining powdered sugar and beat until smooth. Add additional Kahlua if needed to get the right icing consistency.
13. Pipe icing onto cupcakes
14. Drizzle cupcakes with caramel sauce and a sprinkle of sea salt.

APPLE CUPCAKES

INGREDIENTS

- 1½ cups cake flour
- 1 cup all-purpose flour
- 3 tsp. baking powder
- ¼ tsp. salt
- 1 cup butter, room temperature
- 1½ cups brown sugar
- 4 eggs, room temperature
- ½ cup buttermilk
- 1½ cups apple sauce
- 1 tsp. vanilla
- 1½ tsp. cinnamon
- ½ tsp. ground ginger
- ¼ tsp. nutmeg

FILLING

- 2 apples, cored and cubed
- 1 tbsp. brown sugar
- 1 tbsp. butter
- Salt
- ¼ tsp. cinnamon
- 1 tsp. all-purpose flour

TOPPING

- ½ cup butter, room temperature
- ½ cup old-fashioned oats
- ¼ cup all-purpose flour
- ½ tsp. cinnamon

BUTTERCREAM

- ¾ cup butter, room temperature
- 1½ cups confectioners' sugar
- 1 tsp. vanilla

- ¼ cup brown sugar
- 1-2 tbsp. heavy whipping cream

DIRECTIONS

FILLING

1. Heat butter in a small saute pan over medium heat. Once melted, stir in sugar, salt, cinnamon, and apples. Stir constantly until apples are tender, about 5 minutes. Mix in flour and cook for another minute or two. Remove from heat and cool.

TOPPING

1. Combine all the topping Ingredients into a bowl and mix until well combined.

CAKE

2. In the bowl of a stand mixer, add the butter and sugar. Beat until light and fluffy, about 5 min. Beat in the eggs one at a time, making sure to combine well before adding the next. Add vanilla and applesauce: mix well.
3. Sift together the flours, baking powder, cinnamon, ginger, nutmeg, and salt.
4. With the mixer on low, add in the flour mixture and buttermilk alternatively, always starting and ending with the dry Ingredients. Mix until just combined.
5. Preheat the oven to 350F.
6. Line a cupcake tray with cupcake liners. Add a bit of batter to the bottom of each liner, maybe ⅓ of the way. Evenly place the filling into each liner. Top with remaining batter. This should make about 12 cupcakes. Spread out the topping onto each cupcake.
7. Place tray into the oven and bake for 18-20 minutes, or until toothpick comes out clean. Allow to cool slightly in tray and then move cupcakes to wire rack to finish cooling.
8. If decorating with buttercream, add the butter to the bowl of a stand mixer. Cream, on medium speed, until pale and fluffy (about 5 minutes.)

9. Sift in confectioners' sugar and add brown sugar.
10. Pour in vanilla and heavy whipping cream, mixing until combined. Mix on medium/high speed until whipped and fluffy, a good 3-4 minutes.
11. Decorate cupcakes and serve.

MINT ICE CREAM CUPCAKES

INGREDIENTS

CUPCAKES

- 24 chocolate cupcakes, baked and cooled
- 1/2 carton (about .75 quart) mint chip ice cream
- Mint Chip Frosting
- Mini Chocolate Chips, for garnish

MINT FROSTING

- 12 tablespoons unsalted butter, softened
- 3 cups powdered sugar
- 1 teaspoon vanilla
- 1/4-1/2 teaspoon peppermint extract
- 4-6 tablespoons heavy whipping cream
- 4-5 drops green food coloring, optional
- 1/2 cup mini chocolate chips

DIRECTIONS

1. Start with 24 cupcakes that have been baked and completely cooled. You can use a chocolate box mix, or your favorite from scratch recipe.
2. Place the cupcakes on a cookie sheet lined with wax paper. Make room for a second cookie sheet lined with wax paper in your freezer.
3. To prep the cupcakes: use a pairing knife to cut a large circle in the top of the cupcake. Cut down almost to the bottom of the cupcake, then lift out the cut part. You should end up with a cone shaped chunk of cake. Slice the cone off of each of the cupcake pieces. (You need to make the piece of cake smaller, because the cupcake will be filled with ice cream.) See this post for photo DIRECTIONS.
4. prepare all the cupcakes for the ice cream, then place your second cookie sheet in the freezer. Work in batches of 3-4 cupcakes, filling with ice cream, then placing on the cookie

sheet that's in the freezer. That way the ice cream won't melt out of the cupcakes.

5. Scoop about 1-2 tablespoons of ice cream into the center of each cupcake. Place the top back on and press gently. Put the cupcake on the cookie sheet in the freezer. Continue until all the cupcakes are filled and in the freezer.

6. Cover the cupcakes with plastic wrap (leaving them on the cookie sheet) and freeze for at least 4 hours before serving. You can place them in a single layer in large Ziploc bags and freeze for up to 1 month before serving.

7. To make the frosting: beat butter with a hand or a stand mixer until smooth. Mix in powdered sugar slowly, then add vanilla and peppermint extract. Start with 1/4 teaspoon peppermint extract then taste and add more as desired. Mix in 1 tablespoon of heavy whipping cream at a time, mixing well, until you've reached your desired consistency.

8. When ready to serve, have your frosting ready. Remove a cupcake from the freezer, frost as desired, and serve immediately. Top with additional mini chocolate chips for garnish.

CLASSIC CUPCAKES WITH CHOCOLATE BUTTERCREAM

INGREDIENTS

CUPCAKES

- 1/2 cup unsalted butter (1 stick), melted
- 1 large egg plus 1 egg yolk
- 1 cup granulated sugar
- 6 ounces (about 1/2 cup) Greek yogurt
- 2 teaspoons vanilla extract
- 1 1/2 cups all-purpose flour
- 1 1/2 teaspoons baking powder
- 1/4 teaspoon salt, optional and to taste

CHOCOLATE BUTTERCREAM FROSTING

- 1/2 cup unsalted butter (1 stick), softened
- 1/2 heaping cup unsweetened natural cocoa powder, sifted
- 2 1/2 to 3 cups confectioners' sugar, sifted is ideal
- 1 teaspoon vanilla extract
- splash cream or milk, only as needed for consistency
- chocolate sprinkles, optional for garnishing

DIRECTIONS

1. Preheat oven to 350F. Line a Non-Stick 12-Cup Regular Muffin Pan with paper liners; set aside.
2. Cupcakes - In a large, microwave-safe bowl, melt the butter, about 1 minute on high power.
3. Allow the butter to cool momentarily, and add the egg plus yolk, sugar, yogurt, vanilla, and whisk to combine.
4. Stir in the flour, baking powder, optional salt, and mix until just combined and free from large lumps; don't overmix or cupcakes will be tough.

5. Using a medium 2-inch cookie scoop, place about 2 tablespoons of batter per cupcake into each of the 12 cavities so they're solidly ¾ full

6. Bake for 18 to 19 minutes, or until tops are golden, set, slightly domed, and springy to the touch. A toothpick inserted in the center should come out clean or with a few moist crumbs, but no batter. Allow cupcakes to cool in pan for 5 to 10 minutes before transferring to a wire rack to cool completely. While they cool, make the frosting.

7. Frosting - To the bowl of a stand mixer fitted with the paddle attachment, add the butter and beat on medium-high speed until pale, light and fluffy, about 5 minutes. Stop to scrape down the sides of the bowl as necessary.

8. Add the cocoa, 2 1/2 cups confectioners' sugar, vanilla, and beat on medium-high speed until fluffy, about 5 minutes. Stop to scrape down the sides of the bowl as necessary.

9. Based on texture and taste preferences, optionally add ½ cup additional sugar. Transfer frosting to a piping bag and frost the cooled cupcakes.

10. Optionally, garnish each cupcake with a pinch of sprinkles.

AVOCADO CUPCAKES

INGREDIENTS

MILK CHOCOLATE CUPCAKES

- 1 cup cake flour
- ⅔ cup sugar
- ⅓ cup cocoa powder
- 1 pinch of baking soda
- 1 pinch of salt
- ¾ cup water
- ⅓ cup oil
- 1 egg, beaten
- 1 teaspoon vinegar

AVOCADO BUTTERCREAM

- ½ an avocado
- ½ tablespoon butter, softened
- 1¼ cup powdered sugar
- ½ teaspoon vanilla

DIRECTIONS

1. Whisk the dry Ingredients together until well mixed.
2. Add the wet Ingredients and stir until moistened. The batter will be thinner than typical cake batter.
3. Pour into a lined muffin pan, filling each cupcake about ¾ of the way full. They pop straight up, so you can fill them up closer to the top if you want.
4. Bake at 350 for about 12 minutes.
5. Avocado Buttercream
6. With an electric mixer, blend the avocado and butter together. Add the vanilla and powdered sugar. If it's too thick, add a tbs. of milk. If it's too thin, add more sugar.
7. To put the frosting neatly on the cupcakes, scoop it into a snack-size plastic bag, cut off the tip, and squeeze out the frosting into nice little spirals on top of the cupcakes.

CARAMEL CHEESECAKE

INGREDIENTS

- butter 70g, melted
- digestive biscuits 150g
- full-fat soft cheese 400g
- double cream 100ml
- dulce de leche 200g, plus more to serve
- eggs 2, beaten

DIRECTIONS

1. Heat the oven to 170C/fan 150C/gas 31/2. To make the base, mix the butter and biscuits until they looks like damp breadcrumbs. Butter and line the base of a 22cm springform tin, pack the biscuit mixture into the base and chill.
2. For the filling, mix the cheese, cream, dulce de leche and eggs to a smooth paste. Put this mix in the tin with the biscuit base and cook for 45 minutes until it is set, but still has a slight wobble. Cool to room temperature, then chill until ready to serve. Spread more dulce de leche on top.

THE NEW 2015 BROWNIES RECIPE

INGREDIENTS

- ¼ cup (1/2 stick) unsalted butter
- ¼ cup unsweetened applesauce
- ¾ cup white sugar
- 2 large eggs
- ½ cup unsweetened cocoa powder
- ½ tsp salt
- ½ tsp baking powder
- ½ tbsp vanilla extract
- ¾ cup unbleached all-purpose flour
- ¼ cup semisweet chocolate chips

DIRECTIONS

1. Preheat oven to 350 F.
2. In medium bowl, add cocoa, applesauce, eggs, salt, baking powder, and vanilla and whisk until all blended and smooth. Add chocolate chips on top, but do not stir in yet.
3. In a separate small bowl, microwave butter until melted (30 seconds). Add sugar, and microwave again for 30 seconds.
4. Pour melted butter and sugar over chocolate chips sitting on cocoa mixture and stir.
5. Add flour and stir until everything is well blended and smooth.
6. Pour melted butter and sugar over chocolate chips sitting on cocoa mixture and stir.
7. Add flour and stir until everything is well blended and smooth.

THE ULTIMATE BLUEBERRY CAKE

INGREDIENTS

- 1 (15.25 oz) box of yellow cake mix
- 4 cups of fresh blueberries
- 3 tbsp cornstarch
- 3/4 cup white granulated sugar
- 1/2 cup butter (1 stick) cut into 1/2 inch chunks

DIRECTIONS

1. Preheat oven to 350F. Grease a 9 x 13 inch baking pan. Add 3 cups of blueberries to the pan, spreading evenly across. Sprinkle cornstarch evenly across. Sprinkle sugar evenly across.
2. Sprinkle cake mix on top of blueberries, trying to spread evenly across. Spread butter chunks evenly on top. Sprinkle remaining 1 cup of blueberries on top.
3. Bake for 45-55 minutes or until cake mix is golden brown and no raw cake mix remains. Let cake cool for about 30 minutes before serving and eating.

APPLE CAKE WITH CARAMEL

INGREDIENTS

APPLE CAKE

- 3 granny smith apples, peeled and cored
- 2 cups all purpose flour
- 1 tablespoon baking powder
- 1 tablespoon cinnamon
- 1 teaspoon nutmeg
- 1 teaspoon salt
- ½ cup (1 stick) unsalted butter, softened
- ½ cup light brown sugar
- ⅓ cup honey
- ½ cup sour cream
- ½ cup unsweetened almond milk
- 2 large eggs
- 2 teaspoons vanilla

CARAMEL

- 1 cup granulated sugar
- 6 tablespoons unsalted butter, cut into pieces
- ½ heavy cream
- 1 teaspoon salt

DIRECTIONS

1. Preheat oven to 350 degrees. Lightly grease an 8 inch springform pan.
2. Slice all three apples, with two of the apple chop them in until you have a large dice.
3. In a bowl, mix the flour, baking powder, cinnamon, nutmeg and salt. Set aside.
4. In a stand mixer, beat the butter until smooth. Add the sugar and honey and beat until fluffy.
5. Next add the sour cream and beat until combined, followed by each egg, one at a time, mixing well after each addition.

6. Scrape down your bowl, add vanilla and beat an additional time.
7. Finally, beat in the milk. The batter may appear to be curdled, but that's perfectly normal.
8. Stir in the flour mixture, beating until you get a smooth, creamy, beige batter.
9. Stir in the chopped apples and spread into the prepared pan. Arrange the remaining apple slices over top, overlapping them slightly, in a circular patter over the batter.
10. Put the pan on the top rack of the oven for 40-50 minutes. Once a toothpick or skewer is inserted and comes out dry, the cake is done.
11. Allow the cake to cool completely.
12. Heat sugar in a medium saucepan over medium heat, stirring constantly with a rubber spatula, The sugar will start to form hard clumps but will eventually melt into a thick brown amber liquid. Be careful not to burn.
13. Once the sugar has completely melted, immediately add the butter. The butter will bubble rapidly so be careful. Stir the butter into the caramel until it is completely melted, about 2 minutes.
14. Very slowly, pour the heavy cream into your pan. Again, this will bubble and splatter so be careful. Allow the mixture to boil for one minute.
15. Remove from the heat and stir in salt.
16. Allow to cool slightly before drizzling over the apple cake. If done over the entire cake, serve immediately. If serving over a longer period of time, drizzle over each slice individually as served.

FLOURLESS CHOCOLATE BLENDER CAKE

INGREDIENTS

- 1 extra-large or 2 small ripe banana(s), peeled
- 1 large egg
- heaping 1/2 cup creamy peanut butter
- 3 tablespoons honey
- 1 tablespoon vanilla extract
- 1/4 teaspoon baking soda
- pinch salt, optional and to taste
- heaping 1/2 cup mini semi-sweet chocolate chips, plus more for sprinkling on top

DIRECTIONS

1. Preheat oven to 350F and spray a 9-inch round cake pan with cooking spray; set aside.
2. To the canister of a blender, add all Ingredients except chocolate chips and blend on high speed until smoothy and creamy, about 1 minute.
3. Add chocolate chips and stir in by hand; don't use the blender because it will pulverize them.
4. Turn batter out into prepared pan, smoothing the top lightly with a spatula if necessary.
5. Evenly sprinkle with a tablespoon or two of extra chocolate chips.
6. Bake for about 25 minutes, or until the cake is set in the center, springy to the touch, and a toothpick inserted into the center comes out clean, or with a few moist crumbs, but no batter. Due to variances in moisture levels in bananas, peanut butter, oven and climate variances, baking times will range. Start watching closely at 20 minutes, and always bake until done. Allow cake to cool in pan for about 15 minutes, or until it's firmed up and is cool enough to remove from pan.

THE ULTIMATE BANANA CAKE

INGREDIENTS

FOR THE CAKE

- 1 1/2 cups sugar
- 1/2 cup (1 stick) unsalted butter, softened
- 2 large eggs
- 1 teaspoon vanilla extract
- 3 medium ripe bananas
- 2/3 cup milk
- 1 teaspoon baking soda
- 1/8 teaspoon salt
- 2 1/4 cups all-purpose flour

FOR THE CREAM CHEESE FROSTING

- 2 oz. cream cheese, softened
- 3/4 cup confectioners' sugar
- 6 tablespoons unsalted butter, melted
- 1/2 teaspoon vanilla extract

TOPPINGS

- Caramel sauce
- 1/4 cup semisweet chocolate chips, melted or chocolate syrup
- 1/4 cup mini chocolate chips
- 1/4 cup salted peanuts
- 1/2 jar Maraschino cherries, cut in half
- sprinkles

DIRECTIONS

1. Preheat oven to 350 degrees F. Spray an 8-x-8-inch baking pan with nonstick spray.
2. In a stand mixer, combine sugar, butter, eggs, and vanilla. Mix on medium speed for 3 minutes or until well incorporated.

3. Meanwhile, smash 3 large bananas (use a potato masher) and add to the mix.
4. Slowly add milk, soda, salt, and flour and mix until well combined.
5. Pour batter into the prepared baking pan and put into oven. Bake for 30 minutes or until a toothpick inserted in the middle comes out clean. Let cake cool completely.
6. Once cake is cooled, prepare the cream cheese frosting by mixing together the cream cheese, confectioners' sugar, butter and vanilla until smooth and creamy. Spread evenly over the top. Drizzle caramel sauce over the cream cheese frosting (as much as desired), followed by melted chocolate or chocolate syrup. Add cherries, mini chocolate chips, peanuts and sprinkles. Place in the fridge for 2 hours or until cream cheese frosting is set. Cut into squares and serve.

COFFEE AND CHOCOLATE CAKE

INGREDIENTS

FOR THE CAKE

- 2 cups cake flour
- ¾ cup cocoa
- 1½ teaspoons baking soda
- ¾ teaspoon salt
- ¾ cup butter, room temperature
- 2 cups golden brown sugar
- 3 large eggs
- 1½ teaspoons vanilla extract
- 1 cup buttermilk
- 4 teaspoons instant espresso powder dissolved in ¾ cup hot water

FOR THE PEANUT BUTTER FROSTING

- 1½ cups butter, softened
- 1½ cup creamy peanut butter
- 4½ cups powdered sugar
- 4 tsp dark rum
- 3 tsp vanilla
- 6 Tbsp heavy cream

FOR THE RUM DRIZZLE

- ¾ cup brown sugar
- ½ cup Dark Rum
- 1 tablespoon unsalted butter

DIRECTIONS

CAKE LAYERS

1. Position rack in center of oven; preheat to 325. Generously butter two 9-inch cake pans; dust with cocoa, tapping out excess. Line bottom of pan with parchment paper.
2. Sift 2 cups cake flour, cocoa, baking soda and salt into medium bowl.
3. Using electric mixer, beat butter in large bowl until smooth. Add brown sugar and beat until well blended, about 2 minutes.
4. Add eggs, 1 at a time, beating well after each addition. Mix in vanilla.
5. Add flour mixture in 3 additions alternately with buttermilk in 2 additions, beating just until blended after each addition.
6. Gradually add hot espresso-water mixture, beating just until smooth.
7. Divide batter between pans; smooth tops. Bake cakes until tester inserted into center comes out clean, about 40 minutes. Cool cakes in pans on rack 15 minutes. Run small knife around sides of pans to loosen cakes. Invert cakes onto racks; lift pans off cakes and remove parchment. Place wire rack atop each cake, invert again so top side is up.
8. Cool completely.
9. Mark each cake layer with toothpicks halfway up the sides; use the toothpicks as a guide to cut each cake layer in half.

FROSTING

1. In the bowl of a stand mixer, cream together the peanut butter and butter for 2-3 minutes.
2. Add the powdered sugar, scrape the sides of the bowl and mix on high for one minute.
3. Add the rum and vanilla and mix in.
4. Add the heavy cream and beat until smooth; scraping the sides. Beat for 3 minutes on high. Use immediately

RUM DRIZZLE

1. Put all of the Ingredients into a medium size saucepan. Heat until bubbly and cook for one minute. Cool completely.
2. Putting it all together:
3. Spread a tablespoon of frosting in the middle of your cake plate to help hold cake in place. Brush crumbs from one cake layer and put in the middle of the plate. Drizzle one

Tablespoon of rum drizzle over cake layer and spread 1 and ½ cups of frosting on cake, smoothing to edges. Repeat with all layers

4. Swirl frosting over top of cake and either pipe rosettes in the center of the cake on the top or dollop additional frosting and swirl in center.

5. Gently pour rum drizzle over cake; letting pool on top and drip down the sides. Serve.

LEMON AND CHEESE CREAM CAKE

INGREDIENTS

FOR THE CAKE

- 2 cups sugar
- 2 1/2 cups cake flour
- 1 1/2 teaspoons baking powder
- 1 1/2 teaspoons baking soda
- 1 teaspoon kosher salt
- 1 tablespoon pure vanilla extract
- 2 eggs
- 1/2 cup oil
- 1 cup milk
- 1 cup boiling water
- 2 1/2 teaspoons lemon extract
- zest & juice of 1 lemon

FOR THE FROSTING

- 1 cup unsalted butter, room temperature
- 8 ounces cream cheese, room temperature
- 1 teaspoon pure vanilla extract
- 1 1/2 teaspoons lemon extract
- 3 1/2 cups powdered sugar

FOR THE MIDDLE BIT

- 1/2 cup baker's choice of jam

FOR THE CANDIED LEMON TOPPING

- lemon, cut in 1/4 inch slices
- 1/2 cup sugar
- 1/2 cup water

1. In a small saucepan, stir the sugar and water together until the mixture becomes clear.
2. Drop in your slices of lemon and allow to cook in the syrup for 1 minute before taking the mixture off of the heat.
3. Refrigerate until you are ready to frost your cake Heat oven to 350°F. Grease and flour two 9-inch round baking pans.
4. In a large bowl, combine all dry Ingredients. Add eggs, milk, oil, vanilla, lemon extract, and lemon zest and juice.
5. Beat with a hand mixer on medium speed for 2 minutes. Stir in boiling water (batter will be thin). Pour into 2 prepared cake tins.
6. Bake for 30-35 minutes, or until a knife comes out clean in the center.
7. In a large bowl, beat the cream cheese, butter, vanilla, lemon extract, and salt with a hand mixer on medium high speed.
8. Add in the powdered sugar in 3 additions, beating in between each time.
9. Place a dollop of frosting on a cake stand (this will hold the cake and prevent it from sliding). Place a layer of cake on the stand, frost the top with the lemon cream cheese frosting, then a thick layer of jam.
10. Place the second layer of cake on top. Frost the sides before frosting the top. Add on your candied lemon babies.

BASIC CHOCOLATE PUDDING CAKE

INGREDIENTS

- 2 1/2 cups all-purpose flour
- 2 1/4 cups packed light brown sugar, divided
- 3 teaspoons baking powder
- 1 teaspoon baking soda
- 1/2 teaspoon salt
- 1 cup chocolate chips
- 2 tablespoons unsalted butter
- 2 ounces unsweetened chocolate
- 2 cups buttermilk
- 1 teaspoon vanilla extract
- 1/2 cup plus 2 tablespoons unsweetened
- 2 1/2 cups boiling water

DIRECTIONS

1. Preheat the oven to 350 degrees F. Grease a 9 x 13-inch baking pan and set aside.
2. In a large mixing bowl, combine flour, 1 cup of the brown sugar, baking powder, baking soda, and salt. Whisk until well combined. If there are lumps of brown sugar, use your hands to break them up. Stir in chocolate chips and set aside.
3. In a small saucepan, melt the butter and chocolate together over medium-low heat.
4. In a separate small saucepan, heat buttermilk over low heat until barely warmed. You don't want it to bubble or boil. Remove from heat.
5. Remove chocolate and butter mixture from heat and stir in the vanilla. Pour mixture over dry Ingredients. Add the buttermilk and stir until combined. Spread into the prepared pan.
6. Combine the remaining 1 1/4 cups brown sugar with the cocoa in a small bowl. Whisk until smooth, using your hands to break up any brown sugar clumps. Sprinkle mixture evenly over the chocolate cake batter.
7. Pour the boiling water evenly over the cake.

8. Carefully transfer the pan to the oven. Bake for 30-35 minutes or until the center is firm to the touch.
9. Remove cake from oven and cool on a cooling rack for at least 30 minutes before serving. To serve, invert each serving on a plate so that the fudge sauce on the bottom becomes a topping. Spoon any extra sauce in the pan over the top. You can serve the cake at room temperature or warm. Top with ice cream, if desired.

THREE COLORS CAKE

INGREDIENTS

- 101 g all-purpose flour
- 31 g unsweetened cocoa powder
- 2.5 g baking soda
- 0.5 g baking powder
- 1 g kosher salt
- 56 g eggs
- 126 g granulated sugar
- 2 g vanilla paste
- 86 g mayonnaise
- 105 g water, at room temperature

GRAHAM STREUSEL

- 50 g almond flour
- 50 g graham crumbs
- 50 g light brown sugar
- 25 g all-purpose flour
- 1 g vanilla powder
- 60 g unsalted butter, cold, cut into 1/2 inch dice

CHOCOLATE CREAM

- 233 g heavy cream
- 100 g whole milk
- 66 g granulated sugar
- 10 g unsweetened cocoa powder
- 1 g salt
- 66 g egg yolks
- 125 g dark chocolate, melted

MERINGUE

- 50 g egg whites
- 75 g granulated sugar
- 1 g vanilla paste

1. To start, line three 3 inch diameter and 1.75 inch tall ring molds with acetate and place on a silpat lined baking sheet. Set aside.
2. For the cake, preheat the oven to 325 F. Line a half sheet pan with a silpat or spray lightly with nonstick spray, line with parchment paper, and spray the parchment.
3. Sift the flour, cocoa powder, baking soda, and baking powder into a medium bowl. Add the salt and stir to combine.
4. Place the eggs, sugar, and vanilla paste in the bowl of a stand mixer fitted with the whisk attachment and mix on medium-low speed for about 1 minute to combine. Increase the speed to medium and whip for 5 minutes, until the mixture is thick and pale yellow. Scrape down the sides and bottom of the bowl, then whip on medium-high speed for another 5 minutes, or until the mixture has thickened. When the whisk is lifted, the mixture should form a slowly dissolving ribbon.
5. Add the mayonnaise and whip to combine. Remove the bowl from the mixer stand and fold in the dry Ingredients and water in 2 additions each.
6. Pour the batter into the prepared pan and, using an offset spatula, spread it in an even layer, making sure that it reaches into the corners. Bake for 10 minutes, until a skewer inserted into the centre comes out sean and the cake springs back when lightly touched. Set on a cooling rack and cool completely.
7. Lay a piece of parchment on the back of a sheet pan. Run a knife around the edges of the cake to loosen it and invert it onto the parchment. Remove the silpat or parchment from the top of the cake. Place in the freezer for at least 30 minutes.
8. Cut out three 3-inch diameter rounds from the cake while it is still frozen and place in the ring molds. Wrap the remainder of the cake in plastic wrap and freeze for up to 2 weeks (this is extra).
9. For the streusel, preheat the oven to 325 F. Line a baking sheet with parchment paper.
10. Combine the almond flour, graham crumbs, sugar, vanilla powder, and flour in a small bowl. Whisk to combine. Add the butter and quickly break it up with your fingertips until the

mixture resembles coarse meal. Spread the streusel on the baking sheet in an even layer and freeze for 10 minutes.

11. Bake for 12 to 15 minutes, stirring the streusel every 4 minutes. Remove from the oven and cool completely. Spoon 40 g of streusel into each ring hold and gently press into the holds Store the remainder in an airtight container at room temperature for up to 4 days or freeze for up to 2 weeks.

12. For the custard, combine the milk and cream in a medium saucepan set of medium-high heat. In a small bowl, whisk together the egg yolks, sugar, and cocoa powder until slightly paler in colour.

13. When the milk mixture has come to a boil, slowly pour a small amount into the yolk mixture, whisking continuously. Continue tempering the yolks with the milk mixture, then transfer all of back into the saucepan. Cook over medium-low heat, stirring continuously with a rubber spatula, until the mixture has thickened enough to coat the back of a spoon and a thermometer reads 82 C.

14. Remove from heat and strain through a fine-mesh sieve into a bowl set over an ice bath. While the mixture is still warm, add the melted chocolate and emulsify with an immersion blender. Place a piece of plastic wrap directly on the surface of the custard and refrigerate for at least 3 hours, or overnight.

15. Fill a piping bag with the chocolate custard and pipe into the molds until it reaches the top of the molds. Smooth the top with an offset spatula and freeze for 4 hours, or overnight.

16. Remove the rings from the cakes, but keep the acetate on. Add a second layer of acetate 0.5 inches higher than the original acetate over top the original acetate. Place the rings back on.

17. For the meringue, combine the egg whites and sugar in the bowl of a stand mixer set over a saucepan of barely simmering water. Whisking constantly, bring the mixture to 60 C, then transfer to the stand mixer and whip on high speed until stiff peaks form, about 8 minutes. Add the vanilla paste and whip for 1 minute to combine.

18. Pipe the meringue into the rings until it reaches the top of the second layer of acetate. Smooth the top with an offset spatula and freeze for 30 minutes.

19. Place into the fridge 4 hours before serving but remove the rings and both layers of acetate while frozen. When ready to

serve, use a handheld torch to toast the meringue while being careful not to scorch the custard.

CHOCOLATE BUTTERCREAM BROWNIES CAKE

INGREDIENTS

- 1 cup chocolate chocolate drink mix
- ¾ cup butter, softened
- 1½ cup flour
- 2½ cups sugar
- 4 eggs
- 1 TB vanilla
- ½ American Heritage chocolate bar
- 1 tsp. salt

FROSTING

- 6 TB unsalted butter, softened
- ¼ cup unsweetened cocoa powder
- ¼ tsp. salt
- 1¼ cups powdered sugar
- 1 TB milk
- ½ tsp. vanilla extract

DIRECTIONS

1. Combine chocolate drink mix, flour, sugar and salt in a bowl and mix. Add softened butter, eggs and vanilla and beat on LOW until well combined. Fold in ½ cup chocolate bar (grated) and mix well.
2. Spread into a greased 9x13. Bake at 350 for 30-35 minutes. Let cool completely.
3. For frosting, mix butter, cocoa, vanilla and salt in a bowl until well combined. Slowly add powdered sugar and milk and beat until well combined. Spread over cooled brownies. Sprinkle with mini M&Ms.

APPLE CAKE WITH CARAMEL V2

INGREDIETNS

APPLE SPICE CAKE

- 1 cup flour
- 1/2 tsp baking soda
- 1 tsp baking powder
- 1/4 tsp salt
- 1/2 tsp cinnamon
- 1/4 tsp cloves
- 1/4 tsp allspice
- 1/2 stick butter, room temperature
- 1/2 cup brown sugar
- 1 egg
- 3/4 cup unsweetened applesauce

VANILLA BUTTERCREAM

- 2 stick butter, room temperature
- 1/2 cup vegetable shortening
- 1 tsp vanilla paste (or extract or vanilla bean pods)
- 5-7 cups powdered sugar

CARAMEL DRIZZLE

- 1/4 cup heavy cream
- 1 tbsp butter, unsalted
- 1/4 tsp salt
- 1/2 tsp vanilla extract
- 6 tbsp sugar
- 1 tbsp light corn syrup
- 1 tbsp water

DIRECTIONS

1. Preheat the oven to 350º F.

2. Using butter, grease the bottom and sides of an 6 inch round cake pan or springform pan and line the bottom with a round piece of parchment paper. To ensure even baking, place a bake even strip around the pan. You can make your own homemade bake even strip by cutting a towel or shirt to fit the size of your pan. Get the fabric really wet, then squeeze out the dripping water but do not squeeze it too dry. Secure the fabric around the pan with a safety pin.
3. In a small bowl combine the flour, baking soda, baking powder, salt, cinnamon, cloves, and allspice. Mix well.
4. In a larger bowl, combine the butter and brown sugar. Beat using an electric mixer until creamy, about 1 minute.
5. Add in the egg, beat again with the mixer.
6. Add in the applesauce, mix by hand with a spatula.
7. Gradually add in the flour mixture, mixing by hand until it's incorporated.
8. Scrape the batter into the prepared cake pan, using a spatula to evenly spread it out.
9. Bake for 23-25 minutes, or until a toothpick inserted in the center comes out clean.
10. Once the cake is done, allow it to cool in the pan on a cooling rack for 10 minutes. After 10 minutes, carefully remove the cake from the pan. If using a springform pan, remove the sides and bottom. Allow the cake to cool completely on a cooling rack. Once cool, remove the parchment paper round from the bottom of the cake. If you need to level the top of your cake, do so now using either a cake lever or knife. Make sure the cake is completely cooled, then wrap the cake in plastic wrap and place it in the refrigerator. This cake is good for up to one week like this.
11. In a mixing large bowl, combine the butter and vegetable shortening, beat using an electric mixer until fluffy, 2 minutes.
12. Add in the vanilla paste, beat using electric mixer.
13. Begin to add the powdered sugar, about 1-2 cups at a time, mixing by hand first, then with the electric mixer. Continue adding powdered sugar until the frosting tastes good to you.
14. Spread a small amount of buttercream on a 6 inch round cardboard cake circle. Place your first layer of cake on top of the cardboard. Put buttercream on top of the first layer and spread it as even as possible with an offset spatula. Decide how much or how little frosting you want in-between each

layer, you can measure the frosting, I'd use 1/3 to 1/2 cup in between each layer.

15. Repeat this process for each layer of cake. Once all of the layers are stacked and frosted, spread some frosting on the top of the cake.

16. Next, go back and fill in the gaps between the cake layers with more frosting. The frosting between the layers does not need to look perfect. Use a small offset spatula to get the frosting in between the layers and to spread it around the cake. Don't completely cover the cake layers as they are suppose to still be visible.

17. Place the entire cake in the freezer or fridge for 20 minutes to harden the buttercream.

18. Once the caramel sauce is cooled, use a spoon to drizzle the caramel around the center and sides of the cake, allowing it to drip down the sides.

19. For decoration, add cinnamon sticks or another garnish to the top of the cake.

CHOCOLATE CHEESECAKE WITH COOKIE DOUGH (NO BAKE)

INGREDIENTS

CRUST

- 4 tablespoons butter, melted
- 2 1/2 cups chocolate cookie crumbs
- Filling
- 4 (8-ounce) blocks cream cheese, softened to room temperature
- 1 cup sugar
- 4 large eggs
- 1 teaspoon all-purpose flour
- 1 teaspoon vanilla
- 1 cup sour cream

COOKIE DOUGH

- ½ cup butter, softened
- ½ cup sugar
- ½ cup packed light brown sugar
- 2 tablespoon water or milk
- 2 teaspoon vanilla extract
- 1 cup all-purpose flour
- 1/4 teaspoon salt
- 1 cup mini chocolate chips
- an additional 1 cup mini chocolate chips to fold into the batter with the cookie dough balls

GARNISH

- 1 cup heavy whipping cream, whipped to stiff peaks
- mini chocolate chips, for sprinkling

DIRECTIONS

1. In a medium bowl, combine the butter and sugars for the cookie dough. Add the water (or milk), vanilla and blend. Mix

in the flour, salt and the chocolate chips. The dough will be fairly soft. Gently roll the dough into small balls and place them on a wax paper lined plate or baking sheet. Place them in the freezer to harden while making the rest of the cheesecake.

2. Lightly grease the bottom and sides of a 10-inch springform pan. In a medium bowl, combine the butter with the chocolate cookie crumbs. Press onto the bottom and about halfway up the sides of the prepared pan.

3. Using an electric mixer on high speed, beat the cream cheese, sugar, eggs and flour until smooth. Add the vanilla and sour cream and mix just until blended.

4. Pour half the batter into the prepared crust. Gently stir in the cookie dough balls and the additional 1 cup mini chocolate chips into the remaining batter. Pour into the pan, spreading the batter to the sides of the pan and evening it out across the top. Wrap your springform pan tightly in a couple layers of foil. Place the pan directly into a bigger pan that's filled about halfway full of water. Obviously, you don't want the water to be higher than the foil, or the water will seep into your cheesecake, and that would be bad news for all.

5. Bake the cheesecake at 325 degrees for one hour. Turn off the oven and prop the door open several inches. Let the cake sit in the oven for an additional 30 minutes. Remove the cake from the oven and let it cool completely on a wire rack. Refrigerate until chilled To serve, cut into slices and top with whipped cream and mini chocolate chips.

CARAMEL AND CHOCOLATE CUPCAKES

INGREDIENTS

CHOCOLATE CUPCAKES

- 1/2 cup salted butter
- 1 cup sugar
- 2 eggs
- 1/2 tsp vanilla extract
- 6 tbsp water
- 6 tbsp cocoa powder
- 1 cup all purpose flour
- 1/2 tsp baking soda
- 6 tbsp Kahlua

KAHLUA ICING

- 1/2 cup salted butter
- 1/2 cup shortening
- 4 cups powdered sugar
- 4-5 tbsp kahlua

CARAMEL SAUCE

- a pinch of salt
- sugar

DIRECTIONS

1. Preheat oven to 350 degrees.
2. Beat butter and sugar until light in color and fluffy, about 2-3 minutes.
3. Add eggs, one at a time, beating just until blended.
4. Add vanilla, water and cocoa powder to another bowl and whisk until smooth.
5. Add chocolate mixture to batter and mix until combined. Scrape down the sides of the bowl as needed to make sure everything is well combined.

6. Combine flour and baking soda in a separate bowl.
7. Alternate adding the flour mixture and kahlua to the batter. Begin by adding half of the dry mix, then mix well. Add the kahlua and mix well, scrapes down the sides as needed. Add the remaining flour mixture and beat until smooth.
8. Fill cupcake liners about half way. Bake for 16-18 minutes, or until a toothpick inserted comes out with a few crumbs.
9. To make icing, beat butter and shortening until smooth.
10. Add 2 cups of powdered sugar and beat until smooth.
11. Add 4 tbsp Kahlua and remaining powdered sugar and beat until smooth. Add additional Kahlua if needed to get the right icing consistency.
12. Pipe icing onto cupcakes.
13. Drizzle cupcakes with caramel sauce and a sprinkle of sea salt.

BASIC CREAM CAKE

INGREDIENTS

FOR THE CAKE

- 1 1/3 cups all-purpose flour
- 1/2 cup unsweetened cocoa powder
- 3/4 teaspoon baking soda
- 1/2 teaspoon baking powder
- 1/4 teaspoon fine salt
- 1 1/4 sticks (10 tablespoons) unsalted butter, room temperature
- 1/2 cup packed light brown sugar
- 1/2 cup granulated sugar
- 3 large eggs, room temperature
- 1 teaspoon vanilla extract
- 2 oz. bittersweet chocolate, melted and cooled
- 1/2 cup buttermilk, room temperature
- 1/2 cup boiling water
- 2/3 cup mini chocolate chips
- 1 tablespoon all-purpose flour

FOR THE FROSTING

- 8 oz. cream cheese, room temperature
- Pinch of salt
- 1/2 cup granulated sugar
- 1 teaspoon vanilla extract
- 2 cups heavy cream, cold
- 3 cups crushed oreos

DIRECTIONS

1. Begin by making the cake. Preheat oven to 350 degrees F. Butter and flour three 8 inch cake pans. Or use my favorite method: spray the pans with cooking spray, line the bottoms with parchment paper, and then spray the parchment paper.

2. In a medium sized bowl, sift together the flour, cocoa powder, baking soda, baking powder, and salt.
3. In a large bowl using an electric mixer, beat the butter on medium speed until creamy. Add the sugars and beat for another couple minutes, until light and fluffy. Add the eggs one at a time, beating after each addition until incorporated. Then beat in the vanilla. Lower the mixer speed to low, and mix in the melted chocolate.
4. Add the dry Ingredients and the buttermilk alternately, beginning and ending with the dry Ingredients (do the dry Ingredients in 3 batches and the buttermilk in 2). Beat after each addition just until incorporated. Use a rubber spatula to scrape down the sides and bottom of the bowl. Still mixing on low speed, add in the boiling water.
5. Toss the chocolate chips with the tablespoon of flour, then use a spatula to stir the chocolate chips in.
6. Divide the batter evenly among the three cake pans, and if necessary use a spatula to spread the batter out in the pans.
7. Bake for 15 to 18 minutes, until a toothpick inserted into the center comes out clean. Let the cakes cool in the pans for about 5 minutes, and then remove them from the pans and place them on wire racks to complete cooling. Once the cakes are completely cooled, wrap them separately in plastic wrap and place them in the freezer for at least an hour.

FROSTING

1. In a large bowl combine the cream cheese, salt, and sugar. Cream together using an electric mixer until smooth and creamy. Then mix in the vanilla.
2. In a separate large bowl, use an electric mixer to beat the cream into stiff peaks. Then use a rubber spatula to gently fold the cream into the cream cheese mixture. Then fold in the crushed oreos.
3. To frost the cake, place one cake layer on the bottom of your cake round or cake plate. Use an offset spatula to spread the top with a layer of frosting. Stack the second layer, then another layer of frosting, then the final layer. (It's best, if you can, to find the most flat layer for the top, and if your layers have risen quite a bit you can use a serrated knife to cut a bit off to make them flatter.) Then spread the top and the sides with frosting. To make the icing smooth, run your spatula under hot water and gently run it over the frosting.
4. Store the cake in the refrigerator until serving.

CHOCOLATE BUNDT CAKE WITH BISCUITS DOUGH (NO BAKE)

INGREDIENTS

- ¼ Dough from Chocolate Chip Cookies
- 1 C M&M's® Milk Chocolate Harvest Candies
- 1 C Unsalted Butter, softened
- 2 C Sugar
- 2 Eggs
- 4 Tbsp Cocoa Powder
- 2 tsp Vanilla Extract
- 1 C Sour Cream
- 2 tsp Baking Soda
- 2½ C All-Purpose Flour
- ¼ tsp Kosher Salt
- 1 C Boiling Water
- 1x Cream Cheese

DIRECTIONS

1. Prepare chocolate chip cookies as directed in the original recipe, swapping out the chocolate chips for the 1 cup of M&M's®. Reserve ¼ of the dough, and wrap the rest in plastic and place in the fridge for later use.
2. Preheat oven to 325 degrees. Grease a bundt pan with shortening or butter, then coat in an even layer of cocoa powder. Tap out the excess and set aside.
3. In a large mixing bowl beat the butter and sugar until light and fluffy, around 5 minutes. Beat in the eggs, one at time, until fully incorporated, then mix in the cocoa powder, vanilla extract, and sour cream.
4. Whisk together the flour, baking soda, and salt and slowly add to the mixture.
5. Gently beat in the boiling water on low speed. Pour the batter into the prepared bundt pan.
6. Roll the cookie dough into small balls and plop them into the cake batter in the bundt cake, pressing down just slightly.

7. Bake for 60 minutes, or until a toothpick inserted into the center of the cake comes out clean.
8. Allow the cake to cool for 10 minutes in the pan before flipping out onto a cooling rack to cool completely.
9. Remove the lid and foil from the icing, then place in the microwave and heat for 15 second intervals until smooth and pourable. Slowly pour over cooled bundt cake, allow to set.

PUMPKIN MOUSSE SWEET CAKE

INGREDIENTS

FOR THE CRUST

- 30-40 ginger snap cookies- crushed into crumbs
- 3 tablespoons of butter, melted
- pinch of salt

FOR THE FILLING

- 1 1/2 cups heavy cream
- 12 oz cream cheese, softened
- 1 cup pumpkin puree
- 1 1/2 teaspoons pumpkin pie spice
- 1 1/4 cup powdered sugar
- 1/4 cup chopped pecans
- 1/4 cup toffee bits
- an extra pinch of cookie crumbs, pecans & toffee for garnish

DIRECTIONS

1. Preheat the oven to 350F. In a large bowl, stir together the cookie crumbs, melted butter and salt. Stir to moisten and then press into the bottom of a 7-inch spring form pan OR a 9 inch pie dish.
2. Freeze crust for 10 minutes and then bake for 10 minutes. Allow to cool on a wire rack while you prep the filling.
3. Whip the heavy cream in a stand mixer with a whisk attachment until medium-stiff peaks form. Scrape the whipped cream into a separate bowl and wipe the mixer bowl out. (No need to wash it.)
4. Switch to the paddle attachment and beat the cream cheese until smooth and creamy. Add the pumpkin, pumpkin pie spice, and powdered sugar, mixing until smooth.
5. Remove the bowl from the mixer and gradually fold in about 2/3 of the whipped cream, saving the rest for the topping. Mixture will be thick and creamy.

6. Fold in the chopped pecans and toffee bits. Spread the filling into the cooled crust. Cover with plastic wrap and chill overnight or until filling has firmed up.
7. Spread the remaining whipped cream over the torte and garnish with a crushed gingersnap, chopped pecans, or toffee.
8. Chill until right before serving

EASY COCONUT AND CHOCOLATE CAKE WITH RUM

INGREDIENTS

- 2 cans coconut milk
- 4 cups maple syrup and/or agave nectar
- 5 tablespoons vanilla
- 8 oz. dark chocolate, around 70%
- 3 cups unsweetened coconut flakes
- 1-1/2 cup pecans
- 1 cup coconut oil
- 2 tablespoons rum
- 2 tablespoons arrowroot powder
- 2-1/2 teaspoon salt
- 1-3/4 cups brown rice flour
- 3/4 cup garbanzo bean flour
- 1-1/3 cup cocoa powder
- 1 tablespoon baking soda

CHOCOLATE CAKE

- 1-3/4 cups brown rice flour
- 3/4 cup garbanzo bean flour
- 1-1/3 cup cocoa powder
- 1 tablespoon baking soda
- 1-1/2 teaspoon salt
- 1 cup coconut oil
- 2 cups maple syrup
- 2 cups water
- 1 tablespoon vanilla

COCONUT FILLING

- 1 can + 1 cup coconut milk
- 1-1/4 cup maple syrup or agave nectar
- 3/4 tsp. salt
- 2 tablespoons arrowroot powder
- 2 tablespoons vanilla
- 3 cups coconut flakes, toasted

- 1-1/2 cups pecans

RUM SYRUP

- 1/2 cup agave nectar
- 1/4 cup water
- 2 tablespoons rum
- 1 tablespoon vanilla

CHOCOLATE GANACHE

- 3/4 cup coconut milk
- 1/4 cup agave or maple syrup
- 1 tablespoon vanilla
- 8 oz. dark chocolate, chopped

DIRECTIONS

1. Preheat the oven to 350F.
2. Grease two 9-inch cake pans and line the bottoms with parchment paper.
3. In a large bowl, whisk together the maple syrup, water, vanilla, and coconut oil. In a medium bowl, sift together the remaining Ingredients and whisk together thoroughly. In a large bowl, whisk together the wet Ingredients. Slowly whisk the dry Ingredients into the wet until there are no lumps.
4. Pour the batter into the pans and bake for about 25-28 minutes, or until somewhat firm. Set the cakes on the counter to cool. Once they are no longer hot, chill them in the fridge until you are ready to assemble the cake. While the cakes are baking and cooling, make the coconut filling, rum syrup, and chocolate frosting.
5. To toast the coconut, spread evenly over a cookie sheet and bake for about 5 minutes at 350F. Take it out, stir it around with a spatula, and put back in the oven, checking and stirring every few minutes, until evenly golden brown.
6. While the coconut is toasting, spread the pecans over another cookie sheet and bake for 7-8 minutes, until well browned and fragrant. Remove from oven and let cool for a few minutes, then transfer to a cutting board and chop.

7. In a stainless steel saucepan, bring the coconut milk, agave, and salt nearly to a boil, then reduce heat to medium-low and simmer uncovered for around 10 minutes. Try not to boil it, because the coconut milk can lose some of its flavor. Mix together the arrowroot and vanilla and whisk in. Cook for another 5 minutes or so, until thickened, whisking often to activate the arrowroot. Remove from heat and stir in the pecans and coconut. It will thicken slightly as it cools.

8. For the syrup, bring all Ingredients to a boil in a small saucepan and simmer for around 10 minutes, until it resembles a thin syrup. It will thicken slightly upon cooling.

9. For the ganache, place the chocolate in a heat resistant bowl. In a small saucepan, heat the coconut milk, agave, and vanilla until it is about to boil. Pour over the chocolate and let it stand a minute. Stir with a spatula until smooth, slowly as to not create air bubbles. Let sit until room temperature, refrigerating if it is not firm enough to spread as frosting.

10. With a plastic spatula or utensil, loosen the cake around the edges of the pan. Remove the cake layers (this is easer if you refrigerate or freeze them for a short while beforehand) and place several toothpicks around the perimeter of the cake, halfway down. Using these as a guide, cut the cake in half horizontally with unflavored dental floss, wrapping it around the cake and tugging the ends toward each other until cut all the way through.

11. Set the first layer on a cake plate and with a pastry brush, douse liberally with the rum syrup. Spread a little less than 1/4 of the coconut frosting over the layer, being sure to reach the sides. Set another layer on top and repeat, brushing each layer with syrup and coconut filling. Be sure to save enough coconut filling for the top; it's okay if there is more frosting on top than in the other layers, but too little frosting on top would be a problem.

12. With a frosting spatula, ice the sides with the chocolate frosting, saving a little to pipe around the edges. Run the spatula under hot water, dry, and use it to smooth the chocolate icing around the sides. With a piping bag and tip, pipe a decorative border of chocolate icing around the top and bottom edges of the cake.

EASY SNACK CAKE WITH LOTS OF BANANA CHUNKS AND CHOCOLATE

INGREDIENTS

CAKE

- 2 cups all purpose flour
- 1 1/2 tsp baking powder
- 1/2 tsp salt
- 3/4 cup unsalted butter, room temperature
- 1 cup sugar
- 2 eggs
- 1 tsp vanilla
- 1/2 cup milk
- 1 cup mashed bananas
- 1 1/2 cups chocolate chunks

FROSTING

- 1 cup butter, room temperature
- 3 cups powdered sugar
- 1/3 cup unsweetened cocoa
- 1 tsp vanilla
- 1 Tbsp milk

DIRECTIONS

1. Preheat oven to 350 F. Grease and flour a 9 X 13 inch baking dish.
2. In a medium bowl, whisk together flour, baking powder and salt until combined. Set aside.
3. In a mixing bowl, cream butter and sugar. Add eggs and vanilla and mix until combined. Add milk, continuing to mix until combined. With the mixer on low, slowly add flour and mix until just combined. Mix in mashed bananas. Stir in chocolate chunks.
4. Pour batter into prepared dish and bake for 30-35 minutes or until done.

5. Remove from oven and cool completely.
6. For frosting: Using a mixer, beat butter and vanilla until smooth. Sift powdered sugar and cocoa together and slowly add to mixer while on low. Increase to medium and beat until completely incorporated. Add milk a teaspoon at a time until desired creaminess.

SIMPLE DUCLE DE LECHE CAKE WITH BANANA LAYERS

INGREDIENTS

TOPPING

- 1 can (14 oz) sweetened condensed milk

LAYERED BANANA CAKE

- 3/4 cup unsalted butter, room temperature
- 1 1/2 cups Extra Fine Granulated Sugar
- 3 large eggs, room temperature
- 3/4 cup plain yogurt
- 2 large ripe bananas, mashed
- 2 teaspoons vanilla extract
- 2 1/2 cups all-purpose flour
- 2 teaspoons baking powder
- 1/2 teaspoon baking soda
- 1/2 teaspoon salt

DULCE DE LECHE FROSTING

- 16 ounces cream cheese, room temperature
- 1 can (14 oz) sweetened condensed milk
- 2 cups Confectioners Powdered Sugar
- 1/2 teaspoon salt

DIRECTIONS

1. Start by making the dulce de leche. Place two 14 ounce cans of sweetened condensed milk (labels removed) on their sides into a large pot of boiling water. Lower heat and simmer for 2 1/2 hours. Make sure water covers top of can at all times (pouring in more water every 30 minutes or so). Allow cans to cool to room temperature before opening. This last step is very important because if you open a hot can the dulce de leche will gush out and burn you.

2. While dulce de leche is cooling, make banana layer cake. Preheat oven to 350°F. Grease three 8-inch cake pans. Set aside.
3. In a large bowl, cream butter and sugar on medium speed. Add in eggs, yogurt, mashed bananas, and vanilla extract, mixing well.
4. In a separate bowl, combine flour, baking powder, baking soda, and salt. Slowly fold into wet Ingredients, mixing until combined.
5. Scoop batter evenly into prepared pans and bake for roughly 35 minutes, until each cake is golden brown and a knife comes out clean when inserted into the center. Allow to cool for at least 10 minutes before removing from pan and cooling completely on a wire rack.
6. While cakes are cooling, prepare dulce de leche frosting. Whip cream cheese, 1 can of prepared dulce de leche, and powdered sugar until smooth. Frost top of each cake layer and stack. Frost sides and top completely. Place in freezer for 5-10 minutes to cool frosting.
7. In a small microwave-safe bowl, stir 1/2 of remaining can of dulce de leche with salt, then heat in microwave for 25 seconds. Remove cake from refrigerator and drizzle warmed dulce de leche over top of cake.

APPLE AND COFFEE CAKE

INGREDIENTS

CAKE

- ½ cup unsalted butter + more to grease pan
- 1½ cups light brown sugar, lightly packed
- 2 large eggs
- 2 cups flour
- 1 tsp baking soda
- 1½ tsp cinnamon
- 1 tsp allspice
- 1 tsp ground ginger
- ½ tsp ground cardamom
- ½ tsp salt
- 1 cup plain Greek yogurt
- 1 tsp vanilla extract
- 2 cups peeled, cored and chopped apples

CRUMBLE

- ½ cup light brown sugar, lightly packed
- ½ cup flour
- ½ tsp cinnamon
- ¼ tsp allspice
- 4 Tbsp unsalted butter, softened

CARAMEL DRIZZLE

- 1 cup light brown sugar, lightly packed
- ½ cup half-and-half
- 4 Tbsp salted butter
- 1 tsp vanilla extract

DIRECTIONS

1. Preheat oven to 350 degrees. Grease a 9"x13" glass baking dish with butter.

2. In a large bowl, cream together the butter and brown sugar until light and fluffy. Add the eggs one at a time, beating well after adding each. Fold in the yogurt and vanilla.
3. In a medium bowl, combine flour, baking soda, cinnamon, allspice, ginger, cardamom and salt. Slowly add dry Ingredients to wet Ingredients until fully combined. Fold in apples. Spread batter evenly across the greased baking dish.
4. In a small bowl, combine crumble Ingredients. Sprinkle over the batter in the baking dish. Bake for 35 minutes.
5. While the cake is baking, prep the caramel sauce. Mix the brown sugar, half-and-half, butter and vanilla in a small saucepan. Cook over medium-low heat, stirring slowly, until the sugar dissolves and the mixture thickens. This should take around 8-10 minutes. Remove from heat and pour sauce into a jar. Refrigerate until cooled.
6. Once the cake is out of the oven, drizzle caramel over the cake. Serve cake warm.

THE BIG CAKE: CHOCOLATE, BUTTERCREAM FROSTING AND GANACHE

INGREDIENTS

TRIPLE LAYER CHOCOLATE CAKE

- 2¼ cups plain flour
- 2¼ cups white sugar
- 1½ cups unsweetened cocoa powder
- 2¼ teaspoons baking soda
- 2¼ teaspoons baking powder
- 1½ teaspoon salt
- 3 eggs, at room temperature
- 1½ cups buttermilk
- ¾ cup canola oil
- 2 teaspoons vanilla extract
- 1 cup + 2 tablespoons hot coffee
- ¾ cup semi-sweet chocolate chunks or chips

SALTED CARAMEL

- ½ cup water
- 1½ cups caster sugar (330g)
- 90g unsalted butter, cubed
- ¾ cup cream
- ½ -1 tsp table salt
- 1 teaspoon vanilla extract

CARAMEL POPCORN

- ½ cup salted caramel
- a few cups of plain popcorn (1/4-1/3 cups of kernels)
- ¼ teaspoon baking soda

SALTED CARAMEL CREAM CHEESE BUTTERCREAM

- 225g unsalted butter, softened at room temperature
- 120g Philadelphia cream cheese

- ½ cup salted caramel, at room temperature
- 1 tsp vanilla
- 3.5-4 cups icing sugar (430-480g)

CHOCOLATE GANACHE

- 200g dark chocolate, very finely chopped
- ½ cup cream

DIRECTIONS

1. Triple Layer Chocolate Cake
2. Preheat the oven to 175°C. Grease and line three x 20cm round cake tins with baking paper.
3. In a bowl, sift together the flour, sugar, cocoa, baking soda, baking powder and salt. Set aside.
4. In a separate bowl, beat together the eggs, buttermilk, canola oil and vanilla until smooth.
5. Gradually add the dry Ingredients to the wet Ingredients on a low speed until almost combined. Add the hot coffee and mix until just combined. Gently fold in the chocolate chunks.
6. Divide the batter among the three cake tins and bake for 20-25 minutes or until the tops are just set and a skewer comes out just clean. Remove from the oven to cool. After 20 minutes or so, remove from the tins and place cakes on cooling rakes or paper-lined flat plates to cool completely. The cakes need to be completely cool before you start frosting - normally a couple of hours.
7. Make the salted caramel and caramel popcorn in the few days before you assemble the cake, and make the buttercream immediately prior to assembly.
8. For the caramel, heat the butter and cream in a small saucepan over a low heat until the butter is melted and the mixture is combined. Remove from the heat.
9. Place the sugar and water in a large pot over a low heat, stirring until the sugar is dissolved. Stop stirring and cook on a high heat until the mixture reaches a dark amber colour (usually about 10 minutes and when it reaches ~175°C/350°F on a candy thermometer).

10. Quickly whisk in the cream and butter mixture, but be careful here as it boils up vigorously with a lot of steam, so you may want to wear an oven mitt or similar to protect your hand.
11. Remove from the heat and add the salt and vanilla extract, stirring to combine. Leave to cool and then taste to adjust the salt.
12. Set aside in a jar or similar - you will be using this caramel in the popcorn, the buttercream and to drip over the finished cake.
13. Preheat the oven to 150°C and line a baking tray with baking paper. Make the popcorn according to packet DIRECTIONS, in a popcorn machine or in a pot
14. Place popped popcorn in a large bowl.
15. Heat the caramel until almost boiling. Add the baking soda, stir as it fluffs up and quickly pour over the popcorn. Toss the caramel through the popcorn until evenly coated and then spread out over the baking tray in an even layer. Bake for 10 minutes, turning once after 5 minutes. Leave to cool. Store in an airtight container.
16. Using a stand mixer fitted with a paddle attachment or a handheld electric mixer, beat the softened butter until pale and creamy, about five minutes.
17. Add the cream cheese, caramel and vanilla and beat at low speed until fully incorporated. Gradually increase speed and continue beating until light and fluffy, scraping down the sides of the bowl with a spatula, about 3-4 minutes.
18. Add the icing sugar in three lots, beating on low speed until combined. Beat on medium high speed until smooth and fluffy while scraping down the sides (about 2 minutes)
19. Make the salted caramel and the salted caramel popcorn. Just before assembly, make the salted caramel cream cheese buttercream.
20. If your cakes have domed at all, cut off the top with a serrated knife to flatten.
21. Place the first layer, flat side up (upside-down) on a cake stand. Cut out few strips of baking paper and slide under the edges of the cake (see picture above) to catch any drips, so when you have finished icing the cake you can pull them out and end up with a clean-edged cake stand/plate.
22. With a knife or offset spatula, spread the top with caramel buttercream (use just under a cup, or enough to make a layer a similar size to in the picture). It doesn't matter if the

buttercream goes over the edge a little as it will be incorporated into the frosting on the sides of the cake. Place the second layer on top and spread evenly with frosting. Repeat with the third layer, but this time also frost the sides of the cake with the remaining frosting.

23. If you are at all worried about the structural stability of your, cut 3-4 wooden skewers to the height of your cake and poke them through the three layers to stop them from sliding over each other.

24. Place in the fridge to set slightly while you make the chocolate ganache.

25. Place very finely chopped chocolate a small bowl. Bring cream to boiling point and pour over the chocolate, making sure the chocolate is all covered. Leave for five minutes then stir with a fork until smooth and glossy.

26. Once you have made the chocolate ganache, remove the cake from the fridge and pour the ganache over the top of the cake. Use a knife or offset spatula to spread it over the top, creating drips down the sides.

27. Leave to set for 10-15 minutes. At this point you can remove the baking paper strips from the cake stand.

28. Just before serving, stack the caramel popcorn on the top of the cake, interspersing handfuls of popcorn with drizzles of extra salted caramel to stick it all together. You will probably end up with extra popcorn.

29. Drizzle any extra salted caramel over the sides of the cake.

PUMKIN CAKE V2

INGREDIENTS

- 1 box yellow cake mix
- 1 can (16 oz.) pumpkin
- 1 can (12 oz.) evaporated milk
- 3 eggs
- 1 1/2 cup sugar
- 4 teaspoons pumpkin pie spice
- 1/2 teaspoon salt
- 1/2 cup chopped pecans
- 1/2 cup chopped walnuts
- 1 cup melted butter
- whipped topping

DIRECTIONS

1. Preheat oven to 350F.
2. Grease bottom of 9X13 pan.
3. Combine pumpkin, evaporated milk, eggs, sugar, pumpkin pie spice and salt in bowl then pour it into your pan.
4. Sprinkle your dry yellow cake mix evenly over pumpkin mixture.
5. Sprinkle chopped pecans and walnuts over the cake mix.
6. Drizzle melted butter evenly over everything.
7. Bake your pumpkin crunch cake for 55 minutes or until top is turning golden brown. Cool completely, cut and serve with whipped topping. Refrigerate leftovers.

THE SIMPLE RECIPE: CHOCOLATE CAKE NEWBIE LEVEL

INGREDIENTS

CAKE

- 1 cup all-purpose flour
- ½ cup whole-wheat or white whole-wheat flour
- 1 ½ cups unsweetened cocoa powder
- ½ cup white sugar
- ½ cup brown sugar, packed
- ½ teaspoon baking soda
- ½ teaspoon baking powder
- ¾ teaspoon salt
- 1 cup sour cream
- ½ cup milk
- 4 eggs, beaten
- ½ cup butter, melted
- ¼ cup maple syrup
- 1 teaspoon vanilla extract
- 1 cup semisweet chocolate chips

FOR THE FROSTING

- 2 cups chocolate chips
- 1 cup sour cream, at room temperature

DIRECTIONS

1. Preheat the oven to 350° F. Butter a 9- x 9-inch baking pan, line it with parchment paper, and butter the paper, too. In a large bowl, mix together all of the dry Ingredients (flour through salt). In another bowl, mix together the wet Ingredients (sour cream through vanilla extract). Make a well in the center of the dry Ingredients, add the wet Ingredients, and fold with a rubber spatula until everything is just incorporated. Fold in the chocolate chips. Bake the cake for about 50 minutes, or until the center is set and a tester comes out clean.

2. Once the cake has cooled completely, melt the chocolate chips in a double boiler or in the microwave. Mix the melted chocolate chips and the room temperature sour cream using either a whisk, a stand mixer, or hand beaters. Let the frosting cool slightly so that it thickens a bit. If it becomes too thick and clumpy for your liking, gently melt it in a double boiler or the microwave and whisk until smooth. Use a rubber or offset spatula to frost the cake.

STRAWBERRY CHEESECAKE (NO BAKE)

INGREDIENTS

- 200g gluten free digestive biscuits
- 100g unsalted butter, melted
- 500g Philadelphia cream cheese
- 1 tsp vanilla extract
- 170g icing sugar
- 135g pack of strawberry or raspberry jelly cubes
- 100ml boiling water
- 200ml evaporated milk
- 400g strawberries
- Zest of 1 orange

DIRECTIONS

1. Put the biscuits into a large bowl and crush into crumbs using the end of a rolling pin, then mix in the melted butter until thoroughly combined. Pour into a 20cm diameter loose bottomed cake tin and push down so you have a tightly packed, level layer covering the bottom of the cake tin. Put in the fridge whilst you start on the vanilla layer.
2. In a bowl, add 300g of the cream cheese and mix with a whisk until the cream cheese has loosened to a smooth consistency. Add the vanilla extract and 100g of the icing sugar then whisk again until combined. Take about 4 or 5 strawberries and chop into chunks, then add them to the mixture and stir in gently. Take the biscuit base out of the fridge and spread this vanilla layer on top. Put back in the fridge.
3. Next make the mousse layer. Chop the jelly into chunks and mix with 100ml of boiling water until dissolved. If the chunks aren't dissolving well, then put it in the microwave for 30 seconds or so and mix again. Set aside to cool slightly. Add the remaining 200g of cream cheese to a large bowl and mix using the whisk until it's smooth. Whisk in the remaining icing sugar, then whisk in the evaporated milk. Finally add the jelly mixture and whisk in. Pour this mixture onto the top of the cheesecake and put back in the fridge to set for at least an hour.

4. Once the mousse layer has set, you can decorate with the strawberries. Take the cheesecake out of the fridge and carefully slide out of the cake tin and onto a plate. Slice the strawberries into thin slices. Arrange the strawberries in a circle around the cheesecake, starting from the outside and working your way in. Overlay the strawberries slightly so you're not left with any gaps. Sprinkle the top with the orange zest and serve.

BLUEBERRY CHEESECAKE V2

INGREDIENTS

CRUST

- 2 cups raw nuts
- 1 cup dates or raisins
- pinch of salt

ORANGE CHEESECAKE

- 3 cups cashews
- 3/4 cup fresh orange juice
- 1/2 cup agave/maple syrup
- 1/2 cup melted coconut oil
- juice of one lemon
- zest of all the oranges you juiced
- pinch of salt

BLUEBERRY LAYER

- 2 cups organic blueberries
- 1/4 cup of the orange cheesecake mixture

DIRECTIONS

1. To make the crust: process the nuts and dates/raisins in your food processor until the nuts have become crumbs and the mixture sticks together when you press it. Press into the bottom of a spring-form pan and put in the fridge.
2. To make the orange cheesecake: blend all Ingredients (except orange zest) in your high speed blender until very smooth, then add in the orange zest with a spoon. Reserve 1/4 cup of this mixture for the blueberry topping – pour the rest onto your crust and put in the freezer.
3. To make the blueberry layer: blend the blueberries and the 1/4 cup of cheesecake mixture in your food processor or blender until creamy but still with small pieces of blueberry

for texture. Spread this over your cheesecake and keep in the freezer or fridge overnight.

DARK CAKE

INGREDIENTS

- ½ cup/50g unsweetened cocoa powder
- ½ cup/100g light brown sugar, packed
- 1 teaspoon instant coffee
- 1 cup/250 ml hot water
- 1 stick/125g softened butter, plus some for greasing
- 1 tablespoon vegetable oil
- ¾ cup/150g superfine/caster sugar
- 1½ cups/225g all-purpose/plain flour
- ½ teaspoon baking powder
- ½ teaspoon baking soda
- 1 tablespoon vanilla extract
- 2 eggs

FOR THE FROSTING

- ½ cup milk
- 2 tablespoons light brown sugar
- 1½ sticks (3/4 cup) butter, cubed
- 11 ounces dark chocolate, chopped

DIRECTIONS

1. Preheat the oven to 350 degrees F/180 C.
2. In a mixing bowl whisk together the coco powder, instant coffee, brown sugar and hot water. Set aside.
3. In a separate bowl, mix the flour, baking powder, and baking soda together and set aside.
4. Cream the butter and sugar together, beating well until pale and fluffy.
5. Add the oil and the vanilla extract.
6. Add eggs, one at a time with a cup of the flour mixture in between eggs.
7. Mix in the rest of the dried Ingredients for the cake and fold in the cocoa mixture.

8. Divide the batter evenly between the two greased 9-inch round pans and bake for about 25-30 minutes, or until a cake tester comes out clean.
9. Take the pans out and put them on a wire rack for 5 to 10 minutes, before turning the cakes out to cool.
10. For the frosting: Put the milk, 2 tablespoons dark brown sugar and butter in a pan over medium heat and bring to a simmer
11. Place the chopped chocolate in a heat proof bowl. Add the simmering milk mixture and leave to sit for 5 minutes or until the chocolate softens enough to whisk and then whisk until smooth and glossy.
12. Let it stand for about 1 hour, whisking now and again occasionally to keep it from becoming too stiff.
13. Frost the cooled cakes starting with topping one with a half a cup of icing and placing the other on top (bottom side up). Use the remaining frosting to frost the rest of the cake. If the frosting is quite soft once you've iced the cake, you can place it in the refrigerator until its set.

CHOCOLATE CHEESECAKE V2

INGREDIENTS

COOKIE DOUGH

- 1/2 cup butter
- 1/3 cup white sugar
- 1/3 cup dark brown sugar
- 1 1/2 tsp vanilla extract
- 1 cup plus 2 tbsp flour
- pinch salt
- 1 cup chocolate chips

COOKIE CRUMB CRUST

- 1 1/3 cups graham cracker crumbs
- 3 tbsp sugar
- 1/3 cup melted butter

VANILLA CHEESECAKE

- 2/3 cup sugar
- 2 eggs
- 2 tsp vanilla extract
- 2 eight ounce packages ounces cream cheese
- 1/2 cup whipping cream

CHOCOLATE GANACHE

- 1/3 cup whipping cream
- 1 1/3 cups chocolate chips

VANILLA WHIPPED CREAM

- 1 cup whipping cream
- 3 rounded tbsp icing sugar (powdered sugar)
- 1 tsp pure vanilla extract

1. For the dough, combine the sugar, butter, vanilla extract and fold in just until a dough forms. Add the flour and salt. Finally mix in the chocolate chips.
2. Chill the dough in the fridge for at least an hour.
3. Break off small nuggets of the dough about the size of the top of your forefinger. Place them on a parchment lined tray and keep chilled in the fridge. About 3/4 of these dough nuggets will go into the cheesecake batter. Reserve the other 1/4 to garnish the cheesecake after it is baked, cooled and glazed.
4. For the crumb crust, in a small bowl, combine the graham cracker crumbs, sugar and the melted butter.
5. Press into the bottom of a lightly greased or parchment lined 9 inch spring form pan. (Grease bottom only!) Parchment paper is ideal here because it makes it very easy to release the cheesecake from the bottom of the pan.
6. For the vanilla cheesecake, cream together the cream cheese, sugar, the eggs(one at at time), vanilla extract. Finally blend in a ½ cup of whipping cream.
7. Fold in 3/4 of the chilled cookie dough pieces. Pour over the prepared base and bake at 300 degrees F for 60 – 70 minutes. The cheesecake does not have to brown at all in order to be fully baked; the surface of the cheesecake should lose any shine when the cake is properly baked. It can still be slightly wobbly just at the center at this point.
8. Remove the cake from the oven and run a sharp knife completely around the edge of the pan. This will allow for the cheesecake to shrink as it cools and hopefully not crack (Allow the cheesecake to cool thoroughly on a wire rack at room temperature. (NOT in the fridge). Refrigerate after fully cooled.
9. Top with chocolate ganache and vanilla whipped cream as well as the reserved cookie dough pieces.
10. In a small saucepan, heat almost to boiling:
11. Remove from heat and pour in
12. Let stand for 5 minutes, then stir until smooth. Pour evenly over the cheesecake when it is still in the pan. Return to the fridge to let the chocolate set.
13. Beat to firm peaks and use to garnish the edges of the cheesecake. If you don't have a piping bag just cut a half inch

opening off the corner of a large Ziploc bag and use that to squeeze the whipped cream onto the cheesecake.

SIMPLE LAVA CHOCOLATE CAKE

INGREDIENTS

- 4 oz. semi-sweet baking chocolate, chopped
- 6 T. butter, cubed
- ⅓ cup granulated sugar
- 2 eggs
- 4 T. all-purpose flour
- 2 tsp Knees peanut butter
- 1 + ½ T. unsweetened cocoa powder

DIRECTIONS

1. Preheat oven to 425 degrees. Spray 2 8 oz. ramekins with non-stick cooking spray. Place 1 tablespoon of cocoa powder in the first ramekin. Swirl the cocoa powder all around the ramekin and tap out the extra in the second ramekin. Add in the remaining ½ tablespoon of cocoa powder and discard the excess cocoa powder once ramekin is covered.
2. In a medium-sized microwave-safe bowl, add in the chopped semi-sweet chocolate and butter. Microwave in 30 second intervals and stir after each 30 seconds. Do this 3 to 4 times until the chocolate is smooth and completely melted.
3. Set aside and let cool for 10 minutes.
4. Add in the granulated sugar and eggs and whisk until thoroughly incorporated.
5. Add in the all-purpose flour. Using a spatula, mix until the flour is barely combined.
6. Pour batter into the 2 ramekins.
7. Place a large teaspoon of the peanut butter in the center of each ramekin. Make sure to press it down a little and cover it with the cake batter.
8. Place the two ramekins on a quarter sheet pan and place in the oven. Bake for about 14 minutes. The outside of the cakes will be baked and the center will still be very jiggly.
9. Serve immediately. If you're feeling crazy, add a scoop of ice cream to the cake.

OREO CAKE

INGREDIENTS

CHOCOLATE LAYER CAKE

- 3/4 cup unsweetened cocoa powder (not dutch process)
- 1 and 1/2 cups granulated sugar
- 1 and 1/2 cups cake flour1
- 1 teaspoon baking soda
- 1/4 teaspoon salt
- 2 large eggs, at room temperature2
- 1/4 cup vegetable or canola oil
- 1 cup full fat sour cream or full fat Greek yogurt, at room temperature
- 2 teaspoons vanilla extract
- 1/2 cup hot coffee or hot water
- 1 cup milk chocolate chopped
- 1 15.25 ounce package Oreos

OREO CREAM

- 1/4 cup unsalted butter, softened to room temperature
- 1/4 cup shortening3
- 2 and 1/2 cups confectioners' sugar
- 2 Tablespoons milk or cream
- 2 teaspoons vanilla extract

CHOCOLATE BUTTERCREAM

- 3/4 cup unsalted butter, softened to room temperature
- 1/2 cup unsweetened cocoa powder
- 1 teaspoon vanilla extract
- 4 cups confectioners' sugar
- 1/4 cup milk or cream
- 16 additional Oreo cookies, pulsed into a fine crumb

DIRECTIONS

1. Position oven rack in the center of the oven. Preheat to 350°F (177°C). Generously spray two 9-inch cake pans with nonstick spray. Line the bottom of the pan with Oreos in a single layer. Set aside.
2. In a large bowl, using a handheld or stand mixer fitted with a paddle attachment, blend the cocoa powder, sugar, cake flour, baking soda, and salt together on low speed for 30 seconds. Add the eggs, oil, sour cream, and vanilla and mix for 1 minute on medium-low speed.
3. Remove the bowl from the mixer and add the coffee and chocolate chips; stir to combine. Some of the chocolate chips will melt as you stir. Try to avoid over mixing the batter.
4. Pour the batter into the prepared cake pans over the Oreos. Bake for 28-32 minutes or until a toothpick inserted in the center of the cakes comes out clean. Allow cakes to cool completely in the pan on a wire rack.
5. While the cake cools, make the Oreo Cream Filling. In a large bowl, using a handheld or stand mixer fitted with a paddle attachment, cream the butter and shortening together on high speed until fluffy. Add the confectioners' sugar, 1 cup at a time, alternating with the milk/cream and vanilla. The filling will be very thick, but you may add more milk/cream if you prefer. Set aside in the refrigerator.
6. While the cake cools, make the Chocolate Buttercream. In a large bowl, using a handheld or stand mixer fitted with a paddle attachment, cream the butter on high speed until fluffy, about 1 minute. Beat in the cocoa powder and vanilla on low speed, then add the confectioners' sugar 1 cup at a time, alternating with the milk/cream. The buttercream will be thick. Set aside in the refrigerator.
7. Once the cakes are cooled, assemble the cake. Place 1 cooled layer on a cake stand or large plate, Oreo cookie side down. Using an offset spatula or knife, cover the top with a 1-inch thick layer of Oreo Cream Filling. Top with the 2nd cake, Oreo cookie side up. Cover the tall layer cake with chocolate buttercream. Working quickly, cover the cake in Oreo crumbs. This will get a little messy, but just pat them up the sides with your hands and all over the top of the cake.
8. Slice and serve cake. Leftover cake can be covered and stored in the refrigerator for up to 3 days.
9. Make ahead tip: The cake layers can be baked, cooled, and covered tightly at room temperature overnight. Likewise, the

frosting and filling can be prepared then covered and refrigerated overnight. Assemble and frost the cake the next day when you are ready to serve. Frosted cake can be frozen up to 2 months if you have room in the freezer. Thaw overnight in the refrigerator and bring to room temperature before serving.

UPSIDE-DOWN MEYER CAKE

INGREDIENTS

- ¾ cup butter, softened
- ⅔ cup packed brown sugar
- 3-4 Meyer lemons
- Zest of 2 large Meyer lemons
- 1 cup granulated sugar
- 2 eggs
- 1 cup all-purpose flour
- ¾ cup cornmeal
- 2 tsp baking powder
- ¼ tsp salt
- ½ cup milk
- 1 tsp vanilla extract

DIRECTIONS

1. Preheat oven to 350°. Spray the inside of a 9-inch springform pan with oil and line the bottom with parchment paper. Spray the inside of the paper; set aside.
2. In a small saucepan over medium heat, bring brown sugar and ¼ cup of the butter to a boil, stirring constantly. Pour mixture into prepared pan and spread evenly.
3. Thinly slice Meyer lemons*, removing any seeds and discarding the ends. Layer lemon slices in pan, starting with one in the centre and working outwards. Slices should overlap by about half.
4. In a small bowl, mix together flour, cornmeal, baking powder, and salt; set aside.
5. In another small bowl, combine milk and vanilla; set aside.
6. Add ⅓ of flour mixture to butter mixture, scraping the sides of the bowl as needed. Add half the milk, mixing until well combined. Continue alternating adding the flour and milk all mixed. Pour batter into pan and spread evenly.
7. Bake until cake has browned and springs back to the touch, 50-55 minutes. Let cool in pan for about 2 hours before running a knife around the edges of the pan and releasing the cake.

8. Flip, cut with a serrated knife, and serve.

LEMON AND BLUEBERRY CHEESECAKE

INGREDIENTS

BLUEBERRY SAUCE

- 2 cups fresh blueberries
- ½ cup water
- ½ cup sugar
- 2 tablespoons cornstarch, mixed with 2 tablespoons cold water
- 1 tablespoons vanilla extract

FOR THE CRUST

- 2 cups graham cracker crumbs
- 8 tablespoons unsalted butter, melted
- 2 tablespoons granulated sugar

CHEESECAKE FILLING

- 4 packages (8 oz.) cream cheese, softened
- 1 cup sour cream
- 2 tablespoons cornstarch
- 3 eggs
- 1⅓ cups sugar
- ½ cup graham cracker crumbs
- juice of one meyer lemon
- zest from one meyer lemon

DIRECTIONS

PREPARING THE BLUEBERRY SAUCE

1. The sauce can be made while the cake is cooking or many days in advance.
2. In a large saucepan over medium heat, combine blueberries, water and sugar. Stir frequently, but careful not to crush the berries, bring to a low boil.
3. In a small bowl, mix the cornstarch with cold water until combined.
4. Slowly stir the cornstarch into the blueberries, careful not to crush them. Simmer until the homemade blueberry sauce is thick enough to coat the back of a metal spoon, about 10 minutes.
5. Remove from heat and gently stir in vanilla.
6. Let the sauce cool at room temperature. Measure ½ cup for your recipe, store the rest in jars in the fridge.

ii.

PREPARING THE CRUST

1. In a large bowl, mix the crumbs with melted butter and granulated sugar with a rubber spatula until combined.
2. Press the mixture into the bottom of a 9inch spring form cake pan and slightly up the sides. Make sure it is tight and compact.
3. Chill the crust for 15 minutes.

CHEESECAKE FILLING

1. Preheat oven to 325F.
2. In the bowl of an electric mixer fitted with the whisk attachment beat cream cheese on medium speed until fluffy. Add the sugar, cornstarch, lemon juice, lemon zest and beat until combined.
3. Add eggs, one at a time, beating until just combined after each addition. On low speed beat in sour cream just until combined.
4. Remove crust from the fridge and pour the batter into the crust.
5. In circles pour the blueberry sauce over the cheesecake and with the edge of a spatula create swirls and mix the blueberry sauce into the cheesecake filling. Carefully not to over mix.
6. Bake for about 1¼ hours or until center is almost set. Cool on a wire rack for 15 minutes. Sprinkle graham crackers on top and

loosen sides of pan and continue cooling on wire rack until the cheesecake is at room temperature.
7. Transfer to the fridge. Refrigerate overnight or at least 6 hours before serving.
8. The cheesecake can be served with warm blueberry sauce.
9. Store in refrigerator.

CHOCOLATE BROWNIE CAKE WITH MASCARPONE

INGREDIENTS

FOR THE BROWNIE LAYERS

- 1 cup unsalted butter, melted
- 2 cup granulated sugar
- 4 large eggs
- 1 cup all-purpose flour
- ½ cup unsweetened cocoa powder
- ½ teaspoon salt
- ½ teaspoon baking soda

FOR THE COCONUT FILLING

- 1 cup walnuts, measure then grind
- 1 cup coconut flakes
- ½ cup heavy cream
- ½ cup sugar
- 1 egg yolk
- 3 tbsp. butter, room temperature

FOR THE VANILLA BUTTERCREAM

- 3 sticks of butter, softened
- 8 oz mascarpone cheese, chilled
- 2½ cups powdered sugar
- 1 vanilla bean
- pinch of salt

FOR THE CHOCOLATE GANACHE

- 8 ounces semisweet chocolate, chopped
- 2 tbsp. light corn syrup
- 3 tablespoons unsalted butter
- 1 cup heavy cream

DIRECTIONS

1. Preheat oven to 350°F.
2. Grease bottom of 3 8inch round pans with melted butter or cooking spray.
3. In the bowl of an electric mixer, whisk together melted butter and sugar until smooth. Add in each egg one at a time on low speed and whisk until well combined.
4. Using a large rubber spatula, gently stir in flour, cocoa, baking soda and salt.
5. Spread batter into the pans and bake for 25-30 minutes until set.
6. Remove and let cool completely before assembling the cake.

FOR THE COCONUT FILLING

1. Place the butter, walnuts and coconut in a large bowl and set aside.
2. In a medium sauce pan, on low/medium heat, stir together the heavy cream, sugar and egg yolk until the mixture begins to thicken and coats the back of a spoon (180 degrees F.). Pour the hot custard immediately onto the walnut-coconut mixture and stir until the butter is melted. Cool completely to room temperature before topping the brownie layers.

FOR THE VANILLA MASCARPONE BUTTERCREAM

1. Place softened butter and mascarpone into the bowl of an electric stand mixer that has been fitted with the whisk attachment. Turn the mixer on a medium setting and cream until it smooth and combined, 2 - 3 minutes.
2. Add sugar, ½ a cup at a time. Add vanilla beans and a pinch of salt and whisk until well-incorporated.
3. If the frosting is too thick add heavy cream one tablespoon at a time until it has reached the desired consistency.

FOR THE CHOCOLATE GANACHE

1. Place the chocolate, corn syrup and butter in a medium bowl. Heat the cream in a small saucepan over medium heat until it just begins to boil. Remove from heat and pour over the

chocolate. Let stand one minute, then stir until smooth. Cool to room temperature.

ASSEMBLE THE CAKE

1. Remove the cooled brownie layers from the pans. Set the first cake layer on a cake plate.
2. Top with a half of the coconut walnut filling, spread it evenly. Top the coconut wittier with ⅓ of the frosting, also spread evenly. Repeat the process with the second brownie cake layer. Third (top) layer, is covered in frosting only, no coconut mixture.
3. Pour the chocolate ganache on top of the cake, distribute evenly and also ice the sides of the cake while the ganache is dripping down.
4. Decorate with frosting if you have any remaining and chocolate sprinkles.
5. Chill the cake for at least 2 hours before serving.

DARK AND WHITE CHOCOLATE TRUFFLE CAKE

INGREDIENTS

CAKE LAYERS

- 6 ounces bittersweet chocolate, finely chopped
- 1 stick unsalted butter
- ½ cup unsweetened cocoa powder
- 1 cup water
- ⅔ cup mascarpone cheese, room temperature
- 3 large eggs
- 3 large egg yolks
- 1 cup granulated sugar
- 1 cup light brown sugar
- 1¼ cups all-purpose flour
- 1 tablespoon baking soda
- 2 teaspoons baking powder
- 1 teaspoon salt

WHITE CHOCOLATE WHIPPED GANACHE

- 1 pound white chocolate, chopped
- ¾ cup heavy cream
- 2 tablespoons unsalted butter
- 2 cups powdered sugar

MILK CHOCOLATE WHIPPED GANACHE

- 1⅓ cups heavy cream
- 10 ounces milk chocolate, chopped
- 3 cups powdered sugar

DARK CHOCOLATE FROSTING

- 4 ounces dark chocolate, chopped
- 3 tablespoons granulated sugar
- ¼ cup corn syrup
- 6 tablespoons unsweetened cocoa powder

- ¼ cup plus 2 tablespoons water
- 1 pound (4 sticks) unsalted butter, softened
- ¾ cup powdered sugar

CAKE TRUFFLES

- 1½ cup milk chocolate ganache
- cake edges and top
- 10 ounces dark chocolate

DIRECTIONS

CAKE LAYERS

1. Preheat the oven to 350°.
2. Spray with non stick baking spray a 18x13 inch sheet cake pan and line with parchment paper, spray the parchment paper with baking spray. Set aside.
3. In a medium saucepan, melt the chopped chocolate with the butter over very low heat, stirring gently. Once chocolate has completely melted, remove the mixture from the heat and let cool slightly.
4. In a small saucepan, combine cocoa powder with the water and bring to a boil, whisking constantly. Let it cool slightly and then whisk the mixture into the melted chocolate. Whisk in the mascarpone cream cheese.
5. In a large bowl or in the bowl of an electric mixer fitted with the whisk attachment, beat the whole eggs, egg yolks and both sugars at medium speed until pale and fluffy, about 5 minutes. Beat in the chocolate mixture.
6. In a medium bowl, whisk together the dry Ingredients: flour, baking soda, baking powder and salt. Using a spatula, gently fold in the dry Ingredients into the cake batter until fully incorporated.
7. Transfer the batter to the prepared pan and bake the cake in the lower third of the oven for 25 to 30 minutes, until the centers spring back when lightly pressed.
8. Let the cake cool completely in the pans.

WHITE CHOCOLATE WHIPPED GANACHE

1. In a medium bowl set over a medium saucepan of simmering water, melt the white chocolate. Remove from the heat and set aside.
2. Discard the water from the sauce pan add the heavy cream and butter to the saucepan and heat until the butter is melted and small bubbles appear around the edges.
3. Whisk the hot cream mixture into the white chocolate. Lumps will start to appear, don't be afraid, continue to quickly mix until the mixtures combine and the lumps disappear. Set the bowl in a cool place for at least 1 hour.
4. Once the ganache has cooled down, using a hand mixer or an electric mixer whisk in the powdered sugar. Once you did this cool the mixture for a few minutes only and start layering it on the cake as if placed in the fridge it will stiffen.

MILK CHOCOLATE WHIPPED GANACHE

1. In a medium saucepan, heat the cream until small bubbles appear around the edges. Put the chopped chocolate in a heatproof bowl and pour the hot cream on top. Let stand for 2 to 3 minutes, until the chocolate has melted, then whisk until shiny and smooth. Set the bowl in a cool place for at least 1 hour.
2. Once the ganache has cooled down, measure 1½ cups of chocolate ganache and set aside for the cake truffles.
3. Using a hand mixer or an electric mixer whisk in the powdered sugar into the remaining chocolate ganache. Once you did this cool the mixture for a few minutes only and start layering it on the cake as if placed in the fridge it will stiffen.

DARK CHOCOLATE FROSTING

1. In a medium saucepan, melt the chocolate over very low heat, stirring frequently. In a small saucepan, whisk together the granulated sugar, corn syrup, cocoa and water and bring to a boil, whisking constantly. Remove from the heat and whisk in the melted chocolate. Let cool completely, about 30 minutes.
2. In the bowl of an electric mixer fitted with a wire whisk, beat the butter at medium speed until light and fluffy. Add the cooled chocolate mixture. With a spatula scrape the bowl and whisk until fully combined. With the mixer on low speed, beat in the confectioners' sugar, scraping and beating until fully combined.

1. Cut out a 5-by-11-inch cardboard rectangle.
2. Carefully transfer the cake from the pan to a working area. You will need someone's help on this one, as its easier if you carefully hold the parchment paper with the cake up and someone is pulling the pan.
3. Once the cake was transferred on a working area, place the cardboard one inch from the left corner and cut a rectangle. Repeat moving to the right, you will end up with 3 rectangles. Using a cake leveler, level the top of the rectangles.
4. Transfer the cake edges and removed tops to a medium bowl and crumble with your hands. Set aside as that is what we will be using for the cake truffles. Using a cake lifter, transfer one of the rectangles to a flat rectangle platter, that is our first layer.
5. Spoon dollops of milk chocolate whipped ganache onto the cake and spread it evenly, make the layer as thick as you want, you must have just a little chocolate whipped ganache leftover.
6. Top with another cake rectangle and top it with white chocolate whipped ganache. Top with the final layer, if you have chocolate whipped ganache left spread it on the top layer.
7. Coat the sides and top of the cake with a thick layer of chocolate frosting and refrigerate to set the frosting.
8. Cake Truffles:
9. Mix cake truffles with chocolate ganache in a bowl using a fork until well combined, you can make small golf ball sized cake balls and place them on parchment paper and refrigerate until firm.
10. Or you can use a silicone petit four cakes or truffles form, press the cake truffle batter which is soft at this point into the form, refrigerate for a few hours and when ready remove from silicone form and top the cake.
11. In a medium bowl set over a medium saucepan of simmering water, melt the dark chocolate. Remove from the heat and set aside for a few minutes to cool down. Pour the melted chocolate over the cake truffles and cake.
12. When serving the cake run a knife thru how water before slicing it while the cake is cold, and let the slices come to room temperature before serving.

PEANUT BUTTER CHEESECAKE WITH BROWNIE BOTTOM LAYER

INGREDIENTS

FOR THE BROWNIES

- 1 package of Brownie Mix
- 15 peanut butter eggs or cups
- For the Cheesecake:
- 16oz cream cheese, at room temperature
- 3 eggs
- 1 cup of sugar
- 2 cups creamy peanut butter
- 1 tbsp. vanilla extract

FOR THE CHOCOLATE GANACHE

- 1 semi sweet chocolate bar
- ½ cup of heavy cream

TOPPINGS

- 2 small packages of peanut M&Ms
- 1 small package of mini peanut butter cups

DIRECTIONS

1. Preheat the oven to 325 degrees F , butter a 9″ springform pan and set aside.
2. To make the brownies: follow the DIRECTIONS on the box, once the batter is prepared pour it into the pan and cover with a layer of peanut butter cups
3. To make the cheesecake: beat the cream cheese and peanut butter together on medium speed until smooth. Add the sugar, vanilla extract and continue to beat on medium speed until well combined. Reduce the speed to low and add the eggs one at a time, beating until combined after each addition. Using a spatula, scrape the bowl and mix on low for another 30

seconds. Pour the cheesecake filling on top of the brownies & PB cups.

4. Bake for 45 minutes to one hour or until the sides of the cheesecake are set and the middle just slightly jiggles. Turn of the oven, open the door slightly and let the cheesecake cool inside for one hour. Transfer the cake to a wire cooling rack and cool at room temperature for 2 hours.

5. To make the ganache: Chop the chocolate and place in a medium bowl. In a sauce pan, on medium heat, bring the heavy cream to a boil, pour over chocolate and stir well until the chocolate is melted and well combined with the heavy cream. Pour the mixture on top of the cheesecake, using a spatula distribute it evenly. Decorate with mini peanut butter cups and peanut M&M's.

6. Refrigerate the cheesecake before serving for at least 4 hours or overnight, until thoroughly chilled.

DARK AND WHITE CAKE WITH MASCARPONE & CARAMEL BUTTERCREAM

INGREDIENTS

FOR CAKE LAYERS

- 1 Vanilla Cake Mix
- 1 Triple Chocolate Cake Mix
- 6 eggs
- 2 cups water
- ⅔ cups vegetable oil
- 4 tbsp butter, melted (to grease the pans)

FOR VANILLA MASCARPONE BUTTERCREAM

- 2 sticks unsalted butter, softened
- 4 oz chilled mascarpone cheese
- 2 vanilla beans
- 2 cups confectioners sugar, sifted
- 2 tbsp. heavy cream
- 1 cup fresh strawberries, washed and sliced

FOR CARAMEL BUTTERCREAM

- 2 sticks unsalted butter, softened
- 3 cups confectioners sugar, sifted
- ½ cup caramel sauce

DIRECTIONS

FOR CAKE LAYERS

1. Preheat oven to 350°F.
2. Grease sides and bottom of 4 8inch foil pans with butter. Flour lightly.
3. Open the vanilla mix, and empty the box mix into a medium bowl. Add 3 eggs, 1 cup water and ⅓ cup of vegetable oil. Stir

using a spatula until well incorporated. Divide the mixture equally into 2 pans. Set aside.

4. Open the chocolate mix, and empty the box mix into a medium bowl. Add 3 eggs, 1 cup water and ⅓ cup of vegetable oil. Stir using a spatula until well incorporated. Divide the mixture equally into 2 pans. Bake for 25-30min or until a toothpick inserted in the middle of the cake comes out clean, or with only a few moist crumbs attached to it, the cake is done.

5. Let the cakes completely cool, when cooled using a sharp kitchen knife level the surface of the cakes.

FOR VANILLA MASCARPONE BUTTERCREAM

1. Place softened butter into the bowl of a stand mixer that has been fitted with the paddle attachment. Turn the mixer on a medium setting and cream the butter until it is smooth and has lightened in color, about 2 minutes.

2. Add the mascarpone cheese, specs from vanilla beans and sugar ½ cup at a time, beating 15 sec on medium after each addition.

3. Add heavy cream one tbsp. at a time, beating on medium until desired consistency is achieved.

4. Set the bowl aside and let the frosting chill for 30 minutes.

FOR THE CARAMEL BUTTERCREAM

1. Place softened butter into the bowl of a stand mixer that has been fitted with the paddle attachment. Turn the mixer on a medium setting and cream the butter until it is smooth and has lightened in color, about 2 minutes.

2. Add sugar ½ cup at a time, and mix on medium until well incorporated.

3. Add caramel, and mix until desired consistency is achieved.

ASSEMBLE THE CAKE

1. On a cake stand, start with a leveled vanilla layer, top with vanilla mascarpone buttercream and fresh strawberries, followed by a chocolate layer topped with caramel buttercream, another vanilla layer topped with vanilla mascarpone buttercream and fresh strawberries. Finish with a top layer of chocolate cake, cover the entire cake in caramel

buttercream. Decorate with vanilla mascarpone buttercream and sprinkles.

BROWNIE CHOCOLATE CAKE WITH VANILLA BUTTERCREAM

INGREDIENTS

FOR THE BROWNIE LAYERS

- 2 packages Brownie Mix
- 4 eggs
- ½ cup of water
- ¾ cup vegetable oil

FOR THE COCONUT FILLING

- 1 cup heavy cream
- 1 cup granulated sugar
- 3 egg yolks
- 5 tbsp. unsalted butter, cut into small pieces
- 1 cup pecans, grinded
- 1½ cups unsweetened coconut

FOR THE VANILLA BUTTERCREAM

- 1 cup unsalted butter/2 sticks, softened
- 4 cups confectioner's sugar
- 1 vanilla bean
- 3 tbsp. heavy cream
- pinch of salt

FOR THE CHOCOLATE GANACHE

- 8 ounces semisweet chocolate, chopped
- 2 tbsp. light corn syrup
- 3 tablespoons unsalted butter
- 1 cup heavy cream

DIRECTIONS

FOR THE BROWNIE LAYERS

1. Preheat oven to 350°F , 325°F.
2. Grease bottom of 3 8inch round pans with shortening or cooking spray.
3. In a large bowl mix brownie mix, eggs, oil and water. Stir until well blended. Spread evenly into the greased pans and bake immediately.
4. Brownies are done when toothpick inserted 1 inch from edge of pan comes out clean. About 25 minutes. Cool completely in pan on wire rack before assembling the cake.

FOR THE COCONUT FILLING

1. Place the butter, pecans and coconut in a large bowl and set aside.
2. In a medium sauce pan, on low/medium heat, stir together the heavy cream, sugar and egg yolks until the mixture begins to thicken and coats the back of a spoon (180 degrees F.). Pour the hot custard immediately into the pecan-coconut mixture and stir until the butter is melted. Cool completely to room temperature before topping the brownie layers.

FOR THE VANILLA BUTTERCREAM

1. Place softened butter into the bowl of a stand mixer that has been fitted with the paddle attachment. Turn the mixer on a medium setting and cream the butter until it is smooth, 2 - 3 minutes.
2. Add sugar, ½ a cup at a time.
3. Add vanilla beans and a pinch of salt and combine until well-incorporated.
4. Add heavy cream a tablespoon at a time until the frosting has reached the preferred consistency.

FOR THE CHOCOLATE GANACHE

1. Place the chocolate, corn syrup and butter in a medium bowl. Heat the cream in a small saucepan over medium heat until it just begins to boil. Remove from heat and pour over the chocolate. Let stand one minute, then stir until smooth. Cool to room temperature.

1. Remove the brownie layers from the pans. Set the first cake layer on a cake plate.
2. Spread with a generous amount of buttercream first and add top the buttercream with ¾ cup of the coconut filling over the cake layer, making sure to reach to the edges.
3. Set another cake layer on top and repeat with all three layers including the top one.
4. Ice the sides with the chocolate ganache, add coconut topping to the middle, and create a border with Ferrero chocolates.

FRENCH CAKE WITH BLUEBERRIES

INGREDIENTS

CUSTARD CAKE FILLING

- 2 cups (500 grams) heavy cream
- 3½ tablespoons (50 grams) butter
- 1 teaspoon vanilla extract
- ¾ cup (100 grams) all-purpose white flour
- 1¼ cups (250 grams) white granulated sugar
- 2 whole large eggs + 2 egg yolks
- ½ teaspoon salt
- zest of one lemon
- 1¾ cups (550 grams) of blueberries
- Extra butter for the mold

BISCOFF CRUST

- 3 cups (750 grams) biscoff crumbs
- 10 tablespoons (140 grams) unsalted butter, melted
- ⅔ cup (85 grams) granulated sugar
- Blueberry Sauce:
- 6 cups fresh blueberries (frozen work too)
- 1½ cups (375 ml) water
- 1½ cups (300 grams) sugar
- 6 tablespoons cornstarch, mixed with 6 tablespoons cold water
- 2 tablespoons vanilla extract

MASCARPONE LEMON BUTTERCREAM

- 1 sticks (113 grams) of butter, softened
- 5 oz. (140 grams) mascarpone cheese, chilled
- 2½ cups (225 grams) powdered sugar
- zest of one lemon
- pinch of salt

DIRECTIONS

CUSTARD CAKE FILLING

1. In a large bowl, whisk by hand until well combined eggs, egg yolks, flour, sugar, lemon zest and salt. Set aside.
2. In a small sauce pan, place heavy cream on medium heat until it starts to boil, remove from heat and mix in vanilla extract.
3. Slowly pour ⅓ of the heavy cream into the egg mixture and whisk constantly. Do not pour all the heavy cream at once, since the high temperature will make the eggs cook.
4. Slowly pour the ½ of the remaining heavy cream, whisk until combined. Repeat with the remaining boiled heavy cream.
5. Cover the bowl with a plastic wrap and let it cool on the counter for 20 minutes, before transferring to the fridge for one hour.

BISCOFF CRUST

1. Preheat oven to 350F.
2. In a food processor or blender to grind the biscoff cookies until you get 3 cups of crumbs.
3. Mix the crumbs with melted butter and granulated sugar with a rubber spatula in a medium bowl until combined.
4. Press the mixture into the bottom of a 10inch spring form cake pan and slightly up the sides. Make sure it is tight and compact, otherwise the custard will leak.
5. Pre-bake the crust for 7 minutes at 350°F (177°C), before adding the custard filling.
6. Note: For a no-bake dessert, chill the crust for 2 hours before using in your recipe.
7. Butter the edges of the spring form pan. Place the blueberries on the biscoff crust.
8. Remove the custard from the fridge and pour it into the pan. Bake for 50 minutes, until golden brown.
9. Remove cake from the oven and place on a wire rack to cool completely.
10. Blueberry Sauce:
11. The sauce can be made while the cake is cooking or many days in advance.
12. In a large saucepan over medium heat, combine blueberries, water and sugar. Stir frequently, but careful not to crush the berries, bring to a low boil.
13. In a small bowl, mix the cornstarch with cold water until combined.

14. Slowly stir the cornstarch into the blueberries, careful not to crush them. Simmer until the homemade blueberry sauce is thick enough to coat the back of a metal spoon, about 10 minutes.
15. Remove from heat and gently stir in vanilla.
16. If making the buttercream frosting, let the sauce cool completely before topping the cake.
17. Note: this makes a lot of sauce, save the rest for other recipes, or cut it in half.
18. Mascarpone Lemon Buttercream:
19. Place softened butter and mascarpone into the bowl of an electric stand mixer that has been fitted with the whisk attachment. Turn the mixer on a medium setting and cream until it smooth and combined, 2 - 3 minutes.
20. Add sugar, ½ a cup at a time. Add lemon zest and a pinch of salt and whisk until well-incorporated.
21. If the frosting is too thick add heavy cream one tablespoon at a time until it has reached the desired consistency.
22. Top the cooled cake with the lemon mascarpone buttercream, and pour the cooled blueberry sauce on top of the frosting.

STRAWBERRY CREAM CREPE CAKE

INGREDIENTS

FOR CREPES

- 4 large eggs
- 1½ cups milk
- 1 cup water
- 2 cups flour
- 6 tablespoons melted butter
- 4 tablespoons sugar
- 1 teaspoons vanilla extract or 3 vanilla beans
- Butter - coat the pan between making each crepe
- 3 - 4 cups of fresh strawberries, sliced

FOR THE MASCARPONE BUTTERCREAM

- 1 stick of butter, softened at room temperature
- 6 oz mascarpone cheese, chilled
- 2 cups powdered sugar
- 1 vanilla bean
- pinch of salt

FOR THE CHOCOLATE GANACHE

- 8 ounces semisweet chocolate, chopped
- 2 tbsp. light corn syrup
- 3 tablespoons unsalted butter
- 1 cup heavy cream

DIRECTIONS

FOR THE CREPES

1. Place all the liquid Ingredients in a blender and mix on low - medium speed. If you don't have a blender just whisk by had until well combined. Add flour one cup at a time and mix/whisk

until well combined. Place batter in the refrigerator for at least 1 hour.

2. Place an 8-inch non-stick pan on low heat and when hot and add a little butter to coat it (less than half of a tablespoon).

3. Pour ⅓ cup of crepe batter into the center of the pan and swirl to spread evenly. Cook for roughly 30 seconds or until the edges of the crepe appear loosened from the pan.

4. Flip the crepe and cook for another 10 seconds, until slightly golden brown.

5. Remove crepe and stack on a plate. Continue with the remaining batter and stack crepes on the plate.

6. When done cooking cover the crepes with a kitchen towel to avoid the edges from drying out.

FOR THE MASCARPONE BUTTERCREAM

1. Place softened butter and mascarpone into the bowl of an electric stand mixer that has been fitted with the whisk attachment. Turn the mixer on a medium setting and cream until it smooth and combined, 2 - 3 minutes.

2. Add sugar, ½ a cup at a time. Add vanilla beans and a pinch of salt and whisk until well-incorporated.

3. If the frosting is too thick add heavy cream one tablespoon at a time until it has reached the desired consistency.

4. Refrigerate for 30 minutes before assembling the cake.

FOR THE CHOCOLATE GANACHE

1. Place the chocolate, corn syrup and butter in a medium bowl. Heat the cream in a small saucepan over medium heat until it just begins to boil. Remove from heat and pour over the chocolate. Let stand one minute, then stir until smooth. Cool to room temperature before assembling the cake.

ASSEMBLE THE CAKE

1. Take one crepe from the stack, place on a flat surface, using a soup spoon, take 1 - 2 spoons of chocolate ganache, place it in

the center of the crepe and coat it avoiding the edges, it should be covered in chocolate ½ inch from the edges.

2. In a line, place the strawberries in the middle of the crème on top of the chocolate ganache, from one edge to the other.

3. From your side, flip the bottom of the crepe to cover the strawberries, secure with your hand just where the strawberries are (like you would do when rolling sushi) and roll into a tube.

4. Place the filled crepe on the bottom of a glass baking pan, starting from one side, not the middle.

5. Repeat this technic with the rest of the crepes until the bottom of the pan is covered. This is your first layer.

6. Now, cover your crepe layer with a good amount of mascarpone buttercream, even it out. Start filling the rest of the crepes and stacking them on top of the cream, your second layer must be smaller than the first one, aiming for a pyramid.

7. Once you are done with your layers, pour the leftover chocolate ganache on top of the cake.

8. Refrigerate the cake for at least 3-4 hours or overnight before serving.

STRAWBERRY, CHAMPAGNE & ROSE CAKE

INGREDIENTS

FOR THE SPONGE

- 125g unsalted butter, softened
- 400g caster sugar
- 350g plain flour
- 3 tsp baking powder
- ¼ tsp salt
- 350ml milk
- 3 medium eggs
- 1 tsp vanilla extract

FOR THE SYRUP

- 140g caster sugar
- 1 tsp rose water

FOR THE DECORATION

- 400g white chocolate
- 5 Waitrose British Strawberries
- Dr Oetker Hot Pink Gel Food Colour
- Waitrose Cooks' Homebaking Freeze Dried Strawberries and Cooks' Ingredients Rose Petals

FOR THE BUTTERCREAM FILLING

- 250g unsalted butter, softened
- 500g icing sugar
- 125ml Champagne or Prosecco
- 6 tbsp Waitrose Duchy
- Organic Strawberry Preserve

DIRECTIONS

1. Grease and line 3 x 20cm round baking tins with baking parchment, and preheat the oven to 170ºC, gas mark 3.
2. Place the butter, sugar, flour, baking powder and salt into the bowl of a stand mixer with paddle attachment. Mix on low until all the butter is rubbed into the dry mixture and it has a sandy texture.
3. In a small jug, beat together the milk, eggs and vanilla. Keeping the mixer on a low speed, pour the mixture down the side of the flour and butter bowl. When all the liquid has been added, beat on a high speed for 2 minutes until it is light and fluffy.
4. Divide the mixture evenly between the prepared tins and bake in the preheated oven for 25-30 minutes until golden brown.
5. While the cake is baking, place the sugar into a saucepan with 100ml of water and bring to the boil. Simmer for 2 minutes, then remove from the heat and stir in the rose water.
6. When the cakes are cooked, leave them to cool in the tins for 10 minutes, then liberally brush with the cooled rose syrup. Leave to cool completely.

CHOCOLATE DECORATIONS

1. Melt the chocolate over a bowl of simmering water until smooth. Dip the strawberries into the chocolate and place them onto baking parchment to set.

SHARDS

1. Take a quarter of the remaining white chocolate and mix in the food colouring until it is one uniform colour, then transfer this mixture into a piping bag.
2. Pour the rest of the white chocolate into a large, lined baking tray, then drizzle with the pink chocolate and scatter over dried strawberries and rose petals.
3. Leave to set at room temperature for 30 minutes, then score 12 large triangles into it with a sharp knife. Chill until completely solid.

FOR THE BUTTERCREAM

1. Beat the soft butter and icing sugar in a stand mixer until it clumps together.
2. Add the Champagne, a few tablespoons at a time, until the icing loosens up and becomes fluffy. Beat on a high speed for 3-4 minutes to get air in.

ASSEMBLE THE CAKE

1. Place the bottom layer of sponge onto a large plate.
2. Spread the top with buttercream and 3 tbsp strawberry jam, repeat with the second layer of sponge, then add the third on top.
3. Cover the whole cake with a thin layer of buttercream, then place in the fridge for 20 minutes to solidify. Then, using a large palette knife, coat the chilled cake with more buttercream to achieve a smooth, clean finish.
4. Arrange the chocolate shards and strawberries on top, then sprinkle over some dried berries and rose petals.

CHOCOLATE & POMEGRANATE LAYER CAKE

INGREDIENTS

FOR THE LAYERS

- 200g plain flour
- 70g cocoa powder
- 1 tsp bicarbonate of soda
- 1 tsp baking powder
- ¼ tsp salt
- 120ml sunflower oil
- 340g caster sugar
- 2 medium Eggs
- 200ml pomegranate juice

FOR THE GANACHE

- 200g butter
- 280g dark chocolate (60-70% cocoa solids), chopped
- 2 tbsp golden syrup
- 250ml double cream
- 110g pack pomegranate seeds, to decorate

INTRUCTIONS

1. Preheat the oven to 180°C, gas mark 4. Grease and line the bases of 3 x 20cm tins with baking parchment.
2. Combine the flour, cocoa powder, bicarbonate of soda, baking powder and salt together in a bowl. In a separate bowl, whisk together the oil, sugar and eggs until smooth.
3. Add the pomegranate juice and the flour mixture to the oil, sugar and egg mixture. Pour in half the juice, and then add half the flour, then the remaining juice and the remaining flour. Make sure you mix well after each addition to avoid any lumps.

4. Divide the mixture between the 3 tins and bake in the preheated oven for 20-25 minutes, or until the cakes are springy to touch and,
when inserted, a skewer comes out clean. Leave to cool in the tins for 10 minutes, then transfer to a wire rack to cool completely.

FOR THE GANACHE

1. Place the butter, chocolate and golden syrup into a heatproof bowl over a pan of boiling water. Stir until the
mixture is melted and smooth – about 7-8 minutes. Pour in the
double cream and mix until combined, then place into the fridge and chill until cool but not set – about 35-40 minutes. Use an electric hand whisk to whip the ganache until it turns from dark to pale brown – about 2-3 minutes.

ASSEMBLE THE CAKE

1. Place one layer of the sponge on to a plate and spread with quarter of the ganache. Top with the second layer of sponge and another quarter of the ganache.
2. Add the final layer of sponge. Crumb coat the top and sides of the completed cake with a thin layer of ganache.
3. Place in the fridge for around 30 minutes to set. Cover the cake with the remaining ganache and then top with the pomegranate seeds.

CHOCOLATE CINNAMON CAKE

INGREDIENTS

- 225 g organic butter
- 225 g organic golden caster sugar
- 4 Range Medium Eggs
- 175 g organic self raising flour
- 1 tsp baking powder
- 50 g Cocoa Powder
- 1 tsp ground cinnamon
- ½ x 265g jar
- 150ml double cream, whipped
- Extra cocoa for dusting

DIRECTIONS

1. Preheat the oven to 180C, gas mark 4.
2. Place the butter, sugar and eggs together in a large mixing bowl. sift in the flour, baking powder, cocoa and cinnamon and beat until thoroughly mixed.
3. Spoon into 2 greased and base-lined round 20cm sandwich tins and levels the surface.
4. Bake for 30 minutes until well risen and a metal skewer emerges clean from the centre of the cakes.
5. Turn out and cool on wire racks.
6. Sandwich the 2 cakes together with the damson jam and whipped cream and dust with cocoa.

CHOCOLATE GANACHE CAKE

INGREDIENTS

FOR THE FILLING

- 150g Country Life Butter
- 150g Sugar
- 200g plain chocolate, broken into small chunks
- 200g ground almonds
- 6 medium Free Range Eggs, separated
- 4 tbsp brandy or milk

FOR THE GANACHE

- 200g plain chocolate
- 200ml double cream

DIRECTIONS

1. Preheat the oven to 150°C, gas mark 2. Base line 2 x 20cm sandwich tins with non-stick baking parchment.
2. Melt the butter, sugar and chocolate in a pan until melted. Cool slightly and fold in the almonds, egg yolks and brandy or milk.
3. Whisk the egg whites until they hold stiff peaks and fold into the chocolate mixture. Pour into the tins and bake for 40-45 minutes until firm. Cool slightly before turning out onto wire racks. Discard the paper and allow to cool.
4. Meanwhile, make the ganache by melting the chocolate and cream in a bowl over a pan of simmering water until melted. Whisk until glossy and thickened and allow to cool.
5. Place one half of the cake upside down on a serving plate, spread with ¼ of the ganache and put the other cake on top. Spread the rest of the ganache on the top and sides with a palate or round bladed knife until smooth and shiny.

CHOCOLATE PISTACHIO CAKE

INGREDIENTS

- 100g pack pistachio nuts
- 200g bar White Chocolate, chopped
- 450ml essential Waitrose Double Cream
- 250g tub ricotta cheese
- 2 tsp vanilla bean paste or extract
- 330g Double Chocolate Loaf
- 3 tbsp Kirsch, optional
- 200g bar Plain Chocolate, chopped
- 2 tbsp golden syrup

DIRECTIONS

1. Put the nuts in a heatproof bowl and cover with boiling water. Leave to stand for 30 seconds, then drain well and tip the nuts onto several sheets of kitchen paper. Cover with more layers of paper and rub under the palms of your hands to release the skins.
2. Peel away the skins. Roughly chop the nuts, either by hand or in a food processor.
3. Put the white chocolate and 100ml of the cream in a heatproof bowl over a pan of gently simmering water. Leave until melted, stirring occasionally. Remove from the heat and beat in the ricotta and vanilla.
4. Slice the cake as thinly as possible. Arrange a third of the slices in a base-lined 20cm spring-release or shallow, loose-based cake tin, cutting the slices to fit. Drizzle with 1 tbsp of the Kirsch, if using.
5. Whip a further 200ml of the cream until firm, and stir into the white chocolate mixture, along with all but 2 tbsp of the nuts.
6. Spread half the mixture in the tin and level the surface. Arrange half the remaining cake slices on top and drizzle with another tbsp of the Kirsch. Spread with the remaining filling, then the remaining cake slices and Kirsch.
7. Cover and chill for at least 2 hours.
8. Melt the plain chocolate in a heatproof bowl over a saucepan of simmering water.

9. Remove from the heat and add the golden syrup, then the remaining 150ml of cream, stirring until smooth. Leave until cooled but not thickened. Run a knife around the edges of the cake and release the cake from the sides of the tin.
10. Invert onto a serving plate and peel away the lining paper.
11. Spread the chocolate mixture over the top and sides with a palette knife and scatter with the reserved nuts.

FLOURLESS CHOCOLATE PRALINE CAKE

INGREDIENTS

- 175g unsalted butter, softened, plus extra for greasing
- 100g whole blanched hazelnuts
- 175g caster sugar
- 200g dark chocolate (70% cocoa), chopped
- 5 eggs, separated
- ½ tsp salt

DIRECTIONS

1. Preheat the oven to 180°C, gas mark 4.
2. Grease a 23cm cake tin and line with baking parchment.
3. Put the hazelnuts in a roasting tray and roast for 10 minutes until golden. Set aside and, once cool, blitz in a food processor with 25g sugar until finely ground.
4. Meanwhile, melt the chocolate in a bowl set over a pan of barely simmering water.
5. Using electric beaters, cream the butter and 100g sugar in a bowl for 5 minutes, until pale and fluffy. Beat in the egg yolks one at a time, then the melted chocolate and salt. Fold through the ground hazelnuts.
6. Reduce the oven to 160°C, gas mark 2.
7. In a separate bowl, whisk the egg whites to stiff peaks. Whisk in the remaining 50g sugar until stiff and glossy. Stir $^1/_3$ the egg white into the chocolate mixture to loosen, then carefully fold in the remaining egg white, a third at a time, trying to retain as much air as possible. Carefully tip into the tin, gently smooth the top and bake for 50-55 minutes until just set.
8. Cool in the tin for 20 minutes, then remove the sides (leave the base on) and cool completely on a wire rack.

FLOURLESS CHOCOLATE AND ALMOND CAKE

INGREDIENTS

FOR THE CAKE

- 265g Waitrose Belgian dark chocolate
- 6 eggs, 5 separated + 1 whole
- 210g caster sugar
- 150g ground almonds

FOR THE TOPPIN

- 3 tbsp apricot jam
- 120ml double cream
- 120g Waitrose Belgian dark chocolate

DIRECTIONS

CAKE LAYERS AND FILLING

1. Pre-heat your oven to 180°C, gas mark 4.
2. Grease and base line a 21cm round loose bottom cake tin.
3. Melt the chocolate in a bowl over a pan of simmering water and then allow to cool a little.
4. Whisk the egg whites in a large bowl until stiff.
5. In another bowl using an electric whisk, beat the egg, egg yolks and sugar together until thick and pale. The mixture should leave a trail on the surface when the beaters are lifted.
6. Whisk the ground almonds, melted chocolate and 1tbsp of egg white into the egg yolk mixture. Using a metal spoon carefully fold the remaining egg whites into the chocolate mixture. Pour the mixture into the prepared tin.
7. Bake for 45-50 minutes, until the crust that forms on top of the cake is firm and the sides shrink away from the tin.
8. Leave the cake to cool in the tin for at least 10 minutes. Then turn it out, upside down onto a clean tea towel on a wire rack.
9. Remove the parchment from the cake and leave to cool completely. Turn the cake the right way up on the rack and remove the tea towel.

10. Gently heat the jam and brush it evenly over the top and sides of the cake.

TOPPING

1. Melt the cream and chocolate in a bowl over a pan of simmering water. Stir occasionally until smooth and glossy. Allow to cool so the topping begins to thicken, but don't let it set.
2. Pour onto the centre of the cake and allow it flow over the top and the sides of the cake.
3. Use a palette knife to spread around the sides and completely coat the cake. Leave to set before serving.

BLACK FOREST CAKE

INGREDIENTS

FOR THE SPONGE

- 8 large Eggs
- 2 large Egg yolks
- 200g golden caster sugar
- 1 tbsp vanilla bean paste
- 90g cocoa powder
- Pinch of salt

FOR THE CHOCOLATE ICING

- 35g cocoa powder
- 120g golden syrup
- Pinch salt
- 100g plain chocolate, finely chopped
- 25g unsalted butter

FOR THE FILLING AND TOPPING

- 250g jar Opies Black Cherries With Kirsch
- 4 tbsp kirsch
- 600ml double cream
- 50g icing sugar, sifted
- 2 tsp vanilla bean paste
- 8-10 whole cherries with stems
- 25g pack Dark Chocolate Curls

DIRECTIONS

1. Preheat the oven to 180°C, gas mark 4.

2. Grease and line two 23cm round cake tins with baking parchment.
3. Separate the eggs and combine the yolks (plus extra yolks), sugar and vanilla bean paste in a large bowl. Use an electric hand whisk to whisk until pale and doubled in volume. Sift over the cocoa powder and fold in. In a clean bowl, whisk the egg whites and salt to stiff peaks then carefully fold into the egg yolk mixture.
4. Divide between the lined tins and bake for 30 minutes. Cool on a wire rack. Cut each cake in half horizontally.
5. For the icing, put the cocoa powder, syrup and salt into a saucepan with 125ml hot water, whisk until smooth then bring to the boil. Reduce the heat to a simmer and cook for 2 minutes, whisking constantly, until smooth and glossy. Remove from the heat and whisk in the chocolate and butter until smooth. Set aside to cool.
6. Drain the cherries, reserving the syrup, and set aside. Pour the syrup into a saucepan, bring to the boil and reduce by two thirds. Remove from the heat and stir in the kirsch.
7. Whip the cream, icing sugar and vanilla to soft peaks then fold in the drained cherries.

ASSEMBLE THE CAKE

1.

Put a small spoonful of cream onto a serving plate or cake stand and lay a sponge on top. Spoon over a quarter of the kirsch syrup, spread over a thin layer of the chocolate icing and top with a third of the cream. Repeat this layer with the next two sponges. Top with the final sponge, soak with the remaining syrup and spread over the remaining icing. Top with the fresh cherries and chocolate curls. Chill for 1 hour before serving.

VELVET MOCHA CHEESECAKE

INGREDIENTS

- 85 g unsalted butter
- 250 g double chocolate cookies, crushed
- 4 eggs
- 150 g caster sugar
- 1 vanilla pod, split
- 400 g full fat cream cheese
- 300 g light cream cheese
- 2 tbsp cornflour, sifted
- 300 ml creme fraiche
- 2 tbsp hot coffee
- 350g dark chocolate, 300g melted, 50g chopped
- 5 tbsp golden syrup
- 2 tbsp cocoa powder
- 2 tsp instant coffee granules

DIRECTIONS

- Preheat the oven to 180C/gas 4.
- Melt 70g butter and mix with the crushed cookies; press into a base-lined 23cm springform tin. Bake for 10 minutes until just firm. Leave to cool slightly, then wrap the tin in two large sheets of tinfoil, double-wrapping it around the outsides (it needs to be watertight), but leaving the top open.
- To make the cheesecake, whisk the eggs with the sugar for several minutes, until thick and airy. Scrape in the vanilla pod seeds; beat in all the cream cheese, the cornflour, crème fraîche, coffee and melted chocolate; pour into the tin.
- Set the cake tin in a large roasting tin or dish. Pour boiling water into the roasting dish to reach halfway up the cake tin. Bake for about 1 hour 20 minutes until just firm. Turn the oven off and leave for 15 minutes
- Meanwhile, make the sauce. In a pan, melt the syrup, 15g butter, cocoa, coffee granules and chopped chocolate over a very low heat with 80ml water. Whisk together until smooth. Keep in the fridge for up to 1 week and warm through gently before serving

- Chill the cheesecake overnight, or for up to 4 days, before serving with a drizzle of chocolate sauce

FLOURLESS CHOCOLATE CAKE

INGREDIENTS

- 250g soft unsalted butter, plus extra for greasing
- 100g roasted chopped hazelnuts
- 365g light brown muscovado sugar
- 300g 70% dark chocolate, broken into pieces
- 50g ground almonds
- 85g cocoa powder
- 6 large Eggs, lightly whisked
- 1 tsp vanilla bean paste or 1 vanilla pod, split and
- seeds scraped out
- 1 heaped tsp sea salt
- 190g fresh raspberries, to serve

DIRECTIONS

1. Preheat the oven to 180°C, gas mark 4.
2. Grease and line the sides and bottom of a 23cm loose-bottomed cake tin.
3. Grind the hazelnuts with 1 tsp of the sugar in a small food processor to a fine powder.
4. Gently melt the butter and chocolate in a large bowl over a pan of simmering water. Remove from the heat and stir to combine. Add the sugar, gently whisk until there are no lumps, then fold in the ground almonds and hazelnuts and cocoa powder. Gradually add the eggs, vanilla paste and salt, giving it all a good stir.
5. Pour the batter into the prepared tin and bake in the oven for 35 minutes. Remove and leave to cool for 20 minutes in the tin before carefully removing from the tin to cool.
6. Top with fresh raspberries. Serve in slivers with a dollop of crème fraîche, if you like, and an espresso or glass of amaretto on the side.

1. Make the cake: Preheat the oven to 350 F. Spray three 6-inch round cake pans (or two 8 inch pans) with baking spray and line bottoms with parchment paper.
2. In the bowl of a stand mixer, beat together the eggs, sugar and vanilla until it has tripled in volume - about 10 minutes. Mixture should be thick, creamy and pale. Add the lemon zest.
3. Sift the flour and salt (preferably three times) into a separate bowl or a large parchment paper on the counter. Stir into stand mixer using a plastic or metal spoon, preferably in batches.
4. Add the melted butter and gently fold it in to the cake batter mix.
5. Divide the batter evenly between the pans and gently smooth the tops. Tap the cake pans on the counter to remove any air bubbles.
6. Bake in preheated oven for 21-25 minutes or until the sponges are evenly golden and come away from the sides of the baking pans.
7. Allow the cakes to cool in their pans for 10 minutes. After 10 minutes, turn them onto the wire rack carefully and allow the cakes to cool completely.
8.
    Meanwhile, make the whipped cream: In a small pan, combine gelatin and cold water and allow to sit for 5 minutes until thick. Place over low heat, stirring constantly, just until the gelatin dissolves.
9. Remove from heat and allow to cool slightly (but do not let it to set).
10. Using a stand mixer, whip the heavy cream with the icing sugar until soft peaks form.
11. While slowly beating, add the gelatin to the whipping cream. Whip at high speed until stiff peaks form.

ASSEMBLE THE CAKE

1. Place your first layer of cake on top of a cardboard circle, serving plate or cake stand.
2. Spoon a generous layer of whipped cream and spread evenly using an offset spatula.

3. Place an even layer of sliced strawberries and berries on top of the whipped cream.
4. Add the second layer of cake and repeat until all of the layers are on the cake.
5. For the top layer, spread on with a generous layer of whipped cream and spread evenly using an offset spatula.
6. Garnish with fresh strawberries, blueberries and blackberries. Dust with powdered sugar.

CHEESECAKE BROWNIES

INGREDIENTS

- 1 boxed brownie mix or homemade brownie recipe
- 8 ounces cream cheese, softened
- 2 tbsp butter, softened
- 1 tbsp cornstarch
- 14 ounces sweetened condensed milk
- 1 egg
- 1 tsp vanilla extract
- 16 ounce container chocolate frosting

DIRECTIONS

1. Preheat oven to 350oF. Grease a 9x13 baking dish with nonstick cooking spray.
2. Prepare brownie mix according to directions on package. Pour batter in the baking dish.
3. Beat the cream cheese, butter, and cornstarch until fluffy. Gradually beat in the sweetened condensed milk, egg, and vanilla until smooth. Pour cream cheese mixture over the brownie batter.
4. Bake for 45 minutes. Allow to cool. Spread frosting over top. Store covered in the refrigerator.

MUDSLIDE CAKE

INGREDIENTS

FOR CAKE

- 2 cups granulated sugar
- 2 large eggs, room temperature
- 1 cup hot water
- 1/2 cup unsweetened cocoa powder
- 1 teaspoon instant coffee
- 1 teaspoon salt
- 2 1/2 cups sifted all-purpose flour
- 2 teaspoons baking soda
- 1 teaspoon baking powder
- 1 cup vegetable oil
- 1 cup buttermilk, room temperature
- 1 tablespoon vanilla extract

FOR FILLING

- 1/2 teaspoon gelatin
- 2 cups heavy cream, cold
- 1/2 cup confectioners sugar
- 4-5 tablespoons bourbon, to taste
- For Ganache
- 6 ounces chopped semisweet chocolate
- 1/2 cup heavy cream, room temperature

FOR GARNISH

- 1 cup chopped or crumbled chocolate wafer or sandwich cookies

DIRECTIONS

1. Preheat oven to 350 degrees F. Line the bottoms of 3 9-inch round cake pans with parchment paper; butter parchment and sides of pan.
2. In a large mixing bowl or the bowl of a stand mixer fitted with a whisk attachment, beat sugar and eggs on high speed for 2 to 3 minutes until lightened in color.

3. Combine the hot water, cocoa powder, instant coffee, and salt; stir to combine. With mixer on low speed, slowly pour into mixer bowl. Continue to mix on low speed until incorporated.
4. Add flour, baking soda, and baking powder and mix on low speed until just incorporated. Mix in oil, buttermilk, and vanilla, scraping down the sides of the bowl as necessary. Do not overmix. The batter will be quite thin.
5. Divide batter among prepared pans. Bake for 22 to 25 minutes or until a toothpick inserted near the center comes out clean.
6. Let cool on wire racks. If necessary, run a thin metal knife around the edges of the pans to loosen, then invert onto wire racks. Cakes should come out cleanly. Let cool completely. At this point you can wrap cakes in plastic wrap and seal inside zip-top bags, store in the freezer overnight or until ready to use.
7. To prepare whipped cream, fill a small dish with 2 tablespoons cold water. Sprinkle over gelatin and let sit for 5 minutes to soften. Microwave for 5 seconds to melt, stirring gently to smooth out any chunks, then set aside to cool.
8. In a cold metal mixing bowl, whip cream on high speed until frothy. Add sugar and cooled gelatin and continue to whisk until cream holds soft peaks. Add bourbon to taste and whisk until cream holds stiff peaks. Refrigerate until ready to use.
9. To prepare ganache, combine chopped chocolate and cream in a microwave-safe bowl. Microwave on half power for 15 seconds at a time, stirring well after each interval. Continue to microwave until chocolate is just melted; the residual heat of the mixture should be enough to melt it completely. Let cool until slightly thickened but still pourable. If the ganache is on the thick side, whisk in a tablespoon or two of butter, cut into small cubes, to thin out the ganache as desired.
10. To assemble, place one layer on a cake stand or serving plate. Top with 1/3 of whipped cream, spreading to within 3/4" of the edge. Drizzle with 1/3 of ganache, and sprinkle with crumbled cookies. Repeat with second and third layers, finishing with the remaining whipped cream, ganache, and crushed cookies. Refrigerate until ready to serve.

VEGAN CAKE

INGREDIENTS

- 1 1/2 cups almond milk
- 2 teaspoons apple cider vinegar
- 1 cup plus 2 tablespoons vegan granulated sugar
- 1/3 cup plus 2 tablespoons vegetable oil
- 1 tablespoon vanilla bean paste
- 1/4 teaspoon almond extract
- 2 cups unbleached all-purpose flour
- 3 tablespoons cornstarch
- 3/4 teaspoon baking soda
- 1 teaspoon baking powder
- 3/4 teaspoon salt

FROSTING

- 3/4 cup non-hydrogenated margarine
- 3/4 cup non-hydrogenated shortening
- 3 1/2 cups vegan powdered sugar
- 1 tablespoon pure vanilla extract
- pinch of salt
- 1/4 cup almond milk

DIRECTIONS

1. Preheat oven to 350 degrees, grease (2) 9-inch cake pans. In a large bowl, whisk together almond milk and vinegar and let stand 4 or 5 minutes.
2. Whisk in sugar, oil, almond and vanilla paste, and mix until frothy. Sift together flour, cornstarch, baking soda, baking powder, and salt.
3. Add the flour mixture to the almond and vanilla mixture and blend until flour disappears. Don't over mix! Pour half of the batter into each 9 inch pan and bake for about 25 minutes, or until a toothpick inserted into the center of the cake comes out clean. Cool completely before frosting.

4. In a mixer, add margarine and shortening and beat at medium speed for about 2.
5. Stir in powdered sugar, add vanilla extract and salt and beat on medium for 1 minute. Add almond milk slowly until just spreadable.

TO ASSEMBLE

1. Place first layer on stand, cardboard round or platter and frost.
2. Add second layer and frost evenly and flat.
3. Decorate with raspberries, blueberries, lingonberries, and baby strawberries and a bit of mint.

GLUTEN FREE BROWNIES

INGREDIENTS

- 23 oz almond flour
- 1 teaspoon salt
- 1 tablespoon cocoa powder
- 6 oz. dark chocolate, coarsely chopped
- 1 cup (4 oz.) coconut oil
- 1 cup coconut sugar
- 2 eggs
- 1 teaspoon vanilla extract
- 1 cup dark chocolate chips

DIRECTIONS

1. Preheat oven to 350oF. Line with parchment and lightly grease an 8x8" baking pan.
2. In a medium bowl, whisk the almond flour, salt, and cocoa powder together.
3. Put the chocolate and coconut oil in a large glass bowl and microwave for 30 seconds. Stir, and repeat until the chocolate and coconut oil are completely melted and smooth. Add the coconut sugar. Whisk until completely combined. The mixture should be room temperature.
4. Add 2 eggs to the chocolate mixture and whisk until combined. Add the vanilla and stir.
5. Sprinkle the flour mixture over the chocolate mixture. Using a rubber spatula, fold the flour mixture into the chocolate until just a bit of the flour mixture is visible. Fold in the chocolate chips.
6. Bake in preheated oven for 28-32 minutes or until a toothpick comes out with moist crumbs attached.
7. Cool brownies completely.

M&M'S BROWNIES

INGREDIENTS

- 1/2 cup butter, softened
- 2 cups brown sugar
- 2 eggs
- 2 teaspoons almond extract
- 1/2 teaspoon salt
- 2 teaspoons baking powder
- 1 3/4 cups flour
- 1/2 cup dark cocoa powder
- 1 1/2 cups mini M&M's candies, divided

DIRECTIONS

1. Beat the butter and sugar until creamy. Add the eggs and extract and beat again.
2. Stir together the salt, baking powder, flour, and cocoa powder. Slowly beat into the butter mixture until combined. Add 1 cup mini M&M's and stir gently.
3. Spoon into a greased 9x13 glass baking dish. Top with the remaining candies. Bake at 350 degrees for 25 minutes. Remove and let cool completely before cutting.

CINNAMON CHEESECAKE BARS

INGREDIENTS

CAKE

- 1 large egg
- 1 cup light brown sugar
- 1 cup natural sweetener/or sugar of choice
- 1 cup pure pumpkin puree, canned or homemade
- 1 cup oil
- 1 tablespoon honey
- 1 tablespoon vanilla extract
- 11 cups plain flour
- 1 tablespoon baking powder
- 11 teaspoons ground cinnamon
- Pinch of salt
- 1 cup white chocolate chips

CHEESECAKE

- 1x 250g | 8.8oz packet low fat/fat free cream cheese, at room temp
- 2 tablespoons flour
- 1 teaspoon ground cinnamon
- 4 tablespoons natural sweetener/sugar of choice

DIRECTIONS

1. Preheat oven to 180c | 350F. Grease a 9x11-inch baking pan with cooking spray; line with baking/parchment paper and set aside.
2. In a large bowl, whisk the egg, brown sugar, sweetener/sugar, pumpkin, oil, honey and vanilla until smooth and creamy.
3. Add the flour, baking powder, cinnamon and salt, and stir until just combined.
4. Fold through chocolate chips, set aside and make the cheesecake layer

CHEESECAKE

1. Combine cream cheese, flour, cinnamon and sweetener/sugar in a medium sized bowl, and beat until smooth.

2. Pour the cake batter into prepared pan and evenly smooth the top lightly with a spatula.
3. Pour the cheesecake mixture over the top, and using the back of a knife, swirl small amounts of the blondie batter gently into the cheesecake mix until a marble effect is created on the top.
4. Bake for about 38 - 45 minutes, or until done. A toothpick inserted in the center should come out mostly clean/slightly dirty, with a few moist crumbs but no batter. Allow cake to cool in pan for at least 30 minutes before slicing and serving.

PUMPKIN & CHOCOLATE CAKE

INGREDIENTS

PUMPKIN LAYER

- 1 cup sugar
- 1 cup canola oil
- 2 large eggs
- 1 cup all-purpose flour
- 1 tsp baking soda
- 1 tsp ground cinnamon
- 1 tsp baking powder
- 1 tsp salt
- 1 cup pumpkin purée

CHOCOLATE LAYER

- 6 Tbsp unsweetened cocoa powder, plus more for pans
- cup all-purpose flour
- cup sugar
- 1 tsp + pinch baking soda
- tsp + pinch baking powder
- tsp + pinch salt
- 1 large eggs
- Tbsp buttermilk
- 6 Tbsp water
- Tbsp canola oil
- 1 tsp vanilla extract

WHIPPED BROWN SUGAR ICING

- 7 Tbsp all-purpose flour
- 1 1 cup milk
- 1 1 Tbsp pure vanilla extract
- 1 1 cup salted butter, at room temperature
- 1 1 cup brown sugar, packed
- Pinch of salt

DIRECTIONS

1. Preheat oven to 350oF. Butter 2 – 8" layer round pans. Dust one with flour and one with cocoa.

PUMPKIN LAYER

1 Combine sugar, canola oil and eggs in a mixing bowl; mix well.
2 Whisk flour, baking soda, cinnamon, baking powder and salt in another bowl.
3 Stir into oil mixture; beating well. Stir in pumpkin.
4 Pour into the flour prepared pan. Bake for 35-40 minutes. Cool completely before turning out.

CHOCOLATE LAYER

1 Combine cocoa, flour, sugar, baking soda, baking powder and salt into the bowl of a mixer. Beat on low until combined.
2 Add eggs, buttermilk, water, oil and vanilla. Increase speed to medium and beat until very smooth, about 3 minutes.
3 Pour into cocoa prepared pan. Bake until set about 30-35 minutes. Let cool completely before turning out.
4 When both layers are fully cooled, take the one pumpkin layer and cut it in half, then the one chocolate layer and cut it in half so you have 4 sections of cake. Frost with Whipped Brown Sugar Icing alternating one chocolate section, pumpkin, chocolate and finish with pumpkin.

WHIPPED BROWN SUGAR ICING

1 In a small saucepan, whisk flour into milk and heat, stirring constantly, until it thickens.
2 Remove from heat and let it cool to room temperature. Stir in vanilla.
3 While the mixture is cooling, cream the butter, sugar, and salt together until light and fluffy on medium high, about 3 minutes. Add the completely cooled milk mixture.
4 Beat for 5 minutes on medium-high to high until it looks like whipped cream.

CHOCOLATE BUNDT CAKE

INGREDIENTS

- 1/4 Dough from Chocolate Chip Cookies
- 1 C M&M's Milk Chocolate Harvest Candies
- 1 C Unsalted Butter, softened
- 2 C Sugar
- 2 Eggs
- Tbsp Cocoa Powder
- 2 tsp Vanilla Extract
- 1 C Sour Cream
- 2 tsp Baking Soda
- 2 1/2 C All-Purpose Flour
- 1/4 tsp Kosher Salt
- 1 C Boiling Water
- 1 Container Cream Cheese Icing

DIRECTIONS

1. Prepare chocolate chip cookies as directed in the original recipe, swapping out the chocolate chips for the 1 cup of M&M's. Reserve 1/4 of the dough, and wrap the rest in plastic and place in the fridge for later use.
2. Preheat oven to 325 degrees. Grease a bundt pan with shortening or butter, then coat in an even layer of cocoa powder. Tap out the excess and set aside.
3. In a large mixing bowl beat the butter and sugar until light and fluffy, around 5 minutes. Beat in the eggs, one at time, until fully incorporated, then mix in the cocoa powder, vanilla extract, and sour cream.
4. Whisk together the flour, baking soda, and salt and slowly add to the mixture.
5. Gently beat in the boiling water on low speed. Pour the batter into the prepared bundt pan.
6. Roll the cookie dough into small balls and plop them into the cake batter in the bundt cake, pressing down just slightly.
7. Bake for 60 minutes, or until a toothpick inserted into the center of the cake comes out clean.
8. Allow the cake to cool for 10 minutes in the pan before flipping out onto a cooling rack to cool completely.
9. Remove the lid and foil from the icing, then place in the microwave and heat for 15 second intervals until smooth and pourable. Slowly pour over cooled bundt cake, allow to set.

ANGEL CAKE

INGREDIENTS

- 13 cups sugar, divided
- 1 teaspoon salt
- 1 cup cake flour, sifted
- 12 egg whites
- 1 cup warm water
- 1 teaspoon vanilla extract
- teaspoons cream of tartar
- 1 can of vanilla frosting, optional

DIRECTIONS

1. Preheat oven to 350 degrees F.
2. In medium mixing bowl, combine half of the sugar with the salt and cake flour.
3. In a large mixing bowl, use a balloon whisk to thoroughly mix egg white, water, vanilla, and cream of tartar. After 2 minutes, switch to a hand mixer. Slowly add the remaining half of the sugar sugar, beating continuously at medium speed.
4. Once you have achieved medium peaks, sprinkle enough of the flour mixture to dust the top of the fluffy egg whites. Using a rubber spatula to gently fold in the flour mixture until almost fully incorporated.
5. Repeat until all of the flour mixture is incorporated into the egg whites. You want to mix in the flour in as few folds as possible.
6. Carefully spoon mixture evenly into an ungreased tube pan. Bake for 35 minutes.
7. Check that the cake is done by inserting a wooden skewer into the cake halfway between the middle tube and the outer wall..
8. Cool upside down in the pan on cooling rack for at least an hour. Run a knife around the outer wall of the pan to release the cake. Then run the knife around the center tube and under the cake to finish releasing the cake from the pan.

RED VELVET CAKE

INGREDIENTS

CAKE BATTER

- 31 cups all-purpose flour
- 2 cups sugar
- 3 tablespoons unsweetened cocoa powder
- 2 teaspoons baking soda
- 3 teaspoon salt
- 13 cups buttermilk
- cups vegetable oil
- 3 large eggs
- 1 teaspoon distilled white vinegar
- 1 bottle liquid red food coloring

FROSTING

- 1 pound cream cheese, room temperature
- 1 cup butter, softened
- cups confectioners' sugar

BLOODY GANACHE

- 12 ounces white chocolate bark
- 2 tablespoons heavy cream
- red food coloring

DIRECTIONS

1. To make cake, preheat oven to 350 degrees and spray 3 9-inch cake pans with baking spray with flour.
2. In a large mixing bowl combine flour, sugar, cocoa powder, baking soda, and salt.
3. In a medium bowl, whisk together buttermilk, vegetable oil, eggs, and vinegar.
4. With the mixer on low, add the buttermilk mixture to the flour mixture. Once all buttermilk mixture has been added, turn to medium speed and beat until smooth.
5. Add food coloring and beat until mixed evenly.
6. Divide batter evenly between the prepared pans and bake about 22 to 25 minutes. Let cool in pans for 10 minutes and then remove to wire rack to cool completely.

7   For frosting, beat cream cheese and butter with an electric mixer until smooth. Gradually beat in confectioners' sugar.
8   Spread frosting between layers of cakes and on top and sides.
9   Refrigerate cake to firm up frosting before adding bloody ganache.
10 Melt white chocolate bark with cream cheese in a heavy-bottomed pan over low heat, stirring continuously.
11 Once melted, add food coloring to get desired color. Drizzle on top of cake to resemble blood.

LEMON AND BLUEBERRY CHEESECAKE

INGREDIENTS

BLUEBERRY SAUCE

- 2 cups fresh blueberries
- ½ cup water
- ½ cup sugar
- 2 tablespoons cornstarch, mixed with 2 tablespoons cold water
- 1 tablespoons vanilla extract

CRUST

- 2 cups graham cracker crumbs
- 8 tablespoons unsalted butter, melted
- 2 tablespoons granulated sugar

CHEESECAKE FILLING

- 4 packages (8 oz.) cream cheese, softened
- 1 cup sour cream
- 2 tablespoons cornstarch
- 3 eggs
- 1⅓ cups sugar
- ½ cup graham cracker crumbs
- juice of one meyer lemon
- zest from one meyer lemon

DIRECTIONS

BLUEBERRY SAUCE

1. The sauce can be made while the cake is cooking or many days in advance.
2. In a large saucepan over medium heat, combine blueberries, water and sugar. Stir frequently, but careful not to crush the berries, bring to a low boil.

3. In a small bowl, mix the cornstarch with cold water until combined.
4. Slowly stir the cornstarch into the blueberries, careful not to crush them. Simmer until the homemade blueberry sauce is thick enough to coat the back of a metal spoon, about 10 minutes.
5. Remove from heat and gently stir in vanilla.
6. Let the sauce cool at room temperature. Measure ½ cup for your recipe, store the rest in jars in the fridge.

CRUST

4. In a large bowl, mix the crumbs with melted butter and granulated sugar with a rubber spatula until combined.
5. Press the mixture into the bottom of a 9inch spring form cake pan and slightly up the sides. Make sure it is tight and compact.
6. Chill the crust for 15 minutes.

CHEESECAKE FILLING

10. Preheat oven to 325F.
11. In the bowl of an electric mixer fitted with the whisk attachment beat cream cheese on medium speed until fluffy. Add the sugar, cornstarch, lemon juice, lemon zest and beat until combined.
12. Add eggs, one at a time, beating until just combined after each addition. On low speed beat in sour cream just until combined.
13. Remove crust from the fridge and pour the batter into the crust.
14. In circles pour the blueberry sauce over the cheesecake and with the edge of a spatula create swirls and mix the blueberry sauce into the cheesecake filling. Carefully not to over mix.
15. Bake for about 1¼ hours or until center is almost set. Cool on a wire rack for 15 minutes. Sprinkle graham crackers on top and loosen sides of pan and continue cooling on wire rack until the cheesecake is at room temperature.
16. Transfer to the fridge. Refrigerate overnight or at least 6 hours before serving.
17. The cheesecake can be served with warm blueberry sauce.
18. Store in refrigerator.

CHOCOLATE BROWNIE CAKE WITH MASCARPONE

INGREDIENTS

FOR THE BROWNIE LAYERS

- 1 cup unsalted butter, melted
- 2 cup granulated sugar
- 4 large eggs
- 1 cup all-purpose flour
- ½ cup unsweetened cocoa powder
- ½ teaspoon salt
- ½ teaspoon baking soda

FOR THE COCONUT FILLING

- 1 cup walnuts, measure then grind
- 1 cup coconut flakes
- ½ cup heavy cream
- ½ cup sugar
- 1 egg yolk
- 3 tbsp. butter, room temperature

FOR THE VANILLA BUTTERCREAM

- 3 sticks of butter, softened
- 8 oz mascarpone cheese, chilled
- 2½ cups powdered sugar
- 1 vanilla bean
- pinch of salt

FOR THE CHOCOLATE GANACHE

- 8 ounces semisweet chocolate, chopped
- 2 tbsp. light corn syrup
- 3 tablespoons unsalted butter
- 1 cup heavy cream

7. Preheat oven to 350°F.
8. Grease bottom of 3 8inch round pans with melted butter or cooking spray.
9. In the bowl of an electric mixer, whisk together melted butter and sugar until smooth. Add in each egg one at a time on low speed and whisk until well combined.
10. Using a large rubber spatula, gently stir in flour, cocoa, baking soda and salt.
11. Spread batter into the pans and bake for 25-30 minutes until set.
12. Remove and let cool completely before assembling the cake.

FOR THE COCONUT FILLING

3. Place the butter, walnuts and coconut in a large bowl and set aside.
4. In a medium sauce pan, on low/medium heat, stir together the heavy cream, sugar and egg yolk until the mixture begins to thicken and coats the back of a spoon (180 degrees F.). Pour the hot custard immediately onto the walnut-coconut mixture and stir until the butter is melted. Cool completely to room temperature before topping the brownie layers.

FOR THE VANILLA MASCARPONE BUTTERCREAM

4. Place softened butter and mascarpone into the bowl of an electric stand mixer that has been fitted with the whisk attachment. Turn the mixer on a medium setting and cream until it smooth and combined, 2 - 3 minutes.
5. Add sugar, ½ a cup at a time. Add vanilla beans and a pinch of salt and whisk until well-incorporated.
6. If the frosting is too thick add heavy cream one tablespoon at a time until it has reached the desired consistency.

FOR THE CHOCOLATE GANACHE

2. Place the chocolate, corn syrup and butter in a medium bowl. Heat the cream in a small saucepan over medium heat until it just begins to boil. Remove from heat and pour over the

chocolate. Let stand one minute, then stir until smooth. Cool to room temperature.

ASSEMBLE THE CAKE

6. Remove the cooled brownie layers from the pans. Set the first cake layer on a cake plate.
7. Top with a half of the coconut walnut filling, spread it evenly. Top the coconut wittier with ⅓ of the frosting, also spread evenly. Repeat the process with the second brownie cake layer. Third (top) layer, is covered in frosting only, no coconut mixture.
8. Pour the chocolate ganache on top of the cake, distribute evenly and also ice the sides of the cake while the ganache is dripping down.
9. Decorate with frosting if you have any remaining and chocolate sprinkles.
10. Chill the cake for at least 2 hours before serving.

COFFEE CAKE

INGREDIENTS

- ½ cup coconut oil
- eggs
- 1 cup brown sugar
- 1 tsp. vanilla
- 1 cup cooked oatmeal
- cup white whole wheat flour
- cup all-purpose flour
- 1 tsp. cloves
- 1 tsp. salt
- 1 tsp. cinnamon
- 1 tsp. baking soda
- 1 Tbsp. coconut oil
- 1 cup chopped pecans
- 1 cup brown sugar

DIRECTIONS

1   Preheat oven to 350o F. Spray an 8x8" pan with cooking spray.
2   Stir together the coconut oil, eggs, Truvia, vanilla and cooked oatmeal.
3   In a separate bowl, mix together flour, cloves, salt, cinnamon and baking soda. Combine dry Ingredients with wet Ingredients and stir until combined. Pour into prepared pan.
4   Mix 1 Tbsp. coconut oil, pecans and brown sugar in a small bowl and sprinkle over the top of cake. Bake for 25-30 minutes. Cut into squares and serve.

CHOCOLATE CAKE WITH CARAMEL & MASCARPONE

INGREDIENTS

- 150g of flour
- 30g of cocoa powdered Pantaguel
- 1/4 teaspoon of baking powder
- 1/4 teaspoon of baking soda
- 1/4 teaspoon of salt
- 100g of softened butter
- 145g of brown sugar
- 1 egg
- 1 egg yolk
- 75g of melted chocolate
- 1/2 teaspoon of vanilla extract
- 125ml of milk

FOR THE CARAMEL

- 100g yellow sugar
- 60ml of cream
- tablespoon of unsalted butter
- 1 teaspoon of vanilla extract
- pinch of salt

MARSCARPONE CREAM AND CARAMEL

- 250g mascarpone cheese
- 63g powdered sugar
- 100ml fresh cream
- Caramel

CHOCOLATE SHAVINGS

- 100g chocolate

DIRECTIONS

1   Pre-heat the oven at 175oC and prepare two trays with 15cm with a parchment paper base, spread with butter and sprinkle a little of the powdered cocoa.

2   Mix in a bowl the sieved flour with the cocoa, baking powder, baking soda and salt. Reserve.
3   On another bowl, beat the butter with the sugar until it becomes a soft cream.
4   Add the egg and the egg yolk to the butter mixture, whisk well and then add the melted chocolate and the vanilla. Mix well.
5   Alternating between the flour and the milk, keep involving the liquid mixture, ending with the flour.
6   Divide the mixture on the two trays. Seeing as it is a thick mixture, it will be necessary to smooth it out with a spoon.
7   Bring it to the oven for 30-35mins or until the toothpick comes out clean.
8   Take it out of the oven and let it rest for 10mins before taking it out of the tray and letting it cool completely.

CARAMEL

1   On a small pan, bring it to medium heat with the sugar, the butter and the cream.
2   Keep stirring non-stop with a spoon, let it shimmer for 3min. Don't stop stirring to avoid it from sticking to the end of the pan.
3   Take it out of the heat and add the vanilla and the salt. Careful because it might me too hot and start to create bubbles.
4   Pour it on a glass bottle and let it cool down at ambient temperature.

MARSCARPONE CREAM AND CARAMEL

1   Whisk the mascarpone with the sugar and caramel until it becomes a soft and smooth cream.
2   Add the cream and whisk it for 5 more minutes until it becomes smooth again.

CHOCOLATE SHAVINGS

1   Put a tray in the fridge, minimum 15min.
2   To season the chocolate, you're going to need to melt half of the black chocolate in bain-marie and the other half, break into very small pieces.
3   When the chocolate is melted, add the chocolate pieces and mix until it all melts.
4   Pour the chocolate over the tray and spread out a thin layer with the help of a spatula.
5   Wait some minutes until the chocolate dries out, if needed, bring the tray into the fridge again for less than 5min.

6   With the help of a metallic spatula or a knife, make little rolls.

ASSEMBLY

1   Put one of the cakes over a base, take out the top and spread a little bit of the cream, some chocolate shaving and some powdered cocoa.
2   On top of it, put the other half of the cake.
3   Spread the resto f the cream, chocolate shaving and more powdered cocoa.

UPSIDE-DOWN TEA CAKE

INGREDIENTS

UPSIDE-DOWN BITS

- 300 g kumquats
- Tbsp coconut oil, melted (30 ml)
- 1 c coconut sugar, lightly packed (40 g)
- 1 Tbsp boiling water (15 ml)

CAKE

- 1 c coconut oil, semi-firm (115 g)
- 1 c coconut sugar, lightly packed (80 g)
- eggs, at room temperature
- 1 c almond milk (115 ml)
- 1 c orange juice (60 ml)
- 1 tsp vanilla paste
- c whole spelt flour (260 g)
- 2 Tbsp arrowroot flour (16 g)
- 2 tsp baking powder
- 1 tsp baking soda
- 1 tsp sea salt

TOPPING

- handful flaked almonds
- handful shredded coconut

DIRECTIONS

1   Preheat oven to 180°C (350°F). Grease sides of an 8 inch / 20 cm cake tin with a bit of coconut oil.
2   Slice a very thin bit off the end of each kumquat and discard. Cut each kumquat in half — or large ones in thirds — and remove seeds.

PREPARE THE UPSIDE-DOWN BITS

1   Drizzle melted coconut oil into base tin.

2   Combine boiling water and sugar and stir gently, then drizzle over coconut oil.

3   Place kumquat slices over caramel mixture, packing them very tightly together .

MAKE THE CAKE BATTER

1   In a large bowl use a spatula to cream coconut oil and sugar together until smooth. Add eggs and beat well.

2   Combine orange juice, almond milk and vanilla in a jug. Combine dry Ingredients in a separate bowl.

3   Stir a third of the dry Ingredients into the egg mixture followed by half the wet Ingredients. Repeat then end with dry Ingredients. Tip batter over kumquats and smooth top.

4   Bake approximately 25 minutes until cake pulls away from the edges and a skewer inserted into the centre comes out clean. Cool in pan for 5 minutes, run a knife around the edge then shake gently to loosen fruit and tip onto serving plate. Set aside to cool completely.

MAKE THE TOPPING

1   Toast almonds in oven in a dry pan until just golden, tip into a plate.

2   Repeat with coconut and combine with almonds.

3   Sprinkle over cake to serve.

PUMPKIN CARROT CAKE

INGREDIENTS

CAKE

- large eggs
- 1 cup pumpkin puree
- 3/4 cup granulated sugar
- 1/4 cup light brown sugar, packed
- 1/2 cup canola or vegetable oil
- 1 tablespoon pumpkin pie spice
- teaspoons vanilla extract
- 1 teaspoon cinnamon
- 1/4 teaspoon ground cloves
- 1 cup grated carrots, loosely packed
- 1 cup all-purpose flour
- 1 teaspoon baking powder
- 1/2 teaspoon baking soda
- 1/2 teaspoon salt, or to taste
- 1 cup raisins, optional (or 1 cup chopped nuts, or 1/2 cup raisins and 1/2 cup chopped nuts)

FROSTING

- ounces cream cheese, softened
- 1/4 cup (half of 1 stick) unsalted butter, softened
- 1 1/2 cups confectioners' sugar, sifted
- 1/2 teaspoon vanilla extract
- 1/2 teaspoon salt, or to taste

DIRECTIONS

CAKE

1   Preheat oven to 350F. Spray a 9-inch springform pan with floured cooking spray or grease and flour the pan; set aside.
2   To a large bowl, add the eggs, pumpkin, sugars, oil, pumpkin pie spice, vanilla, cinnamon, cloves, and whisk to combine.
3   Add the carrots and stir to combine.

4   Add the flour, baking powder, baking soda, salt, and stir until just combined.

5   Optionally add the raisins and/or nuts and stir to combine. Turn batter out into prepared pan, smoothing the top lightly with a spatula.

6   Bake for about 45 minutes or until center is set and a toothpick inserted in the center comes out clean or with a few moist crumbs, no batter.

7   In the last 10 minutes, loosely drape a sheet of foil over the top of the springform pan to prevent the top from becoming overly browned.

8   Allow cake to cool completely in pan on a wire rack before frosting it so the frosting.

FROSTING

1   To a large bowl add the cream cheese, butter, and beat with an electric mixer on high-speedy until fluffy, about 2 minutes.

2   Add the confectioners' sugar, vanilla, salt, and beat until smooth and incorporated, about 2 minutes.

3   Turn frosting out onto cake and spread into a smooth, even, flat layer using a spatula or knife. Unlatch springform pan, slice, and serve.

CREPE CHEESECAKE

INGREDIENTS

CREPES

- 1 cup all-purpose flour
- tablespoon sugar
- 1 teaspoon salt
- cups whole milk
- large eggs
- tablespoons unsalted butter, melted
- 1 teaspoons vanilla extract or 1 vanilla bean, halved and seeds removed
- Butter - to coat the pan

RICOTTA CREPE FILLING

- cup ricotta cheese
- tablespoons sugar
- 1 egg
- 1 tablespoon flour
- 1 cup chocolate chips

CHEESECAKE FILLING

- (8 ounce) packages cream cheese
- cup white sugar
- ½ or 1 cup whole milk
- eggs
- 1 cup sour cream
- 1 cup all purpose flour
- 1 teaspoons vanilla extract or 1 vanilla bean, halved and seeds removed

GARNISH

- baking spray
- ounces dark chocolate, chopped
- 1 lb. fresh raspberries
- powdered sugar

CREPES

1. Place eggs, milk and melted butter in a blender and mix on low - medium speed.
2. Add sugar, salt, vanilla bean seeds and flour - one cup at a time and mix in the blender/or whisk until well combined. Let the batter sit at room temperature for 15-20 minutes.
3. Place a 12-inch non-stick pan ver low-medium heat and when hot add a little butter to coat it.
4. Pour 1 cup of crepe batter into the center of the pan and swirl to spread evenly. Cook for roughly 1 minute or until the edges of the crepe appear to loosen from the pan.
5. Using a rubber spatula, loosed the crepe edges from the pan, now using your fingertips, quickly flip the crepe and cook for another 1 minute, until slightly golden brown.
6. Remove crepe and stack on a plate. Continue with the remaining batter and stack crepes on the plate. Coat the pan with butter as needed.
7. When done cooking, and the crepes have cooled to room temperature, cover them with a kitchen towel to avoid the edges from drying out.

RICOTTA CREPE FILLING

1. In a medium bowl, mix ricotta cheese with the egg and sugar, when combined mix in the flour, after fully incorporated add the chocolate chips. Set aside.

CHEESECAKE FILLING

1. In the bowl of an electric mixer, fitted with the wire attachment, mix cream cheese with sugar until smooth. Add the milk, and then mix in the eggs one at a time, mixing just enough to incorporate. Stop and scrape the bowl sides and the bottom of the bowl, using a rubber spatula. Mix in sour cream, vanilla bean seeds and flour until smooth.

BAKE

1. Preheat oven to 350F.
2. Spray a 8 inch springform pan with baking spray.
3. Place 2 crepes on the bottom of the bowl and 3 on the sides, to create a crepe crust.
4. Pour half of the New York cheesecake filling into prepared crepe crust.
5. Place a crepe on a working table, place 1 of the ricotta chocolate chip mixture a few inches from the side that is facing you, and spread it over half of the crepe. Roll it

gently into a tube and place it carefully into the pan on top of the cheesecake filling. Repeat with the remaining 3 crepes.

6. Top the crepes with the remaining New York Cheesecake filling.
7. Bake in the preheated oven for 1 hour. Turn the oven off, and let cake cool in oven with the door closed for 4-5 hours, this prevents cracking. If the cake cracks, don't worry since we are covering it in chocolate so it won't be visible.
8. Once you remove the cake from the oven, the crepe edges that are over the pan will be slightly burned, trim them, and bring the crepe crust to the same level as the cake.
9. Keep the cake in the pan.

GARNISH

1. Bring a medium saucepan half filled with water to a boil. Place the chocolate in a medium bowl set over the saucepan of simmering water, let it melt, stir just a few times. Remove from heat and set aside. Pour the chocolate on top of the cheesecake, level the mixture with a spatula or spoon.
2. Top with fresh raspberries and refrigerate for at least 4 - 5 hours or better overnight.
3. Before serving, sift powdered sugar on top of the cake and remove from the springform pan.

MEYER LEMON CHEESECAKE

INGREDIENTS

BLUEBERRY SAUCE

- cups fresh blueberries
- 1 cup water
- 1 cup sugar
- tablespoons cornstarch, mixed with 2 tablespoons cold water
- 1 tablespoons vanilla extract

CRUST

- cups graham cracker crumbs
- tablespoons unsalted butter, melted
- tablespoons granulated sugar

CHEESECAKE FILLING

- packages (8 oz.) cream cheese, softened
- 1 cup sour cream
- tablespoons cornstarch
- eggs
- 1 ½ cups sugar
- 1 cup graham cracker crumbs
- juice of one meyer lemon
- zest from one meyer lemon

DIRECTIONS

BLUEBERRY SAUCE

1   In a large saucepan over medium heat, combine blueberries, water and sugar. Stir frequently, but careful not to crush the berries, bring to a low boil.
2   In a small bowl, mix the cornstarch with cold water until combined.
3   Slowly stir the cornstarch into the blueberries. Simmer until the homemade blueberry sauce is thick enough to coat the back of a metal spoon, about 10 minutes.
4   Remove from heat and gently stir in vanilla.

5   Let the sauce cool at room temperature. Measure 1 cup for your recipe, store the rest in jars in the fridge.

CRUST

1   In a large bowl, mix the crumbs with melted butter and granulated sugar with a rubber spatula until combined.
2   Press the mixture into the bottom of a 9inch spring form cake pan and slightly up the sides. Make sure it is tight and compact.
3   Chill the crust for 15 minutes.

CHEESECAKE FILLING

1   Preheat oven to 325F.
2   In the bowl of an electric mixer fitted with the whisk attachment beat cream cheese on medium speed until fluffy. Add the sugar, cornstarch, lemon juice, lemon zest and beat until combined.
3   Add eggs, one at a time, beating until just combined after each addition. On low speed beat in sour cream just until combined.
4   Remove crust from the fridge and pour the batter into the crust.
5   In circles pour the blueberry sauce over the cheesecake and with the edge of a spatula create swirls and mix the blueberry sauce into the cheesecake filling. Carefully not to over mix.
6   Bake for about 11 hours or until center is almost set. Cool on a wire rack for 15 minutes. Sprinkle graham crackers on top and loosen sides of pan and continue cooling on wire rack until the cheesecake is at room temperature.
7   Transfer to the fridge. Refrigerate overnight or at least 6 hours before serving.
8   The cheesecake can be served with warm blueberry sauce.
9   Store in refrigerator.

PUMPKIN SPICE CAKE

INGREDIENTS

CAKE

- large eggs
- 1 cup granulated sugar
- 1 cup pumpkin puree
- 1/2 cup canola or vegetable oil
- teaspoons pumpkin pie spice
- 1 teaspoon vanilla extract
- 1 cup all-purpose flour
- 1 teaspoon baking powder
- 1/2 teaspoon baking soda
- 1/2 teaspoon salt, or to taste

FROSTING

- ounces cream cheese, softened
- 1/4 cup unsalted butter, softened
- 1 1/2 cups confectioners' sugar
- 1/2 teaspoon vanilla extract
- 1/2 teaspoon salt, or to taste

DIRECTIONS

CAKE

1   Preheat oven to 350F. Line an 8x8-inch pan with aluminum foil and spray with cooking spray; set aside.
2   To a large bowl, add the eggs, sugar, pumpkin, oil, pumpkin pie spice, vanilla, and whisk to combine.
3   Add the flour, baking powder, baking soda, salt, and stir until just combined.
4   Turn batter out into prepared pan, smoothing the top lightly with a spatula. Bake for about 35 to 40 minute or until center is set and a toothpick inserted in the center comes out clean or with a few moist crumbs, no batter. Set cake aside on a cooling rack to cool completely before .

FROSTING

1 To a large bowl add the cream cheese, butter, confectioners' sugar, vanilla, salt, and whisk until smooth and fluffy or beat with an electric mixer.

2 Turn frosting out onto cake and spread into a smooth, even, flat layer using a spatula or knife. Slice and serve

STRAWBERRY UPSIDE DOWN CAKE

INGREDIENTS

- 1 cup sugar
- tbsp corn starch
- cups fresh quartered strawberries
- 1 tsp vanilla extract
- For the cake batter
- cups all-purpose flour
- 1 tablespoon baking powder
- 1 tsp salt
- large eggs, at room temperature
- cups sugar
- 1 cup melted butter
- 1 cup vegetable oil
- 1 cup whole milk, at room temperature

DIRECTIONS

Grease and flour a 10 inch round cake pan very well and preheat oven to 350 degrees F. A large 9 or 10 inch tube pan or an 9x9 square baking pan can also be used.

Cut the strawberries in half.

Mix the corn starch and 1 cup sugar together and sprinkle over the strawberries along with the 1 tsp vanilla extract. Toss together well and spread evenly into the bottom of the prepared pan.

CAKE BATTER

1. Sift together the flour baking powder and salt. Set aside.
2. In the bowl of an electric mixer, beat together the eggs, sugar at high speed until very foamy.
3. Mix together the butter and vegetable oil in a measuring cup with a spout.
4. Slowly add this butter and oil mixture to the egg and sugar mixture as it continues to beat.
5. Fold in the dry Ingredients alternately with the milk. When alternating wet and dry Ingredients, always begin and end with the dry mixture. =
6. Pour the batter over the strawberries in the baking pan.

7   Bake for 50-60 minutes or until a toothpick inserted in the center comes out clean.
8   Cool in the pan for about 10 minutes before inverting onto a heatproof serving plate.
9   Serve with whipped cream or vanilla ice cream.

APPLE CIDER BUNDT CAKE

INGREDIENTS

CAKE

- 1 1/2 cups spiced apple cider
- 1 large apple, peeled, cored, and roughly chopped
- 1/2 cup milk
- 1 teaspoon vanilla extract
- 1/2 cups all purpose flour
- 1 1/2 teaspoons baking powder
- 1/2 teaspoon baking soda
- 1 teaspoon salt
- 1/4 teaspoon nutmeg
- 1 teaspoon cinnamon
- pinch of ground cloves
- 1/2 cup unsalted butter, at room temperature
- 3/4 cup sugar
- 1/2 cup light brown sugar, packed
- large eggs, at room temperature
- 1/4 cup vegetable oil

TOPPING

- tablespoons granulated sugar
- 1 1/2 teaspoons cinnamon
- 1 tablespoon unsalted butter, melted

DIRECTIONS

1 Add the cider and chopped apple to a medium saucepan set over medium-high heat and bring the cider to a boil.
2 Reduce the heat to medium and simmer until half of the cider has been absorbed and the apples can be smashed easily with a fork, about 15 minutes.
3 Remove the saucepan from the heat, and allow to cool for 5 minutes. Pour the mixture into a food processor or blender and blend until pureed and smooth.
4 Measure out 1 cup of the cider mixture and add to a large measuring cup, along with the milk and vanilla extract. Stir with a fork to combine.

5   Preheat the oven to 350 degrees F and position a rack in the middle of the oven. Grease a 10-cup Bundt pan with non-stick spray and dust all over with flour, tapping out the excess.

6   In a medium bowl, whisk together the flour, baking powder, baking soda, salt, nutmeg, cinnamon, and cloves.

7   In the bowl of standard electric mixer fitted with the paddle attachment, beat the butter, granulated sugar, and brown sugar on medium speed until light and fluffy, about 3-4 minutes. Add the eggs, one at a time, beating well after each addition. Scrape down the sides of the bowl with a rubber spatula as needed. Add in the oil, and beat to combine, about 1 minute.

8   Lower the mixer speed to low, and add the flour mixture in three batches, alternating with the cider-milk mixture, beginning and ending with the dry Ingredients. Mix only until incorporated and scrape down the sides of the bowl with a rubber spatula as needed. After the last addition, increase the speed to medium and beat for about 20 seconds to fully combine.

9   Scrape the batter into the prepared pan. Bake the cake until the top is golden brown and a tester inserted into the center comes out clean, about 45 minutes. Transfer the cake to cooling rack set over a baking sheet and let it cool in the pan for 10 minutes, then invert directly onto the cooling rack.

10   While the cake is still warm, combine the granulated sugar and cinnamon to make the topping. Brush the warm cake with melted butter and sprinkle with the cinnamon sugar, using your fingers to rub it onto the sides.

11   Let the cake cool completely.

CHOCOLATE BROWNIE CAKE WITH MASCARPONE

INGREDIENTS

BROWNIE LAYERS

- 1 cup unsalted butter, melted
- cup granulated sugar
- large eggs
- 1 cup all-purpose flour
- 1 cup unsweetened cocoa powder
- 1 teaspoon salt
- 1 teaspoon baking soda

COCONUT FILLING

- 1 cup walnuts, measure then grind
- 1 cup coconut flakes
- 1 cup heavy cream
- 1 cup sugar
- 1 egg yolk
- tbsp. butter, room temperature

MASCARPONE

- sticks of butter, softened
- oz mascarpone cheese, chilled
- 21 cups powdered sugar
- 1 vanilla bean
- pinch of salt

CHOCOLATE GANACHE

- ounces semisweet chocolate, chopped
- tbsp. light corn syrup
- tablespoons unsalted butter
- 1 cup heavy cream

DIRECTIONS

1 Preheat oven to 350°F.
2 Grease bottom of 3 8inch round pans with melted butter or cooking spray.
3 In the bowl of an electric mixer, whisk together melted butter and sugar until smooth. Add in each egg one at a time on low speed and whisk until well combined.
4 Using a large rubber spatula, gently stir in flour, cocoa, baking soda and salt.
5 Spread batter into the pans and bake for 25-30 minutes until set.
6 Remove and let cool completely before assembling the cake.

COCONUT FILLING

1 Place the butter, walnuts and coconut in a large bowl and set aside.
2 In a medium sauce pan, on low/medium heat, stir together the heavy cream, sugar and egg yolk until the mixture begins to thicken and coats the back of a spoon (180 degrees F.).
3 Pour the hot custard immediately onto the walnut-coconut mixture and stir until the butter is melted. Cool completely to room temperature before topping the brownie layers.

MASCARPONE

1 Place softened butter and mascarpone into the bowl of an electric stand mixer that has been fitted with the whisk attachment.
2 Turn the mixer on a medium setting and cream until it smooth and combined, 2 - 3 minutes.
3 Add sugar, 1 a cup at a time. Add vanilla beans and a pinch of salt and whisk until well-incorporated.

CHOCOLATE GANACHE

1 Place the chocolate, corn syrup and butter in a medium bowl.
2 Heat the cream in a small saucepan over medium heat until it just begins to boil.
3 Remove from heat and pour over the chocolate. Let stand one minute, then stir until smooth. Cool to room temperature.

ASSEMBLE

1 Remove the cooled brownie layers from the pans. Set the first cake layer on a cake plate.

2   Top with a half of the coconut walnut filling, spread it evenly. Top the coconut wittier with frosting, also spread evenly.

3   Repeat the process with the second brownie cake layer. Third layer, is covered in frosting only, no coconut mixture.
    Pour the chocolate ganache on top of the cake, distribute evenly and also ice the sides of the cake while the ganache is dripping down.

4   Chill the cake for at least 2 hours before serving.

CHESTNUT CHOCOLATE CAKE

INGREDIENTS

CHESTNUT LAYER

- 1 small egg white
- A pinch of cream of tartar
- 1 table spoon powder sugar
- 1 large egg
- 40 grams (1,4 oz) sugar
- 40 grams (1,4 oz) butter, at room temperature
- 80 grams (2,8 oz) chestnut meal boiled and peeled chestnuts
- 25 grams (0,9 oz) rice flour
- A pinch of salt

CHOCOLATE MOUSSE

- 100 grams (3,5 oz) dark eating chocolate
- 60ml. + 80ml. sweetened heavy whipping cream
- 1 egg yolk
- 20 grams (0,7 oz) sugar
- 1/2 tea spoon vanilla extract
- grams of gelatine
- ml. water

CHOCOLATE GANACHE

- 50 (1,8 oz) grams dark eating chocolate
- 15 grams (0,5 oz) butter
- 15 ml. heavy whipping cream

CARAMELIZED NUTS

- 40 grams (1,4 oz) sugar
- 50 grams (1,8 oz) raw nuts

DIRECTIONS

CHESTNUT LAYER

1. Preheat your oven to 180C, fan-forced (350F, fan-forced). Line a baking sheet with parchment paper
2. Beat the egg white with the cream of tartar in a medium bowl until soft peaks form. Add the powder sugar and continue to beat until meringue turns glossy and light and stiff peaks form. Set aside.
3. In another bowl beat the eggs with muscovado sugar until the mixture becomes fluffy and thickens a bit. Beat in the butter until all is combined.
4. Gently fold in the chestnut meal, rice flour and a pinch of salt. Stir until all Ingredients combine.
5. Gently fold in the egg white.
6. Pour the batter onto the baking sheet and even the top with a spatula.
7. Bake about 7-10 minutes or until the layer turns golden brown.
8. Remove from oven.
9. Cut the chestnut layer while it is still hot.
10. Grease 3 rings with coconut butter or other unflavored oil/butter.
11. Using the rings, cut out of the almond layer 3 circles.
12. Place all rings on a large serving plate with parchment paper. Fit in one cake circle in every ring, press to reach the bottom and stick to the paper. Set aside.

CHOCOLATE MOUSSE

1. In a small bowl combine the chocolate and 60 ml. of heavy whipping cream.
2. Heat t in the microwave oven until cream is so hot that the chocolate will start to melt. Stir with a small spoon until the chocolate melts and the mixture is glossy and smooth. Set aside.
3. In a medium saucepan whisk the egg yolk and sugar until pale.
4. Add vanilla extract and start cooking on medium / medium-low heat. Whisk almost constantly until sugar dissolves and the egg yolk mixture is hot to the touch. Cook egg yolks on medium low heat until you temper them, continue cooking until the mixture thickens. Whisk often to avoid curdling the eggs.
5. Once the sugar dissolves and the mixture is thickened, remove from the heat and add the chocolate-cream mixture. Stir until all combines and the mixture is smooth. Set aside.
6. In a medium-size bowl whip 80 ml. of heavy whipping cream until soft peaks form. Don't over-beat the cream, you need it with soft peaks in order to get a smooth and light as an air mousse. Set aside.
7. Place 5 grams (1/2 sachet) of gelatine in a small heatproof bowl with 10 ml. water and let it sit for a few minutes. Place the bowl with the gelatine over a small saucepan with simmering water. Let the gelatine heats until liquid smooth, crystal clear like water, only little yellowish. Set aside to cool off for a bit. Add it to the

chocolate-egg mixture and stir to combine completely. Fold in the heavy whipping cream and gently stir with a rubber spatula.

8   Fill in the cooking rings with the mousse almost to the edge, leave enough room for a layer of chocolate ganache.

9   Put in the fridge to firm up for about two hours.

CHOCOLATE GANACHE

1   Combine all Ingredients in a small bowl and heat in a microwave oven until the chocolate starts to melt. Stir until the mixture is glossy and smooth.

2   Remove mousse cakes from the fridge and pour a little bit of the chocolate ganache over each mousse cake. Put back in the fridge for 30 minutes.

CARAMELIZED NUTS

1   Add sugar to a small saucepan. Set it over medium heat.

2   Cook until it melts completely and turns golden brown. Pour in the nuts and stir to coat all nuts. Remove from heat and immediately transfer the mixture to a large plate lined with parchment paper. let the nuts cool off completely then crush with a glass/rolling pan or in the food processor.

3   Once cakes are firm enough and the chocolate ganache is set, gently remove each cake from the rings, place on a dessert plate and sprinkle some of the nuts over.

CHOCOLATE CAKE

INGREDIENTS

- egg whites at room temperature
- cups extra fine granulated Imperial sugar
- tablespoons unsweetened cocoa powder
- teaspoons corn starch
- 1 tablespoon lemon juice
- 1 tablespoon vanilla extract
- cups cold heavy whipping cream
- 1 cup powdered Imperial sugar
- 10-12 strawberries, cored and quartered
- chocolate shavings

DIRECTIONS

1 Preheat your oven to 250 degrees F. Line a baking sheet with parchment paper.
2 In the bowl of a stand mixer with the whisk attachment, beat the egg whites and granulated sugar on high, until stiff peaks form.
3 Add the cocoa powder, corn starch, lemon juice and vanilla extract and mix until well blended.
4 Transfer to your lined sheet. Use a spatula to make 6 round rings. Make sure there is an indent in the center of each circle - the centers will rise during baking.
5 Bake for 1 hour and 30 minutes. Turn off the oven and allow the meringues to cool in the oven with the door closed for at least 1 hour. When you remove them from the oven, make sure they are completely cool before assembling your pavlova cake.
6 Beat the whipping cream on high for 3-4 minutes. Slowly add the powdered sugar until the whipped cream is thick and fluffy.

ASSEMBLE

1 Place one meringue on a plate. Top that with whipped cream and repeat until you have used 3 of your meringues.
2 Place several strawberry chunks into the whipped cream and on top of the cake.
3 Sprinkle chocolate shavings on top.

OREO CAKE

INGREDIENTS

- 1 Box Chocolate Cake Mix
- 1 Pack of Oreo Cookies
- 1 Large Box Oreo Instant Pudding
- Cups Milk
- Ounces Cool Whip

DIRECTIONS

1. Preheat oven to 350 F. Roughly chop oreo cookies.
2. Grease a 9x13 inch dish. Prepare chocolate cake according to box directions.
3. Pour cake batter into the prepared pan. Bake for 30-32 minutes or until a tooth pick inserted in the center comes out clean.
4. While the cake is cooling whisk milk and pudding together until smooth.
5. Use a wooden spoon to poke holes in the top of the cake. Evenly pour pudding over the top of the cake.
6. Sprinkle with half of the chopped oreos. Cool cake completely.
7. Frost with cool whip. Sprinkle with remaining oreos. Store in the refrigerator.

CHOCOLATE LAYERED CAKE

INGREDIENTS

LAYERS

- 1 and 3/4 cups (220g) all-purpose flour
- 1 and 3/4 cup (350g) granulated sugar
- 3/4 cup (65g) unsweetened cocoa powder
- 1 teaspoon baking powder
- teaspoons baking soda
- 1 teaspoon salt
- 1 cup (240ml) buttermilk1
- 1/2 cup (120ml) vegetable oil
- large eggs, at room temperature2
- 1 teaspoon pure vanilla extract
- 1 cup (240ml) freshly brewed strong hot coffee

CHOCOLATE FROSTING

- cups (2.5 sticks or 290g) unsalted butter, softened to room temperature
- 3-4 cups (360-480g) confectioners' sugar
- 3/4 cup (65g) unsweetened cocoa powder
- 3-5 Tablespoons (45-75ml) heavy cream
- 1 teaspoon pure vanilla extract
- 1/2 - 3/4 teaspoon salt
- 15 oz (1.5 bags) chocolate chips

DIRECTIONS

CAKE

1 Preheat oven to 350F degrees. Butter & flour two 9 inch round cake pans4, or use non-stick spray.
2 Sift together the flour, sugar, cocoa powder, baking powder, baking soda, and salt in a medium sized bowl. Set aside.
3 Using a handheld or stand mixer on high speed, mix the buttermilk, oil, room temperature eggs, and vanilla in a large bowl until combined. Slowly add the dry

Ingredients to the wet Ingredients with the mixer on low. Add the coffee. The batter will be VERY thin. This is ok.

4   Pour the batter into prepared baking pans and bake for 23-27 minutes or until a toothpick inserted in the center comes out clean. My cakes took exactly 24 minutes. Allow to cool before frosting.

FROSTING

1   Using a handheld or stand mixer fitted with a paddle attachment, beat the butter on high speed until smooth and creamy - about 2 full minutes.

2   Turn speed to low and slowly add 3.5 cups of confectioners' sugar and the cocoa powder. Beat until sugar/cocoa are absorbed into the butter, about 2 minutes. Turn mixer to medium speed and add the vanilla and cream. Once added, turn the mixer to high speed and beat for 1 minute.

3   Taste, and add salt to taste.

ASSEMBLY

1   Place 1 layer, flat side up, on a plate or cake stand. With a knife or offset spatula, spread the top with frosting.

2   Place the second layer on top, rounded side up, and spread the frosting evenly on the top and sides of the cake. Decorate with chocolate chips.

CINNAMON SUGAR CAKE

INGREDIENTS

- cups all-purpose flour
- 1 teaspoon baking powder
- 1 teaspoon baking soda
- 1 teaspoon salt
- 21 teaspoons ground cinnamon
- large eggs
- 1 cup granulated sugar
- 1 cup (1 stick) unsalted butter, softened
- teaspoons vanilla extract
- 1 cup sour cream

BUTTERCREAM FROSTING

- 1 (2 sticks) cup unsalted butter, softened
- cups confectioners' sugar
- Tablespoons 2% milk
- 1 teaspoon ground cinnamon
- 1 teaspoon vanilla extract
- 1 Tablespoon cinnamon-sugar, sprinkle on top of cake

DIRECTIONS

1 Preheat oven to 350F degrees. Spray two 9-on. round baking pans with non-stick cooking spray. Set aside.
2 In a medium bowl, mix flour, baking powder, baking soda, salt and ground cinnamon. Set aside.
3 In a large bowl, using an electric or stand mixer on medium speed, beat eggs and sugar for about 2 minutes, or until light and creamy.
4 Add the butter and vanilla extract and beat on low speed for about 1 minute, or until well blended. Beat in the dry Ingredients on low speed until blended. Add the sour cream and beat until smooth.
5 Divide batter evenly into prepared baking pans. Bake 18 to 20 minutes or until toothpick inserted in center comes out clean. Allow cake to cool before frosting.

FROSTING

1 Mix softened butter on medium speed with an electric or stand mixer. Beat for 30 seconds until smooth and creamy.

2 Add powdered sugar, milk, ground cinnamon and vanilla extract. Increase to high speed and beat for 3 minutes or until smooth.

3 Spread the frosting between layers and over top and sides of cake. Sprinkle with cinnamon-sugar.

DARK CHOCOLATE AND YOGURT CAKE

INGREDIENTS

- tablespoons butter
- 1/2 cup brown sugar
- 1 egg
- 1 teaspoon vanilla extract
- 1 1/2 cups flour
- 1 teaspoon baking powder
- 1/4 teaspoon salt
- tablespoons dark cocoa powder
- 3/4 cup plain greek yogurt
- 1/4 cup milk

DARK COCOA SYRUP

- 1 cup powdered sugar
- 1 tablespoon dark cocoa powder
- 1 teaspoon vanilla extract
- 1 teaspoon water

INSTUCTIONS

1. Preheat oven to 350 degrees. Butter and flour an 8×8 cake pan.
2. Cream butter and sugar together until fluffy. Beat in egg and vanilla. Add cocoa, flour, baking powder and salt and mix until combined. Add yogurt and mix until batter is smooth. Add in milk and mix until batter comes together. Pour into pan.
3. Bake for 18-20 minutes, or until cake is set. Cake will be thin, and appear a bit spongey. Serve with fresh whipped cream and cocoa syrup.

DARK COCOA SYRUP

1. Mix all Ingredients until a smooth glaze forms.

STRAWBERRIES CAKE

INGREDIENTS

STRAWBERRY CAKE

- 1 cup unsalted butter, at room temperature
- cups white sugar
- large eggs
- teaspoons freshly squeezed lemon juice
- cups plus 3 tablespoons flour
- tablespoons cornstarch
- tablespoons strawberry jell-o mix, dry
- 1/2 teaspoon baking soda
- 1/4 teaspoon salt
- 1 cup buttermilk
- 2/3 cup chopped fresh strawberries

FROSTING

- 1/2 cup unsalted butter, softened
- 1 (8 ounces) package of full-fat cream cheese at room temperature
- teaspoons vanilla extract
- 4- 4 and 1/2 cups powdered sugar

TOPPING

- 1 and 1/2 cup sliced strawberries
- 1 and 1/2 tablespoon white sugar

DIRECTIONS

CAKE

1 Preheat the oven to 350 degrees F. Grease and flour a 9 x 13 pan and set aside.
2 Beat the room temperature butter with hand mixers until light and creamy.
3 Slowly add in the sugar until the mixture is light and fluffy,
4 In another bowl, lightly beat the eggs and then add the mixture and mix along with the freshly squeezed lemon juice. Beat in the buttermilk.

5   In a separate bowl, sift together the flour and cornstarch 2-3 times and then add in the jell-o mix, baking soda, and salt.
6   Add the dry Ingredients to the wet and beat at low speed until just combined.
7   Remove the stems from the strawberries and finely chop. Add in the finely chopped strawberries to the cake.
8   Pour the batter evenly in the prepared 9 x 13 pan.
9   Bake for 30-40 minutes or until a toothpick comes out clean when inserted into the center.
10 Cool the cake for at least one hour and then chill in the fridge for another hour.

FROSTING

1   Beat the softened butter and room temperature cream cheese until completely creamy.
2   Beat in the vanilla. Slowly beat in the powdered sugar until smooth and your desired consistency.
3   Spread the frosting over the cake

SUGARED STRAWBERRY TOPPING

1   Stir together the sliced strawberries and sugar in a medium bowl.
2   Let them stand at room temperature for about 20-30 minutes. Add them to the cake when serving and not beforehand.

CARROT CAKE

INGREDIENTS

FOR THE CAKE

- 2 cups shredded carrots
- 8 oz crushed pineapple, drained
- ¾ cup sweetened, shredded coconut
- ½ cup raisins
- 1½ cups sugar
- 1 cup vegetable oil
- 4 large eggs, room temperature
- 2 teaspoons vanilla extract
- 2 cups all purpose flour
- 1½ teaspoons baking powder
- 2 teaspoons baking soda
- 2 teaspoons cinnamon
- 1 teaspoon salt

FOR THE FROSTING

- ½ cup unsalted butter, room temperature
- 5 oz cream cheese, softened
- 1 teaspoon vanilla extract
- ½ teaspoon salt
- 3 cups powdered sugar

DIRECTIONS

1. Preheat oven to 350°F. Grease and flour three 8 inch cake pans and set aside.
2. In a large bowl, combine the carrots, pineapple, coconut, raisins, sugar, vegetable oil, eggs, and vanilla extract. In a separate bowl, combine the flour, baking powder, baking soda, cinnamon, and salt. Incorporate the dry Ingredients into the wet, stirring until well combined.
3. Evenly pour the batter into the prepared pans. Bake for 25 minutes, then allow to cool completely before frosting.

1. Whip the butter and cream cheese until light and fluffy, about 4 minutes.
2. Add in the vanilla extract, salt, and powdered sugar and whip to combine, about 2 minutes more.
3. Place the first cake on a plate, then top with ⅓ of the frosting. Layer the second and third layers, frosting in between each. Be freeform with it, using a flat knife to even the top of each layer. If you'd like, decorate the top with edible flowers! Then make sure you have friends with you when you eat it, or else you'll go nuts.

MOCHA CAKE

INGREDIENTS

- 1 stick + 1 tbsp (125g) butter
- 1 cup (50g) cocoa
- tsp instant espresso powder
- cup (300g) sugar
- 1 cup (150g) plain flour
- eggs

DIRECTIONS

1 Preheat the oven to 180C, and grease and line a 7 inch (18cm) cake tin.
2 Melt the butter in a medium saucepan over a low heat, and then stir in the remaining Ingredients.
3 Scrape the batter into the pan, and bake for 20-40 minutes, or until the edges are set, but the middle is still gooey. Mine took 30 minutes, but start checking at 20.
4 Leave to cool for at least 30 minutes, before removing from the pan and serving with raspberries, and a dollop of creme fraiche.

CHOCOLATE ZUCCHINI CAKE

INGREDIENTS

- 2-1/4c all-purpose flour
- 1/2c cocoa powder
- 1t baking soda
- 1t salt
- 1-3/4c sugar
- 1/2c butter, softened
- 1/2c canola oil
- 2 eggs
- 1t vanilla extract
- 1/2c buttermilk
- 2c zucchini, grated
- 3/4c semi-sweet chocolate chips

DIRECTIONS

1. Preheat oven to 325. Grease and flour a 9x13 inch baking pan.
2. Sift the flour, cocoa powder, baking soda & salt into a medium bowl.
3. In another bowl, beat the sugar, butter and oil in a large bowl until well blended. Add the eggs 1 at a time, beating well after each addition. Add the vanilla extract.
4. Mix in the dry Ingredients alternating with the buttermilk in 3 additions. Mix in grated zucchini.
5. Spread into prepared pan . Sprinkle with chocolate chips. Bake 50 minutes or until toothpick inserted into the center comes out clean. Allow to cool about 15 minutes, slice, and serve warm.

BEFORE YOU LEAVE

I am glad that you stayed till the end of this book. If you've enjoyed reading this book and if you have found it useful, I would like to hear your feedback by writing a review.

Thank you for your support and don't forget that you are AWESOME.

58713418R00189

Made in the USA
Lexington, KY
16 December 2016